Mastering vRealize Operations Manager

Analyze and optimize your IT environment by gaining a practical understanding of vROps 6.0

Scott Norris

Christopher Slater

[PACKT] PUBLISHING enterprise

professional expertise distilled

BIRMINGHAM - MUMBAI

Mastering vRealize Operations Manager

First published: May 2015

Production reference: 1190515

Published by Packt Publishing Ltd.
Livery Place
35 Livery Street
Birmingham B3 2PB, UK.

ISBN 978-1-78439-254-3

www.packtpub.com

Credits

Authors
Scott Norris
Christopher Slater

Reviewers
Steven Bridle
Luke Flemming
Wojciech Marusiak
Mario Russo

Commissioning Editor
Ashwin Nair

Acquisition Editor
Meeta Rajani

Content Development Editor
Riddhi Tuljapurkar

Technical Editor
Pramod Kumavat

Copy Editors
Pranjali Chury
Sameen Siddiqui
Neha Vyas

Project Coordinator
Kinjal Bari

Proofreaders
Safis Editing
Maria Gould
Ameesha Green

Indexer
Rekha Nair

Graphics
Sheetal Aute
Disha Haria
Jason Monteiro
Abhinash Sahu

Production Coordinator
Conidon Miranda

Cover Work
Conidon Miranda

Foreword

When Scott and Chris approached me to write a foreword for their book, I jumped on it right away. As stated in my book, *VMware vRealize Operations Performance and Capacity Management, Packt Publishing*, I excluded a lot of areas in order to stay within the self-imposed page limit. They have read my book, and it gives me sheer joy as an author when another author takes your work and then complements it well. Having read the final product, I am in fact going to change the strategy for my second edition. I am going to refer to this book a lot as they have explained the concepts better than I did. These are indeed "the missing chapters" in my book!

I highly recommend this book to you. Whether you are new to vRealize Operations, or you have a large scale deployment, there is something for you. The book covers the product top-down. I have read the vRealize Operations manuals and white papers, and I think this book stands out. It stands out not because the manuals are not good, but because the book was written by practitioners and field personnel. Just like my book, it was born at the customer's site with real-world input. Scott and Chris have done numerous vRealize Operations implementations, and the content of this book reflects their valuable experience.

Speaking about the product of this book, vRealize Operations has gained the acceptance of many customers globally. It has also gained industry acceptance, as you can see from the many management packs provided by partners. It has evolved from a vSphere-centric management tool to an overall SDDC management tool. vRealize Operations is also undergoing improvement every year. By the time you read this book, there is a good chance that an updated release will be out. The good thing is that the foundation set in this book is required for you to master the new version.

I am certainly glad to see that both the books are published by the same publisher, as this makes future collaboration easier. Together with many bloggers and practitioners out there, we can make a significant contribution toward a great vRealize Operations deployment.

Iwan Rahabok

VCAP-DCD, TOGAF Certified, vExpert, CTO Ambassador, VMware

About the Authors

Scott Norris is currently a senior consultant in VMware's Professional Services Organization (PSO). He specializes in multiple VMware technologies, such as ESXi, vCenter, vRA, vCD, vCOps (vROps), vRO, SRM, and vRealize Automation Application Services.

Prior to VMware, Scott worked for HP Australia and was the VMware SME for the APAC region. In this role, he did everything from breaking and fixing to architecting solutions for clients all over the region. For the last 6 years, Scott has worked exclusively on VMware products and technologies, supporting small environments, from a single server office to large federal government environments with hundreds of hosts.

Scott Norris is a 32-year-old father of two. He has been an IT professional for 11 years minus a small hiatus in which he fought and won the battle against non-Hodgkin's lymphoma. Outside of work, Scott enjoys messing around in his test lab, playing with his children, or kicking back laying the smack down in Halo on the Xbox.

This is his first book, but he runs a popular blog focused on the vRealize Suite at `www.virtualiseme.net.au`.

Scott can be followed on Twitter at `@auScottNorris`.

Christopher Slater is a managing consultant working for VMware as part of the Professional Services Organization (PSO). He specializes in SDDC technologies and methodologies such as vSphere, vRealize Operations Manager, and Infrastructure and Platform as a Service (IaaS/PaaS) through vRealize Automation. He is a VMware Certified Design Expert (VCDX-DV #102) and acquired a bachelor of IT degree from the Australian National University. Chris's primary customer base is the Australian Federal Government, which has allowed him to work in some of the largest vSphere environments in Australia.

He is in his late 20s and is grateful for the support from his wife, Nicola, and two children, Sophia and Daniel. Outside of work, Chris enjoys gaming and watching Hobbit and Frozen (for the 100th time) with his kids.

Chris is glad to join Scott in his first book writing adventure and also blogs on VMware SDDC technologies at `www.definedbysoftware.com`.

He can be followed on Twitter at `@cslater27`.

Acknowledgments

First and foremost, we must express our gratitude to our families for supporting us while writing this book. Both of us wrote and edited the book in our personal time and it is our families that we need to thank for putting up with the time spent on this project. Our gratitude especially goes out to Louise and Nicola for this time.

We would also like to thank our colleagues and managers at VMware, who gave us both the opportunity and support throughout this great experience. A special note of thanks goes out to our editors and reviewers, most of all, Steve Bridle at VMware, who graciously agreed to technically review the book for us.

Finally, we would like to thank our customers and mentors who have given us the opportunity to improve the way their organizations manage a virtualized environment through the use of vRealize Operations Manager.

About the Reviewers

Steven Bridle is a senior consultant for VMware based in Canberra, Australia, with over 7 years of experience working with virtualization software. Working around Canberra in government and commercial organizations, he has vast experience in architecture, design, and support for virtualized environments.

He is a VMware Certified Design Expert - Desktop (VCDX-DT), focusing on VMware End User Computing solutions. He was able to obtain VCDX #179 by demonstrating his ability to gather requirements, architect, design, manage, deploy, and support a factual solution to the VMware VCDX panelists.

Currently, he specializes in VMware End User Computing solutions for large enterprise environments and provides support and tips through various online media, including Twitter (`@virtuallyeuc`) and his blog (`www.virtuallyeuc.com`).

Luke Flemming is an IT professional based in Australia with over 10 years of experience, specializing in VMware Support and Wintel Engineering. He started off his career in an entry-level position and worked his way through the ranks of desktop support and server support. He has worked with various multinational tier 1 companies during his career as well as smaller localized companies. Luke has received several awards and recognitions from his employers for his hardwork ethics, leadership, and dedication and is highly regarded among his peers. Outside of work, he has an affinity for sports, good food, fine wine, and fast cars.

Wojciech Marusiak has more than 8 years of experience as a systems engineer and is currently working for a large financial institution in Frankfurt am Main, Germany. He possesses various industry certifications, including VMware Certified Professional 4 and 5, VMware Certified Advanced Professional 5 - Data Center Administration, Microsoft MCITP Server Administrator, and ITIL V3. In his spare time, Wojciech writes his blog (`http://wojcieh.net`) about VMware products and helps his readers get a better understanding of virtualization. He was listed as a vExpert in 2014 and 2015 for his contributions to the VMware community and his blogging activities.

Mario Russo has worked as an IT architect and a senior technical VMware trainer and has also worked in the presales department. He has been working on the VMware technology since 2004.

In 2005, he worked for IBM on the first large project consolidation for Telecom Italia on the Virtual VMware ESX 2.5.1 platform in Italy, with the Physical to Virtual (P2V) tool.

In 2007, he conducted a drafting course and training for BancoPosta, Italy, and project disaster and recovery (DR Open) for IBM and EMC.

In 2008, he worked for the Project Speed Up Consolidation BNP and the migration P2V on VI3 infrastructure at BNP Cardif Insurance.

In 2014, he worked on Customize Dashboard and Tuning Smart Alert vCOps 5.7 POSTECOM Italy Rm.

He is a VCI Certified Instructor Level 2 of VMware and is certified in VCAP5-DCA, VCP3-4, VCP5-DV, VCP5-DT, and VCP-Cloud.

He is the owner of Business to Virtual, Italy, which specializes in virtualization solutions.

He was also a technical reviewer on *Implementing VMware Horizon View 5.2*, *Implementing VMware vCenter Server*, *Troubleshooting vSphere Storage*, *VMware Horizon View 5.3 Design Patterns and Best Practices*, and *Instant Getting Started with VMware Fusion*, all by Packt Publishing.

I would like to thank my wife, Lina, and my daughter, Gaia. They're my strength.

www.PacktPub.com

Support files, eBooks, discount offers, and more

For support files and downloads related to your book, please visit `www.PacktPub.com`.

Did you know that Packt offers eBook versions of every book published, with PDF and ePub files available? You can upgrade to the eBook version at `www.PacktPub.com` and as a print book customer, you are entitled to a discount on the eBook copy. Get in touch with us at `service@packtpub.com` for more details.

At `www.PacktPub.com`, you can also read a collection of free technical articles, sign up for a range of free newsletters and receive exclusive discounts and offers on Packt books and eBooks.

PACKTLIB™

`https://www2.packtpub.com/books/subscription/packtlib`

Do you need instant solutions to your IT questions? PacktLib is Packt's online digital book library. Here, you can search, access, and read Packt's entire library of books.

Why subscribe?

- Fully searchable across every book published by Packt
- Copy and paste, print, and bookmark content
- On demand and accessible via a web browser

Free access for Packt account holders

If you have an account with Packt at `www.PacktPub.com`, you can use this to access PacktLib today and view 9 entirely free books. Simply use your login credentials for immediate access.

Instant updates on new Packt books

Get notified! Find out when new books are published by following `@PacktEnterprise` on Twitter or the *Packt Enterprise* Facebook page.

Table of Contents

Preface

When were we were originally approached to write this book, the first and most obvious question that we asked was "why should we do that?" However, on reflection, we both thought about our personal experiences with the product and the real world differences it made during times when we needed to troubleshoot performance problems or report on capacity trends. We also thought about our customers for whom we had either demonstrated vROps or run knowledge transfer sessions, and how only after a few hours, the energy in the room changed as people began to grasp the power and concept of how vROps could benefit them on a daily basis.

The second reason for writing this book was because we noticed that in some environments that had the product deployed, many of the concepts, terminology, and settings were not understood well enough. As a result, customers were not getting the maximum value from their investment simply because they weren't familiar enough with the product. There is a lot of great documentation for the product, but like most other product documentation, it is generally very thin on the why aspect. For example, why should I enable some containers for capacity management and not others? Through this book and our blogs, we are making an attempt to fill this gap and to hopefully show the positive impact this product can bring to an environment.

What this book covers

Chapter 1, vROps - Introduction, Architecture, and Availability, begins by taking you through one of the biggest changes in vROps 6.0 from its previous versions, the new clustered platform architecture. This chapter dives straight into the new common platform design and how the controller and analytics components have been modified to work with the new GemFire cluster. We also discuss how high availability has been implemented in vROps 6.0 and how this can affect your design.

Chapter 2, Installing and Migrating vROps 6.0, walks you through a step-by-step guide for migrating (upgrading) from vCOps 5.x to vROps 6.0. We also walkthrough the important initial vApp deployment steps and other important deployment considerations, such as designing vROps for scaling and how to add additional nodes.

Chapter 3, vRealize Operations Manager Badges, discusses in detail the critical concept of Operations Manager 6.0 badges and how they assist in effectively managing your vSphere and non-vSphere environments. We will discover the differences between badges in Operations Manager 5.x and 6.0. We dive into the details of how badges are calculated and tune them to best suit our environment.

Chapter 4, The Merged UI, explains in detail the major improvements in the vROps 6.0 User Interface and the merger of the old vSphere UI and Custom UI. This chapter provides a useful reference for all the major changes and provides a walkthrough for all the relevant components.

Chapter 5, Policies in vRealize Operations Manager 6.0, discusses the virtual topic of creating and modifying policies in vROps 6.0. We show what improvements have been made in vROps 6.0 and how policies can be used to make the smallest change to any object all the way up to an environment-wide change in a few clicks.

Chapter 6, Capacity Management Made Easy, dives into the detail around Operations Manager capacity management, including the major improvements made in version 6.0. We will also cover the capacity management policies in detail and understand how they need to be tuned for your environment to ensure that the recommendations are of the highest quality.

Chapter 7, Dashboard Design, discusses and shows what a custom dashboard is and more importantly, how to create one. This will give you the foundation to create and build custom dashboards that will suit any environment, application, or object being managed.

Chapter 8, Reporting and Views, covers the new vROps 6.0 features of views and reports and how they assist in easily proving any piece of information about your environment at any time. You will discover the major improvements that these features bring in to effectively manage your environment, as well as examples on how to create your own views and reports.

Chapter 9, Super Metrics, discusses the well-proven concept of super metrics and assists in defining the difference between metrics, objects, and attributes. After going through the various types of super metrics, we will walk through a step-by-step guide on how to create your own super metrics.

Chapter 10, Administering vROps 6.0, discusses the importance of how to properly administer vROps 6.0 and leverage role-based access controls (RBAC) to grant the right level of access to the right people. We will also cover how to share items such as dashboards and views for different users within your organization.

Chapter 11, Expanding vROps with Solutions, discusses how to get the most out of vROps 6.0 by expanding the product with solutions (previously known as adapters). We show how to install an additional solution, such as vRealize Hyperic. We will also show the interesting and useful concept of how to import your own metrics via the new REST API.

Chapter 12, Application Management in vROps 6.0, explains the power of applications and how data from different sources can be grouped together into a single application that allows simple navigation and troubleshooting.

Chapter 13, Alerting, Actions, and Recommendations, discusses the major improvements that have been made to alerting and recommendations, as well as the new concept of actions. We show how alerts, actions, and recommendations can be used to provide useful human readable alerts to the right people in real time.

Chapter 14, Just Messing Around, finishes off by showing another interesting way in which dashboards can be used to mix work and pleasure.

What you need for this book

To get the most out of this book, you should have a basic understanding of x86 virtualization, network, storage, VMware vSphere, and, of course, vRealize Operations Manager (or its previous version vCenter Operations Manager). Although vRealize Operations Manager 6.0 is no longer as vSphere-centric as its previous versions, most of the examples and step-by-step guides in this book are based on vSphere objects and concepts.

A useful way to build on the content of this book is to to follow some of the step-by-step guides and theory in your own vROps environment, be it either at work or in your own lab. For those without access to either, or wanting access to a structured practical lab component, we highly recommend checking out the VMware Hands on Labs (HOL) at labs.hol.vmware.com. The catalogs are updated often and always contain at least a few comprehensive labs on vROps with step-by-step online instructions.

Who this book is for

Mastering vRealize Operations Manager aims to help you gain a deep understanding of vROps and learn how to best apply the product to every day operations management use cases. This book aims to move beyond the standard product documentation and explains both why and how vROps should be deployed, configured, and used in your own environment.

Although this book is aimed at mastering vRealize Operations Manager 6.0, expert knowledge of vROps is not a requirement. The chapters in this book range in skill level and expertise, as well as in useful theory versus practical step-by-step content. As such, we expect that this book will be useful for the following people:

- System administrators responsible for the smooth day-to-day running of a virtualized enterprise IT environment
- Infrastructure architects and engineers responsible for designing and building solutions that improve the reliability and maintainability of virtualized environments
- Current customers who want to know how to get the most out of vROps, such as what the badges actually mean, and how capacity management policies should be configured for a typical production environment
- Anyone who is keen to know more about vRealize Operations Manager for specific reference look ups, from badges to capacity planning and the new API

Other resources available

Of course, there is just too much useful information about vROps to capture in a single tech book. For those wondering where further information can be found on how to use and benefit from vROps, there are a few other places to visit to get that extra or missing piece of information.

The first and most obvious source is the product documentation provided by VMware at `www.vmware.com/support/pubs/`. This documentation is especially useful on the subject of the deployment and initial configuration of vROps as well as how to integrate the product with other members of the vRealize suite.

While on the theme of installation and deployment, the vRealize Operations Manager Sizing Guidelines (VMware KB 2093783) includes up-to-date sizing and deployment considerations for various versions of vROps that get released. These knowledge bases also include a very useful sizing calculator that should be the first stop for any designer looking to deploy vROps in their environment.

Last, but certainly not the least, is the VMware Cloud Management for vROps official VMware blog site at `http://blogs.vmware.com/management/vrealize-operations`. The blogs here contain very useful tips and updates on vROps by the people who know it best.

Conventions

In this book, you will find a number of text styles that distinguish between different kinds of information. Here are some examples of these styles and an explanation of their meaning.

Code words in text, database table names, folder names, filenames, file extensions, pathnames, dummy URLs, user input, and Twitter handles are shown as follows: "The Admin UI is available on each node at `https://<NodeIP>/admin`."

A block of code is set as follows:

```
<?xml version="1.0" encoding="UTF-8" standalone="yes"?>
<AdapterKinds>
  <AdapterKind adapterKindKey="VMWARE">
    <ResourceKind resourceKindKey="ClusterComputeResource">
```

When we wish to draw your attention to a particular part of a code block, the relevant lines or items are set in bold:

```
<?xml version="1.0" encoding="UTF-8" standalone="yes"?>
<AdapterKinds>
  <AdapterKind adapterKindKey="VMWARE">
    <ResourceKind resourceKindKey="ClusterComputeResource">
```

Any command-line input or output is written as follows:

```
xsi                    : http://www.w3.org/2001/XMLSchema-instance
xs                     : http://www.w3.org/2001/XMLSchema
ops                    : http://webservice.vmware.com/vRealizeOpsMgr/1.0/
identifier             : 42a2f291-d4be-48c4-b60e-2a8aa3b9d3fa
```

New terms and **important words** are shown in bold. Words that you see on the screen, for example, in menus or dialog boxes, appear in the text like this: "This can be achieved by selecting the **Rebalance GemFire** option that is a far less disruptive process."

> Warnings or important notes appear in a box like this.

> Tips and tricks appear like this.

Reader feedback

Feedback from our readers is always welcome. Let us know what you think about this book—what you liked or disliked. Reader feedback is important for us as it helps us develop titles that you will really get the most out of.

To send us general feedback, simply e-mail feedback@packtpub.com, and mention the book's title in the subject of your message.

If there is a topic that you have expertise in and you are interested in either writing or contributing to a book, see our author guide at www.packtpub.com/authors.

Customer support

Now that you are the proud owner of a Packt book, we have a number of things to help you to get the most from your purchase.

Downloading the example code

You can download the example code files from your account at `http://www.packtpub.com` for all the Packt Publishing books you have purchased. If you purchased this book elsewhere, you can visit `http://www.packtpub.com/support` and register to have the files e-mailed directly to you.

Errata

Although we have taken every care to ensure the accuracy of our content, mistakes do happen. If you find a mistake in one of our books—maybe a mistake in the text or the code—we would be grateful if you could report this to us. By doing so, you can save other readers from frustration and help us improve subsequent versions of this book. If you find any errata, please report them by visiting `http://www.packtpub.com/submit-errata`, selecting your book, clicking on the **Errata Submission Form** link, and entering the details of your errata. Once your errata are verified, your submission will be accepted and the errata will be uploaded to our website or added to any list of existing errata under the Errata section of that title.

To view the previously submitted errata, go to `https://www.packtpub.com/books/content/support` and enter the name of the book in the search field. The required information will appear under the **Errata** section.

Piracy

Piracy of copyrighted material on the Internet is an ongoing problem across all media. At Packt, we take the protection of our copyright and licenses very seriously. If you come across any illegal copies of our works in any form on the Internet, please provide us with the location address or website name immediately so that we can pursue a remedy.

Please contact us at `copyright@packtpub.com` with a link to the suspected pirated material.

We appreciate your help in protecting our authors and our ability to bring you valuable content.

Questions

If you have a problem with any aspect of this book, you can contact us at `questions@packtpub.com`, and we will do our best to address the problem.

1

vROps – Introduction, Architecture, and Availability

vRealize Operations Manager (**vROps**) 6.0 is a tool from VMware that helps IT administrators monitor, troubleshoot, and manage the health and capacity of their virtual environment. vROps has been developed from the stage of being a single tool to being a suite of tools known as vRealize Operations. This suite includes vCenter Infrastructure Navigator (VIN), vRealize Configuration Manager (vCM), vRealize Log Insight, and vRealize Hyperic.

Due to its popularity and the powerful analytics engine that vROps uses, many hardware vendors supply adapters (now known as solutions) that allow IT administrators to extend monitoring, troubleshooting, and capacity planning to non-vSphere systems including storage, networking, applications, and even physical devices. These solutions will be covered later in this book.

In this chapter, we will learn what's new with vROps 6.0; specifically with respect to its architecture components and platform availability.

One of the most impressive changes with vRealize Operations Manager 6.0 is the major internal architectural change of components, which has helped to produce a solution that supports both a scaled-out and high-availability deployment model. In this chapter, we will describe the new platform components and the details of the new deployment architecture. We will also cover the different roles of a vROps node (a node referring to a VM instance of vRealize Operations Manager 6.0) and simplify the design decisions needed around the complicated topics of multi-node deployment and **high availability** (**HA**).

A new, common platform design

In vRealize Operations Manager 6.0, a new platform design was required to meet some of the required goals that VMware envisaged for the product. These included:

- The ability to treat all solutions equally and to be able to offer management of performance, capacity, configuration, and compliance of both VMware and third-party solutions
- The ability to provide a single platform that can scale up to tens of thousands of objects and millions of metrics by scaling out with little reconfiguration or redesign required
- The ability to support a monitoring solution that can be highly available and to support the loss of a node without impacting the ability to store or query information

To meet these goals, **vCenter Operations Manager 5.x** (**vCOps**) went through a major architectural overhaul to provide a common platform that uses the same components no matter what deployment architecture is chosen. These changes are shown in the following figure:

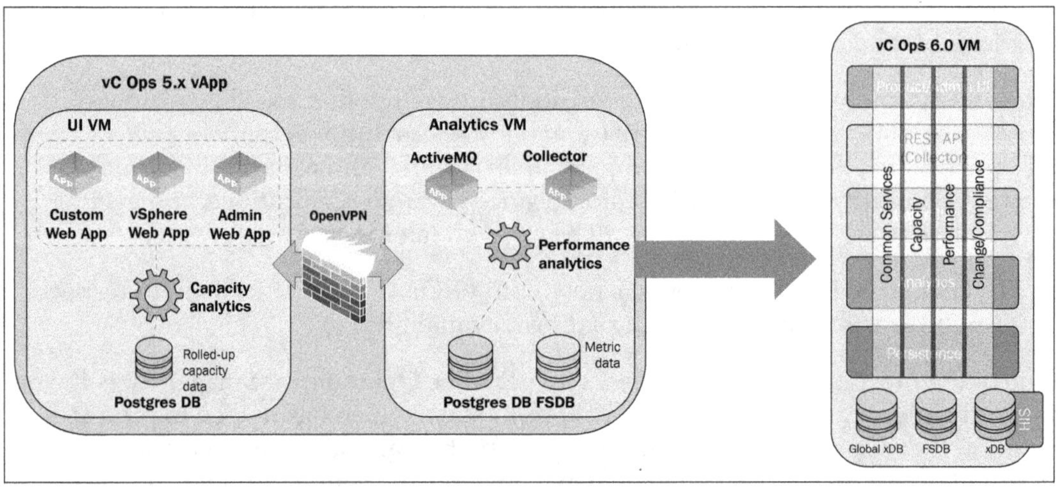

When comparing the deployment architecture of vROps 6.0 with vCOps 5.x, you will notice that the footprint has changed dramatically. Listed in the following table are some of the major differences in the deployment of vRealize Operations Manager 6.0 compared to vRealize Operations Manager 5.x:

Deployment considerations	**vCenter Operations Manager 5.x**	**vRealize Operations Manager 6.0**
vApp deployment	vApp consists of two VMs: • The User Interface VM • The Analytics VM There is no supported way to add additional VMs to vApp and therefore no way to scale out.	This deploys a single **virtual appliance** (**VA**), that is, the entire solution is provided in each VA. As many as up to 8 VAs can be deployed with this type of deployment.
Scaling	This deployment could only be scaled up to a certain extent. If it is scaled beyond this, separate instances are needed to be deployed, which do not share the UI or data.	This deployment is built on the GemFire federated cluster that supports sharing of data and the UI. Data resiliency is done through GemFire partitioning.
Remote collector	Remote collectors are supported in vCOps 5.x, but with the installable version only. These remote collectors require a Windows or Linux base OS.	The same VA is used for the remote collector simply by specifying the role during the configuration.
Installable/ standalone option	It is required that customers own MSSQL or Oracle database. No capacity planning or vSphere UI is provided with this type of deployment.	This deployment leverages built-in databases. It uses the same code base as used in the VA.

Many of these major differences will be discussed in detail in later chapters. However, the ability to support new scaled out and highly available architectures will require an administrator to consider which model is right for their environment before a vRealize Operations Manager 6.0 migration or rollout begins.

The vRealize Operations Manager component architecture

With a new common platform design comes a completely new architecture. As mentioned in the previous table, this architecture is common across all deployed nodes as well as the vApp and other installable versions. The following diagram shows the five major components of the Operations Manager architecture:

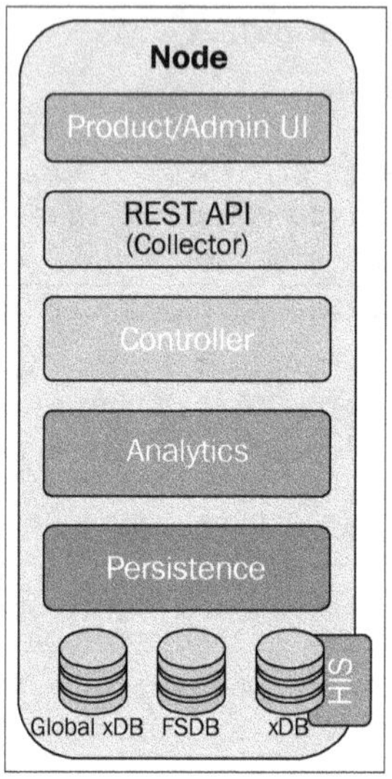

The five major components of the Operations Manager architecture depicted in the preceding figure are:

- The user interface
- Collector and the REST API
- Controller
- Analytics
- Persistence

The user interface

In vROps 6.0, the UI is broken into two components—the Product UI and the Admin UI. Unlike the vCOps 5.x vApp, the vROps 6.0 Product UI is present on all nodes with the exception of nodes that are deployed as remote collectors. Remote collectors will be discussed in more detail in the next section.

The Admin UI is a web application hosted by Pivotal tc Server(A Java application Apache web server) and is responsible for making HTTP REST calls to the Admin API for node administration tasks. The **Cluster and Slice Administrator** (**CaSA**) is responsible for cluster administrative actions such as:

- Enabling/disabling the Operations Manager cluster
- Enabling/disabling cluster nodes
- Performing software updates
- Browsing logfiles

The Admin UI is purposely designed to be separate from the Product UI and always be available for administration and troubleshooting tasks. A small database caches data from the Product UI that provides the last known state information to the Admin UI in the event that the Product UI and analytics are unavailable.

> The Admin UI is available on each node at https://<NodeIP>/admin.

The Product UI is the main Operations Manager graphical user interface. Like the Admin UI, the Product UI is based on Pivotal tc Server and can make HTTP REST calls to the CaSA for administrative tasks. However, the primary purpose of the Product UI is to make GemFire calls to the Controller API to access data and create views, such as dashboards and reports. GemFire is part of the major underlying architectural change of vROps 6.0, which is discussed in more detail later in this chapter.

As shown in the following figure, the Product UI is simply accessed via HTTPS on TCP port 443. Apache then provides a reverse proxy to the Product UI running in Pivotal tc Server using the Apache AJP protocol.

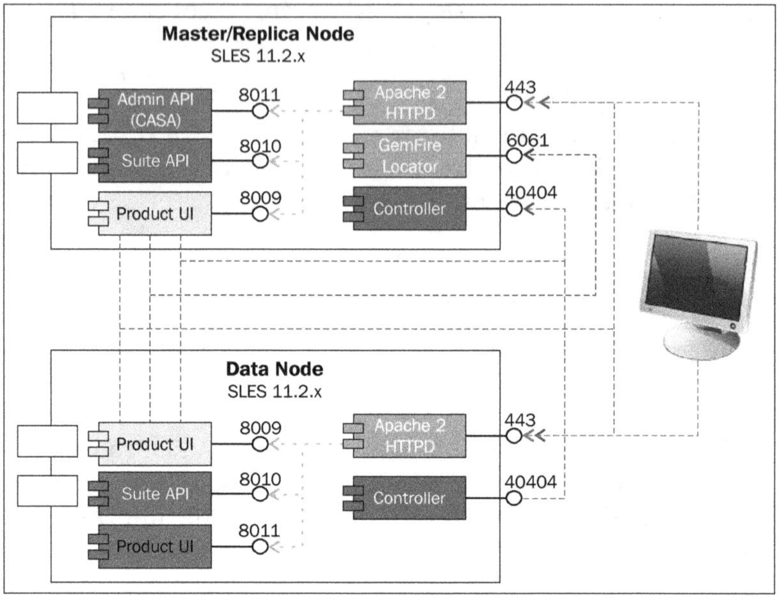

Collector

The collector's role has not differed much from that in vCOps 5.x. The collector is responsible for processing data from solution adapter instances. As shown in the following figure, the collector uses adapters to collect data from various sources and then contacts the GemFire locator for connection information of one or more controller cache servers. The collector service then connects to one or more Controller API GemFire cache servers and sends the collected data.

It is important to note that although an instance of an adapter can only be run on one node at a time, this does not imply that the collected data is being sent to the controller on that node. This will be discussed in more detail later under the *Multi-node deployment and high availability* section.

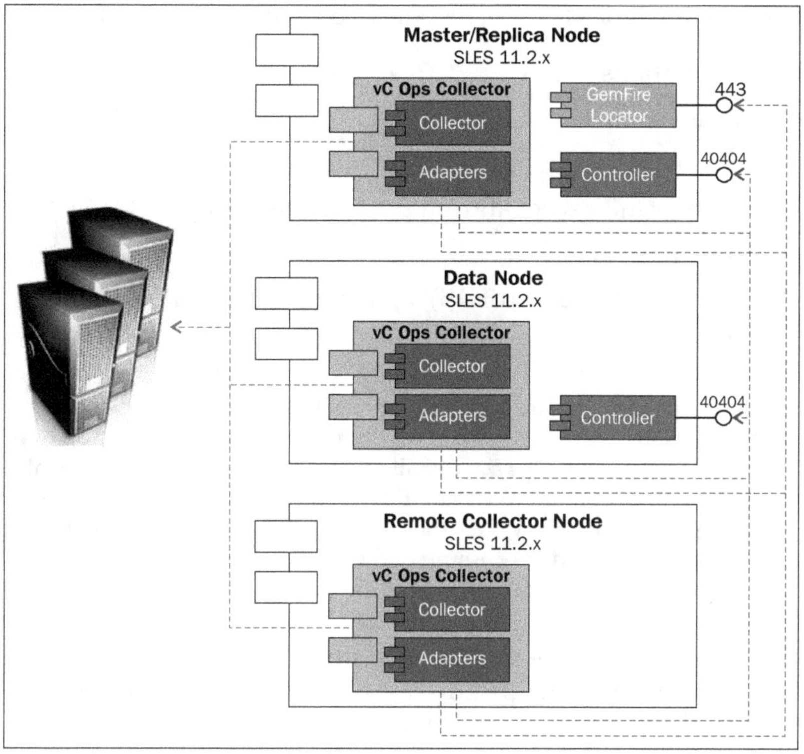

Controller

The controller manages the storage and retrieval of the inventory of the objects within the system. The queries are performed by leveraging the GemFire MapReduce function that allows you to perform selective querying. This allows efficient data querying as data queries are only performed on selective nodes rather than all nodes.

We will go in detail to know how the controller interacts with the analytics and persistence stack a little later as well as its role in creating new resources, feeding data in, and extracting views.

Analytics

Analytics is at the heart of vROps as it is essentially the runtime layer for data analysis. The role of the analytics process is to track the individual states of every metric and then use various forms of correlation to determine whether there are problems.

At a high level, the analytics layer is responsible for the following tasks:

- Metric calculations
- Dynamic thresholds
- Alerts and alarms
- Metric storage and retrieval from the Persistence layer
- Root cause analysis
- **Historic Inventory Server** (**HIS**) version metadata calculations and relationship data

> One important difference between vROps 6.0 and vCOps 5.x is that analytics tasks are now run on every node (with the exception of remote collectors). The vCOps 5.x Installable provides an option of installing separate multiple remote analytics processors for **dynamic threshold** (**DT**) processing. However, these remote DT processors only support dynamic threshold processing and do not include other analytics functions.

Although its primary tasks have not changed much from vCOps 5.x, the analytics component has undergone a significant upgrade under the hood to work with the new GemFire-based cache and the Controller and Persistence layers.

Persistence

The Persistence layer, as its name implies, is the layer where the data is persisted to a disk. The layer primarily consists of a series of databases that replace the existing vCOps 5.x **filesystem database** (**FSDB**) and PostgreSQL combination.

Understanding the persistence layer is an important aspect of vROps 6.0, as this layer has a strong relationship with the data and service availability of the solution. vROps 6.0 has four primary database services built on the EMC Documentum xDB (an XML database) and the original FSDB. These services include:

Common name	Role	DB type	Sharded	Location
Global xDB	Global data	Documentum xDB	No	`/storage/vcops/xdb`
Alarms xDB	Alerts and Alarms data	Documentum xDB	Yes	`/storage/vcops/alarmxdb`

Common name	Role	DB type	Sharded	Location
HIS xDB	Historical Inventory Service data	Documentum xDB	Yes	`/storage/vcops/hisxdb`
FSDB	Filesystem Database metric data	FSDB	Yes	`/storage/db/vcops/data`
CaSA DB	Cluster and Slice Administrator data	HSQLDB (HyperSQL database)	N/A	`/storage/db/casa/webapp/hsqldb`

Sharding is the term that GemFire uses to describe the process of distributing data across multiple systems to ensure that computational, storage, and network loads are evenly distributed across the cluster.

We will discuss persistence in more detail, including the concept of sharding, a little later under the *Multi-node deployment and high availability* section in this chapter.

Global xDB

Global xDB contains all of the data that, for the release of vROps, can not be sharded. The majority of this data is user configuration data that includes:

- User created dashboards and reports
- Policy settings and alert rules
- Super metric formulas (not super metric data, as this is sharded in the FSDB)
- Resource control objects (used during resource discovery)

As Global xDB is used for data that cannot be sharded, it is solely located on the master node (and master replica if high availability is enabled). More on this topic will be discussed under the *Multi-node deployment and high availability* section.

Alarms xDB

Alerts and Alarms xDB is a sharded xDB database that contains information on DT breaches. This information then gets converted into vROps alarms based on active policies.

HIS xDB

HIS xDB is a sharded xDB database that holds historical information on all resource properties and parent/child relationships. HIS is used to change data back to the analytics layer based on the incoming metric data that is then used for DT calculations and symptom/alarm generation.

FSDB

The role of the Filesystem Database is not differed much from vCOps 5.x. The FSDB contains all raw time series metrics for the discovered resources.

> The FSDB metric data, HIS object, and Alarms data for a particular resource share the same GemFire shard key. This ensures that the multiple components that make up the persistence of a given resource are always located on the same node.

vRealize Operations Manager node types

vROps 6.0 contains a common node architecture. Before a node can be added to an existing cluster, a role must be selected. Although deployment will be discussed in detail in the next chapter, from a design perspective, it is important to understand the different roles and which deployment model best fits your own environment.

The master / master replica node

The master or master replica node is critical to the availability of the Operations Manager cluster. It contains all vROps 6.0 services, including UI, Controller, Analytics, Collector, and Persistence, as well as the critical services that cannot be replicated across all cluster nodes. These include:

- Global xDB
- An NTP server
- The GemFire locator

As previously discussed, Global xDB contains all of the data that we are unable to shard across the cluster. This data is critical to the successful operation of the cluster and is only located on the master node. If HA is enabled, this DB is replicated to the master replica; however, the DB is only available as read/write on the master node.

During a failure event of the master node, the master replica DB is promoted to a full read/write master. Although the process of the replica DB's promotion can be done online, the migration of the master role during a failover does require an automated restart of the cluster. As a result, even though it is an automated process, the failure of the master node will result in a temporary outage of the Operations Manager cluster until all nodes have been restarted against the new master.

The master also has the responsibility of running both an NTP server and client. On initial configuration of the first vROps node, you are prompted to add an external NTP source for time synchronization. The master node then keeps time of this source and runs its own NTP server for all data and collector nodes to sync from. This ensures that all the nodes have the correct time and only the master/master replica requires access to the external time source.

The final component that is unique to the master role is the GemFire locator. The GemFire locator is a process that tells the starting or connecting data nodes where the currently running cluster members are located. This process also provides load balancing of queries that are passed to data nodes that then become data coordinators for that particular query. The structure of the master node is shown in the following figure:

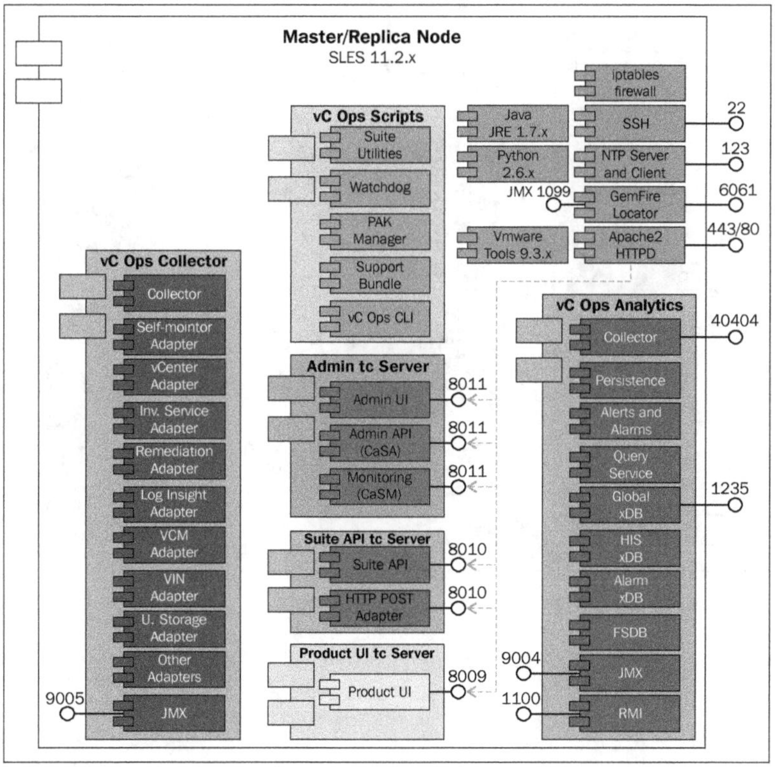

The data node

The data node is the standard vROps 6.0 node type and is the default when adding a new node into an existing cluster. It provides the core functionality of collecting and processing data and data queries as well as extending the vROps cluster by being a member of the GemFire Federation, which in turn provides the horizontal scaling of the platform.

As shown in the following diagram, a data node is almost identical to a master/master replica node with the exception of Global xDB, the NTP server, and GemFire locator:

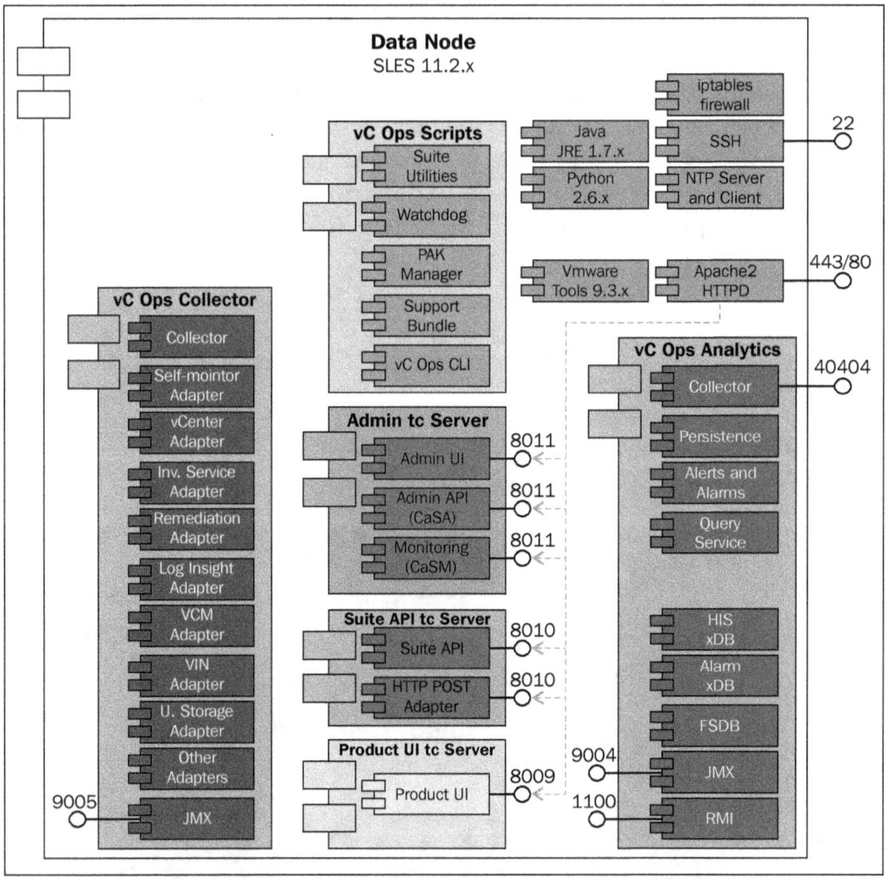

The remote collector node

The remote collector role is a continuation of the vCOps 5.x Installable concept, which includes using a standalone collector for remote sites or secure enclaves. Remote collectors do not process data themselves; instead, they simply forward metric data to data nodes for analytics processing.

Remote collector nodes do not run several of the core vROps components including:

- The Product UI
- Controller
- Analytics
- Persistence

As a result of not running these components, remote collectors are not members of the GemFire Federation, and although they do not add resources to the cluster, they themselves require far fewer resources to run, which is ideal in smaller remote office locations.

> An important point to note is that the adapter instances will fail over other data nodes when the hosting node fails even if HA is not enabled. An exception to this is the remote collectors, as adapter instances registered to remote collectors will not automatically fail over.

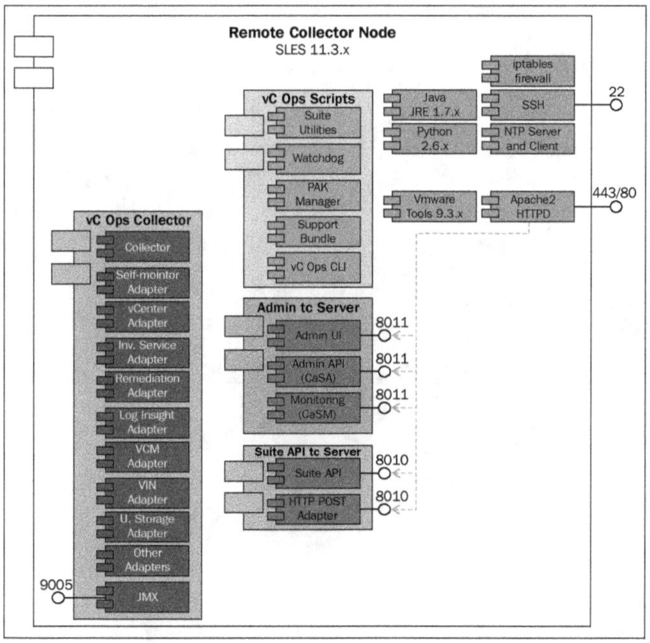

Multi-node deployment and high availability

So far, we have focused on the new architecture and components of vROps 6.0 as well as mentioning the major architectural changes that the GemFire-based controller and the analytics and persistence layers have introduced. Now, before we close this chapter, we will dive down a little deeper into how data is handled in a multi-node deployment and finally, how high availability works in vROps 6.0, and which design decisions revolve around a successful deployment.

The Operations Manager's migration to GemFire

At the core of the vROps 6.0 architecture is the powerful GemFire in-memory clustering and distributed cache. GemFire provides the internal transport bus (replacing Apache ActiveMQ in vCOps 5.x) as well as the ability to balance CPU and memory consumption across all nodes through compute pooling, memory sharing, and data partitioning. With this change, it is better to think of the Controller, Analytics, and Persistence layers as components that span nodes rather than individual components on individual nodes.

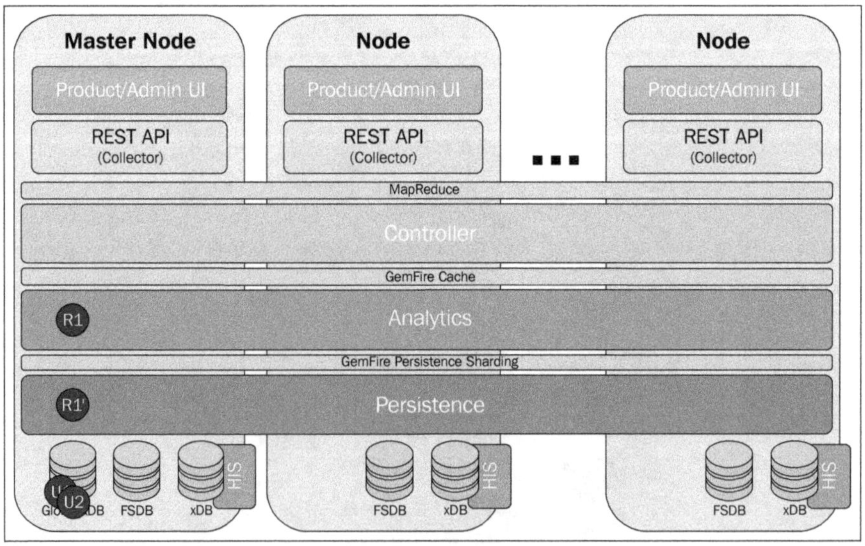

> During deployment, ensure that all your vROps 6.0 nodes are configured with the same amount of vCPUs and memory. This is because from a load balancing point of view, the Operations Manager expects all nodes to have the same amount of resources as part of the controller's round-robin load balancing.

The migration to GemFire is probably the single largest underlying architectural change from vCOps 5.x, and the result of moving to a distributed in-memory database has made many of the new vROps 6.0 features possible including:

- **Elasticity and scaling**: Nodes can be added on demand, allowing vROps to scale as required. This allows a single Operations Manager instance to scale up to 8 nodes and up to 64,000 objects.
- **Reliability**: When GemFire's high availability is enabled, a backup copy of all the data is stored in both the analytics GemFire cache and the persistence layer.
- **Availability**: Even if GemFire's high availability mode is disabled, in the event of a failure, other nodes take over the failed services and the load of the failed node (assuming that the failure was not in the master node).
- **Data partitioning**: Operations Manager leverages GemFire Data partitioning to distribute data across nodes in units called buckets. A partition region will contain multiple buckets that are configured during a startup or that are migrated during a rebalance operation. Data partitioning allows the use of the GemFire MapReduce function. This function is a "data aware query," which supports parallel data querying on a subset of the nodes. The result of this is then returned to the coordinator node for final processing.

GemFire sharding

When we described the Persistence layer earlier, we listed the new components related to persistence in vROps 6.0 and which components were sharded and which were not. Now, it's time to discuss what sharding actually is.

GemFire sharding is the process of splitting data across multiple GemFire nodes for placement in various partitioned buckets. It is this concept in conjunction with the controller and locator service that balances the incoming resources and metrics across multiple nodes in the Operations Manager cluster. It is important to note that data is sharded per resource and not per adapter instance. For example, this allows the load balancing of incoming and outgoing data even if only one adapter instance is configured. From a design perspective, a single Operations Manager cluster could then manage a maximum configuration vCenter with up to 10,000 VMs by distributing the incoming metrics across multiple data nodes.

The Operations Manager data is sharded in both the analytics and persistence layers, which is referred to as GemFire cache sharding and GemFire persistence sharding, respectively.

Just because the data is held in the GemFire cache on one node *does not necessarily result in the data shard persisting on the same node*. In fact, as both layers are balanced independently, the chances of both the cache shard and persistence shard existing on the same node is *1/N*, where *N* is the number of nodes.

Adding, removing, and balancing nodes

One of the biggest advantages of the GemFire-based cluster is the elasticity of adding nodes to the cluster as the number of resources and metrics grow in your environment. This allows administrators to add or remove nodes if the size of their environment changes unexpectedly, for example, a merger with another IT department or catering for seasonal workloads that only exist for a small period of the year.

Although adding nodes to an existing cluster is something that can be done at any time, there is a slight cost incurred when doing so. As just mentioned, when adding new nodes, it is important that they are sized the same as the existing cluster nodes, which will ensure, during a rebalance operation, that the load is distributed equally between the cluster nodes.

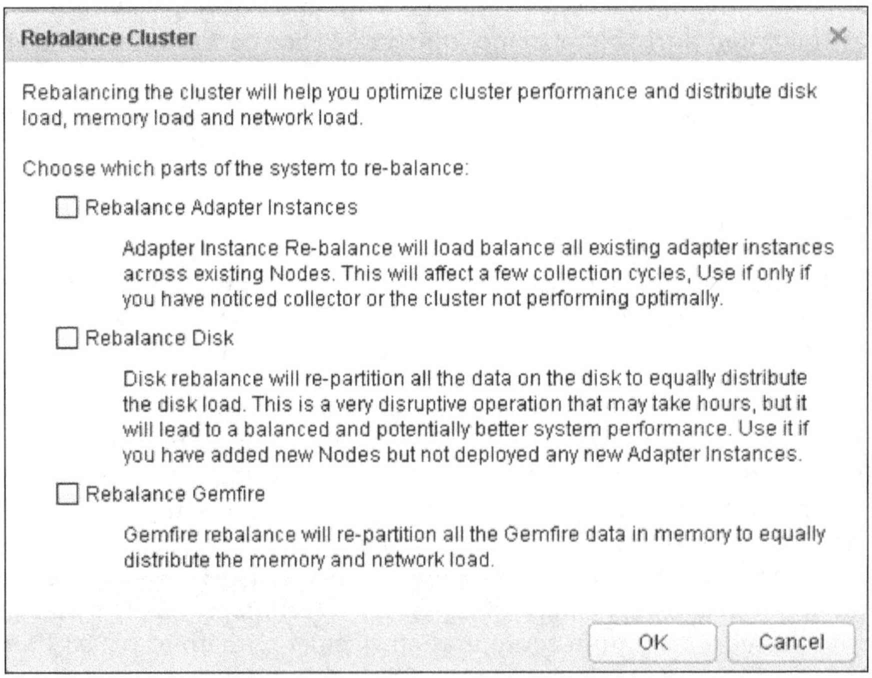

When adding new nodes to the cluster, sometime after initial deployment, it is recommended that the **Rebalance Disk** option be selected under cluster management. As seen in the preceding screenshot, the warning advises that **This is a very disruptive operation that may take hours...**, and as such, it is recommended that this be a planned maintenance activity. The amount of time this operation will take will vary depending on the size of the existing cluster and the amount of data in the FSDB. As you can probably imagine, if you are adding an 8th node to an existing 7-node cluster with tens of thousands of resources, there could potentially be several TB of data that needs to be resharded over the entire cluster. It is also strongly recommended that when adding new nodes, the disk capacity and performance should match with that of the existing nodes, as the Rebalance Disk operation assumes this is the case.

This activity is not required to achieve the compute and network load balancing benefits of the new node. This can be achieved by selecting the **Rebalance GemFire** option that is a far less disruptive process. As per the description, this process repartitions the JVM buckets that balance the memory across all active nodes in the GemFire Federation. With the GemFire cache balanced across all the nodes, the compute and network demand should be roughly equal across all the nodes in the cluster.

Although this allows early benefit from adding a new node into an existing cluster, unless a large amount of new resources are discovered by the system shortly afterwards the majority of disk I/O is persisted, sharded data will occur on other nodes.

Apart from adding nodes, Operations Manager also allows the removal of a node at any time as long as it has been taken offline first. This can be valuable if a cluster was originally well oversized for requirement, and it considered a waste of physical computational resource. However, this task should not be taken lightly though, as the removal of a data node without enabling high availability will result in the loss of all metrics on that node. As such, it is recommended that you should generally avoid removing nodes from the cluster.

> If the permanent removal of a data node is necessary, ensure that high availability is first enabled to prevent data loss.

High availability in vRealize Operations Manager 6.0

One of the most impressive new features that is available as part of vROps 6.0 is the ability to configure the cluster in a HA mode to prevent against data loss. Enabling HA makes two major changes to the Operations Manager cluster:

- The primary effect of HA is that all the sharded data is duplicated by the controller layer to a primary and backup copy in both the GemFire cache and GemFire persistence layers.
- The secondary effect is that the master replica is created on a chosen data node for xDB replication of Global xDB. This node is then taken over by the role of the master node in the event that the original master fails.

Operations Manager 6.0 HA design considerations

Although HA is an impressive new feature in vROps 6.0, from a design perspective, this is not a feature that should simply be enabled without proper consideration.

As mentioned earlier, both cache and persistence data is sharded per resource, not per metric or adapter. As such, when a data node is unavailable, not only can metrics not be viewed or used for analytics, but also new metrics for resources that are on effected nodes are discarded assuming that the adapter collector is operational or failed over. This fact alone would attract administrators to simply enable HA by default and it is easy to do so under vROps 6.0.

Although HA is very easy to enable, you must ensure that your cluster is sized appropriately to handle the increased load. As HA duplicates all data stored in both the GemFire cache and persistence layers, it essentially doubles the load on the system.

> When designing your Operations Manager cluster, as a general rule, you will need to double the number of nodes if you are planning to enable HA. Detailed information on scaling vROps as well as the sizing calculator can be found in KB 2093783: *vRealize Operations Manager Sizing Guidelines*.

It is also important to consider that Operations Manager should not be deployed in a vSphere cluster where the number of vROps nodes is greater than the underlying vSphere cluster hosts. This is because there is little point enabling HA in Operations Manager if more than one node is residing on the same vSphere host at the same time.

> After deploying all your vROps nodes and enabling HA, ensure that a DRS affinity rule is created to keep all nodes on separate vSphere hosts under normal operation. This can be achieved with a DRS "separate virtual machine" or a "Virtual Machines to Hosts" affinity rule.

How does HA and data duplication work?

As we just said, HA duplicates all incoming resource data so that two copies exist instead of one in both the GemFire cache and persistence layer. This is done by creating a secondary copy of each piece of data that is used in queries if the node hosting a primary copy is unavailable.

It is important to note that HA is simply creating a secondary copy of each piece of data, and as such, only one node failure can be sustained at a time (*N-1*) without data loss regardless of the cluster size. If a node is down, a new secondary shard of the data is not created unless the original node is removed from the cluster permanently.

When a failed node becomes available again, a node is placed into the recovery mode. During this time, data is synchronized with the other cluster members and when the synchronization is complete, the node is returned to the active status.

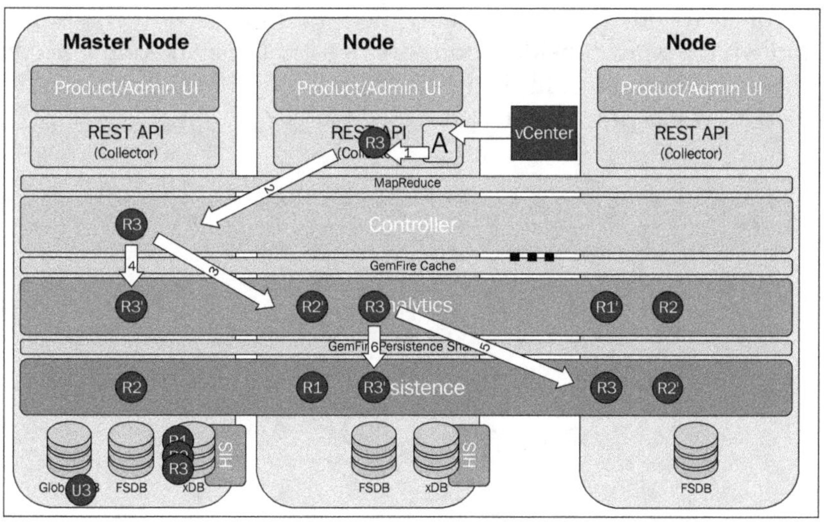

Let's run through this process using the preceding figure for an example of how the incoming data or the creation of a new object is handled in an HA configuration. In the preceding figure, **R3** represents our new resource and **R3'** represents the secondary copy:

1. A running adapter instance receives data from vCenter as it is required to create a new resource for the new object, and a discovery task is created.
2. The discovery task is passed to the cluster. This task could be passed to any one node in the cluster and once it is assigned, that node is responsible for completing the task.
3. A new analytics item is created for the new object in the GemFire cache on any node in the cluster.
4. A secondary copy of the data is created on a different node to protect against failure.
5. The system then saves the data to the persistence layer. The object is created in the inventory (HIS) and its statistics are stored in the FSDB.
6. A secondary copy of the saved (GemFire persistence sharding) HIS and FSDB data is stored on a different node to protect against data loss.

Summary

In this chapter, we discussed the new common platform architecture design and how Operations Manager 6.0 differs from Operations Manager 5.x. We also covered the major components that make up the Operations Manager 6.0 platform and the functions that each of the component layers provide. We then moved on to the various roles of each node type, and finally, how multi-node and HA deployment functions and what design considerations are needed to be taken into account when designing these environments. In the next chapter, we will cover how to deploy vROps 6.0 based on this new architecture.

2

Installing and Migrating vROps 6.0

In the previous chapter, we learned all about what vROps 6.0 is and what makes it tick on the inside. Now, it's time to move on to how to install, or better yet, migrate existing vCOps 5.8.x environments to vROps 6.0.

With vRealize Operations Manager 6.0 there are three different methods to install; this can be done using Linux installable, Windows installable, or a VMware appliance. In this chapter, we will step through the deployment using the appliance.

> There is no functional difference between all these installation types, which was not the case in the previous versions of Operations Manager. Previously, the installable version, for example, supported remote collectors, but did not contain a vSphere UI. Under vROps 6.0, the installation method makes no difference to what features are available for use.

In this chapter, we will guide you through the process of architecting and deploying vROps 6.0. This will include the following topics:

- Installation and migration
- Fresh installation
- Adding additional nodes
- Scaling and high availability

Installation and migration

You may have noticed the term migration is used and not the word upgrade. This is because migration is exactly what is required; due to vROps 6.0 being such a major architectural change, there is no upgrade in place from the previous versions. This is not seen as a significant drawback, however, as the migration process is very simple and gives you the ability to run both vROps 6.0 and vCOps 5.8.x side by side until you feel like decommissioning the previous vCOps 5.8.x servers.

However, this restriction does have its advantages; the biggest advantage being that it will allow administrators time to get used to the new vROps architecture including the look and feel of the new UI, without the worry of not being able to use the older version if an issue arises.

> Running these two instances of vROps side by side is completely up to your discretion. Keep in mind that if a fresh instance of vROps 6.0 is deployed without migrating data, it will take four weeks for dynamic threshold (normal behavior) to be calculated again.

Migration overview

We will just take a quick look at how the migration works under the hood. First up, the vROps 6.0 installation will remotely deliver a ZIP file that contains the migration files on the existing 5.8.x vCOps servers, as shown in the following figure:

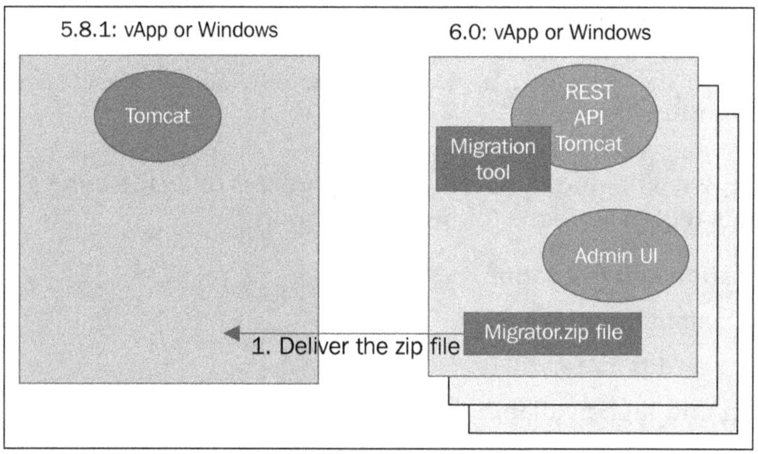

Then, the python installation script is run, which sets up an agent that is required to migrate all of the existing data and settings. This is shown in the following figure:

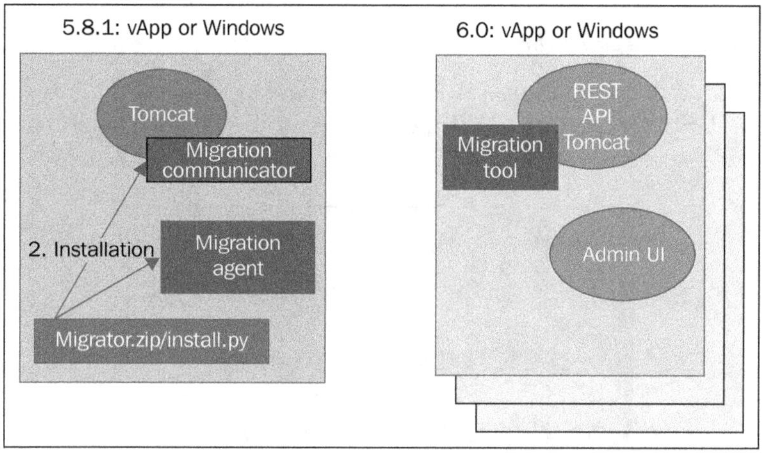

Once the migration agent has been installed and initiated by vROps 6.0, installation will commence with the data transfer, as shown in the following figure:

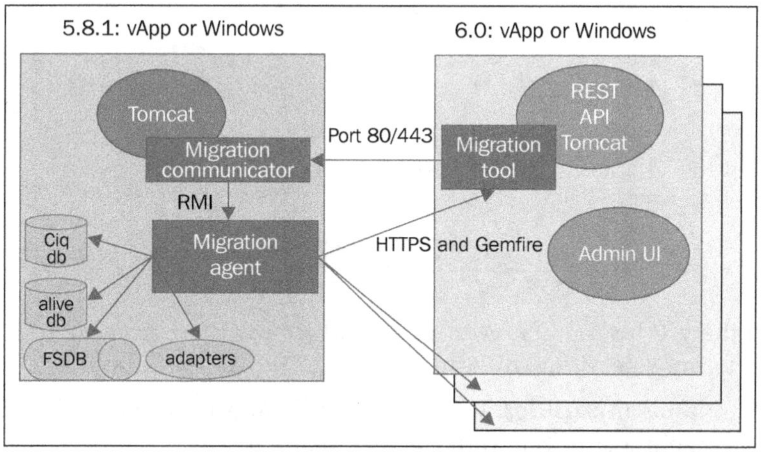

Deploying the vROps 6.0 virtual appliance

Deploying the vROps 6.0 virtual appliance is very similar to any standard OVF/OVA deployment on vSphere. First, download the latest OVA appliance from VMware. Then, deploy it into the environment using the **Deploy OVF Template** wizard.

This can be done either through the *thick* VI client or the vSphere Web Client. For this deployment, the vSphere Web Client will be used as it is the preferred client since vSphere 5.1. Perform the following steps to deploy a vROps 6.0 virtual appliance:

1. Browse to `https://<vCenter Web Client FQDN>:9443`.
2. If you have deployed any OVF or OVA package before, this process is no different. Select **Deploy OVA Template** on the cluster, as shown in the following screenshot:

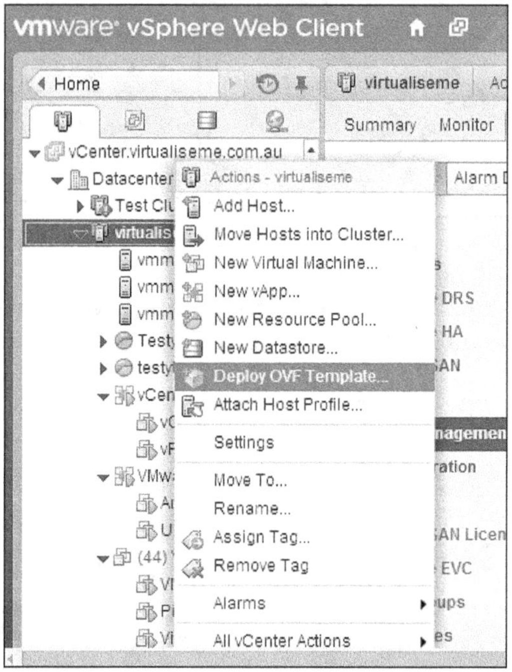

3. Select the vROps 6.0 OVA template and follow the bouncing ball through the different selections. In here we can configure the following:
   - **Name and folder**: In this section, configure the name of the virtual machine and the folder it will reside in.
   - **Configuration**: In this section, configure the Operations Manager 6.0 size. This is where you can select an **Extra Small**, **Small**, **Medium**, or **Large** configuration (as shown in the following screenshot). In our example, we will perform a small deployment that is 4 vCPU and 16 GB RAM.
   - **Storage**: In this section, we find the datastore where the virtual machine will be placed and which disk format it will be placed in (thick or thin).

- ◦ **Networks**: In this section, we configure which port group the virtual machine network card will be assigned.
- ◦ **Customization**: This is where we configure the time zone and networking details.

The following screenshot shows the deployment size of the node. We will discuss more about node sizing toward the end of this chapter.

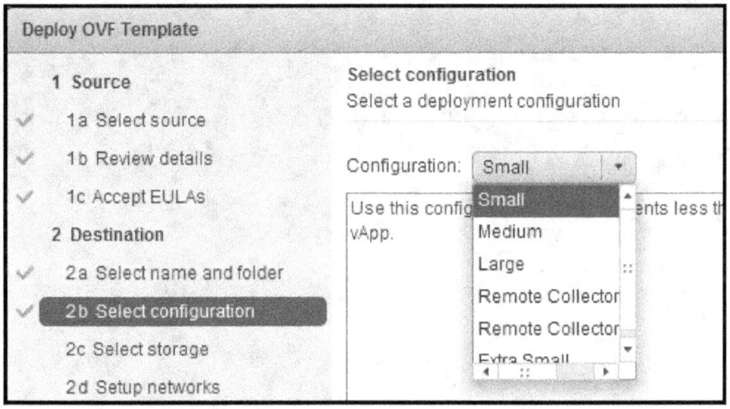

4. Enter all the appropriate networking information as shown in the following screenshot:

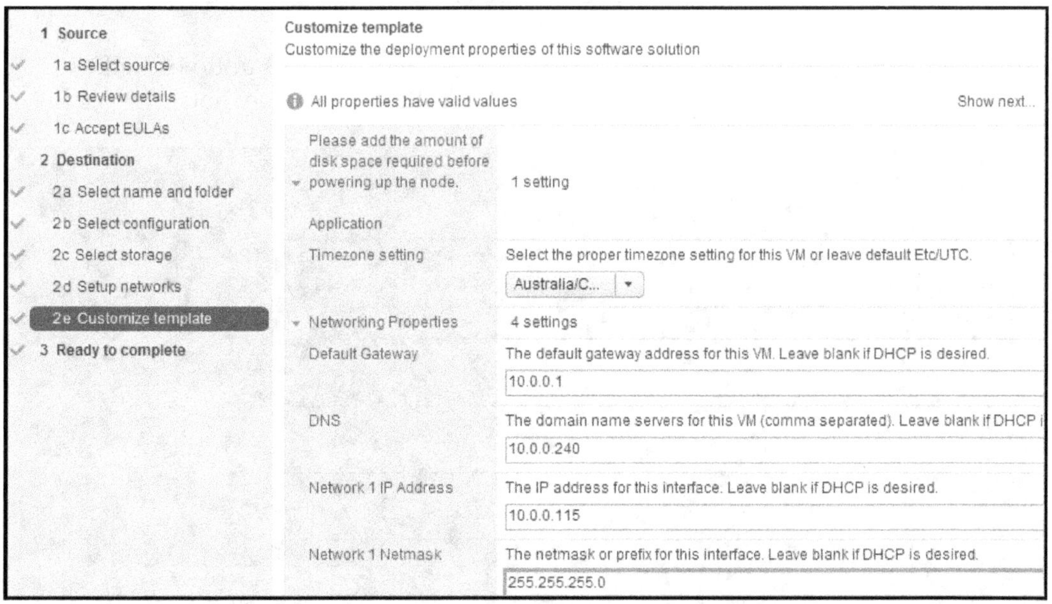

5. Once all the correct information is entered, click on **Finish** and the OVA template will now deploy the first vROps 6.0 node.
6. When the node has been deployed, ensure that it has been powered on. Once the virtual machine has booted up the splash screen, it indicates that you are ready to begin configuring the vROps cluster.

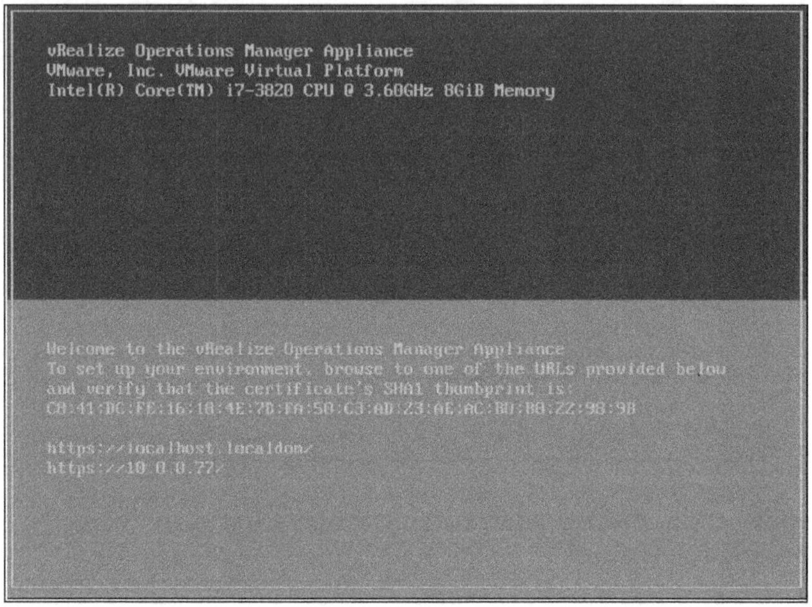

7. As per this example, browse to `https://<ip or fqdn>` and you will be presented with a screen similar to the following screenshot:

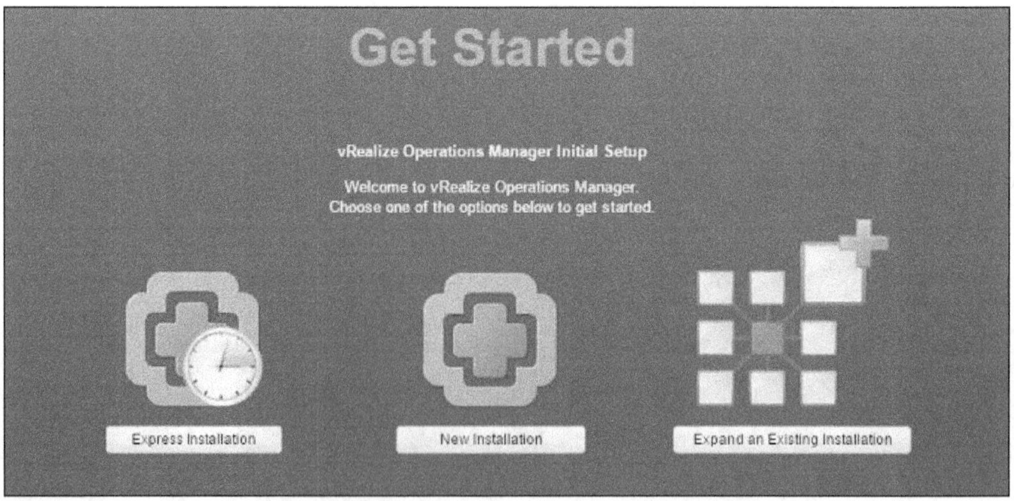

Configuring a new vROps instance

Configuring a new vROps instance is straightforward as it contains the following options:

- **Express Installation**: Just as it sounds, it's an express configuration and only requires a password to be entered. The IP address will be the DHCP assigned and the name of the node will be automatically generated.
- **New Installation**: This option follows a standard installation (we will use this in our example)
- **Expand an Existing Installation**: This adds another vROps 6.0 node to an existing cluster instance.

To configure a new vROps instance, perform the following steps:

1. Since this is the first node in our vROps cluster instance, we will select the **New Installation** option. As soon as you click on **New Installation**, you will be presented with the initial setup wizard.
2. The first section of the wizard is the getting started page, which will show a workflow image of the process of setting up vROps. Click on **Next** to move on to setting the administrator's password.
3. The next section is **Set Administrator Password**. Enter the password that agrees with the minimum requirements listed on the page. Once entered, click on **Next** to move on.
4. The third section on the list is **Choose Certificate**. The certificate applied must be in PEM format and requires the entire chain of certificates, as shown in the following example:

```
-----BEGIN RSA PRIVATE KEY-----
(Your Primary SSL certificate: PrivateKey.key)
—END RSA PRIVATE KEY-----
-----BEGIN CERTIFICATE-----
(Your Primary SSL certificate: Server.crt)
-----END CERTIFICATE-----
-----BEGIN CERTIFICATE-----
(Your Intermediate certificate: Intermediate.crt)
-----END CERTIFICATE-----
-----BEGIN CERTIFICATE-----
(Your Root certificate: TrustedRoot.crt)
-----END CERTIFICATE-----
```

When using certificates, there is a small catch. A certificate is only added to the first node of the cluster. When the cluster is expanded by adding a node, the additional nodes take on the same certificate. This means that the certificate should be planned out with additional SAN names to include future nodes. This however is not a hard requirement if your deployment of vROps is sitting behind a load balancer, which we will cover towards the end of the chapter.

If self-signed certificates are used, the first node becomes the CA for the vROps cluster and will issue certificates to any future nodes.

As this is simply a demonstration environment, self-signed certificates will be used as shown in the following screenshot. It is recommended that all production environments use a certificate from a trusted authority.

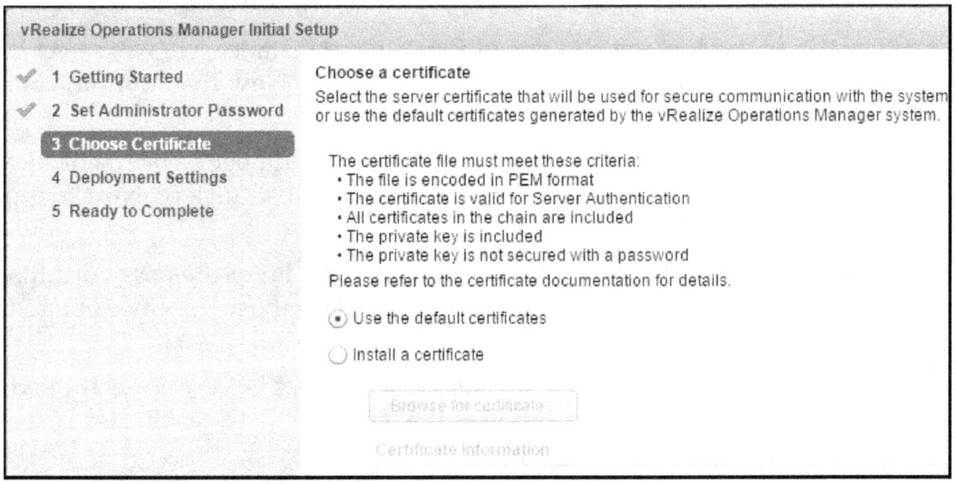

5. The fourth section is **Deployment Settings**. In this section, enter the master node name and enter an NTP server. Even though the first node of a vROps 6.0 cluster is always the master node initially, there is no guarantee it will remain so. This would be the case if a vROps 6.0 cluster was deployed and high availability (HA) was enabled, then at a later time, the first node would fail. As the master is a role that can move between two servers (the master and master replica), it is recommended that you use a name that is relatively generic such as vrops-node1, vrops-node2, and so on.

   The NTP server will only be added if the vROps 6.0 server is able to connect to the service. The master node will become an NTP server itself for other data nodes in the cluster.

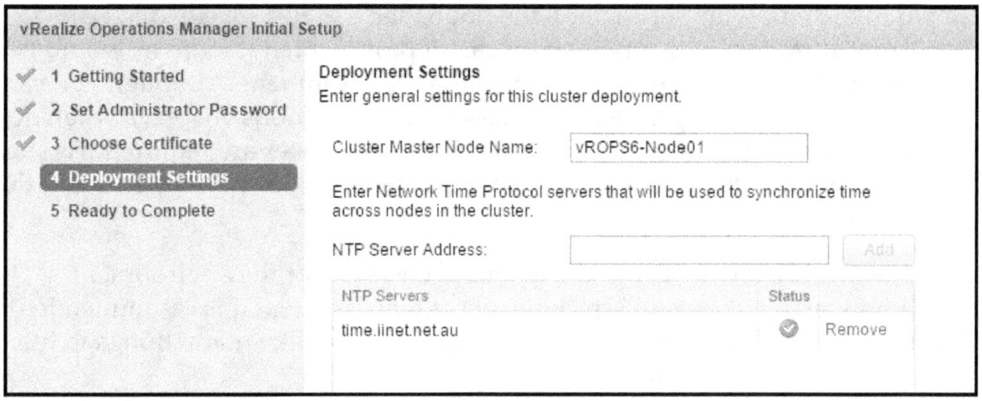

6. The last section is **Next Steps**, but here we don't actually do anything. This lists the next steps involved in configuration of the new vROps 6.0 installation. Click on the **Finish** button.

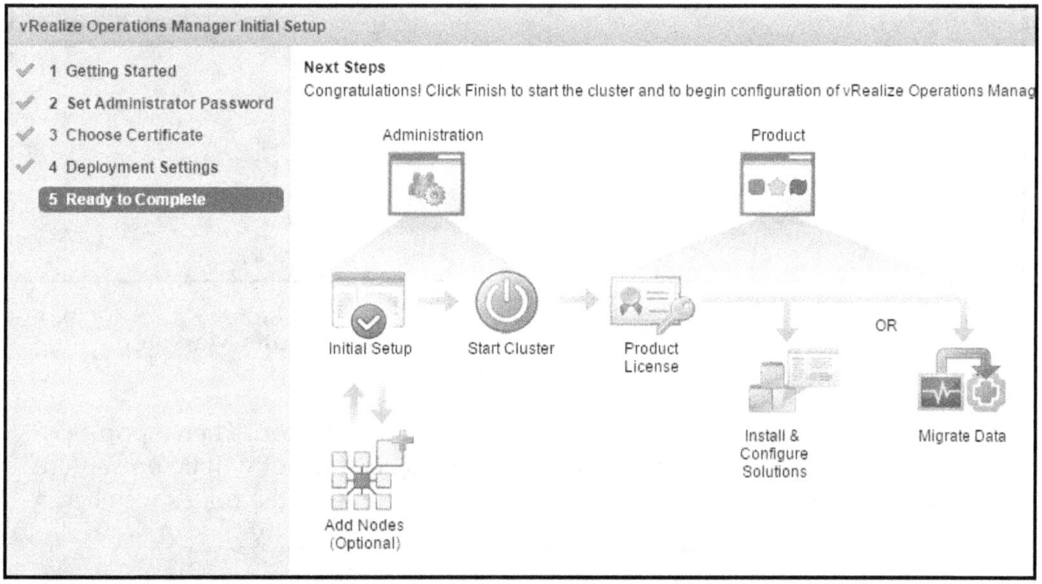

When the **Finish** button is clicked, the web page will be redirected to the admin interface of vROps 6.0. To get to this interface manually, go to `https://<IP or FQDN>/admin`. On this page, we can configure high availability features such as shutting down vROps nodes, adding nodes to the cluster, applying patches, applying updates, and collecting logs if required.

As shown in the following screenshot, the node that was just installed is visible and is currently offline. At this point, you can deploy as many nodes as would be required to meet your desired scale for the target environment. Although you can add additional nodes at any time (as discussed in the previous chapter), when doing so, certain actions such as rebalancing of the GemFire cluster are required. As such, it is highly recommended to aim to size your cluster correctly initially to avoid these tasks in the future.

If you're completely unsure about the eventual end state of the environment regarding how many objects vROps will collect metrics from, it is recommended to start off with a smaller number of nodes. This is because, like many things in life, it is easier to add than take away.

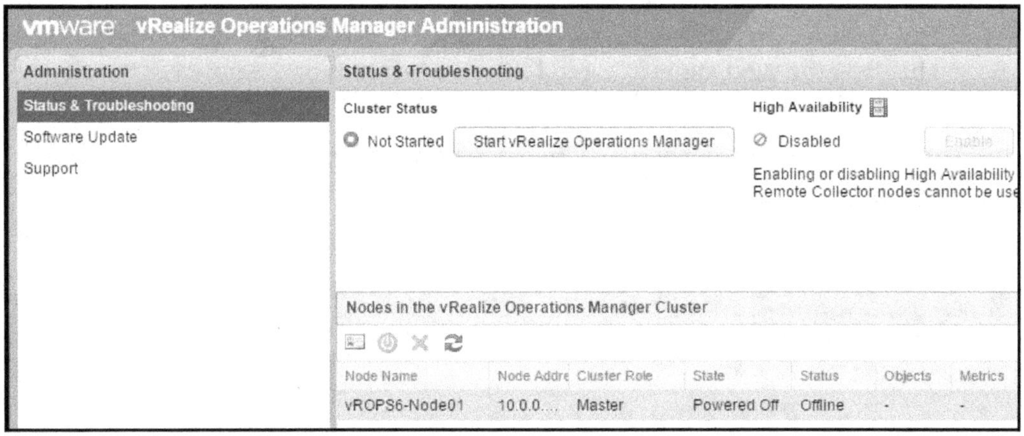

As seen in the preceding screenshot, on the **vRealize Operations Manager Administration** window, we perform the following steps:

1. Click on the **Start vRealize Operations Manager** button. Then a pop-up window like the one shown in the following screenshot will be presented, asking whether we are sure and whether we have all the nodes we need:

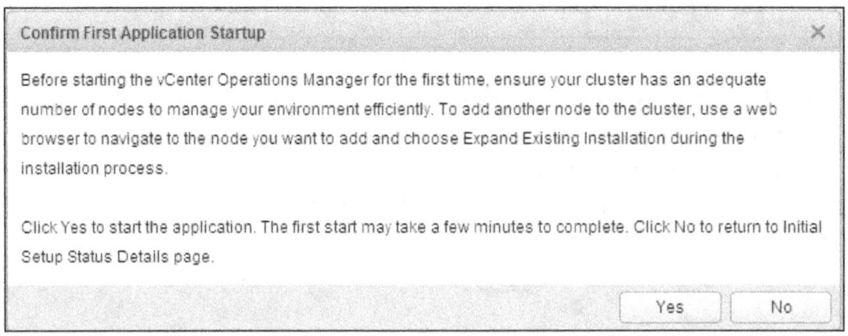

2. Click on **Yes** to move on. vROps 6.0 will take some time to start.

   When vROps starts up, the web page is redirected to the new vROps login page as shown in the following screenshot. The first login is where the final configuration is done but we can configure any of the parts configured after this final configuration.

3. Log in to vROps 6.0 with the username `admin` and the password entered during the first part of the configuration phase, ensuring that **Authentication Source** is set to **Local Users**.

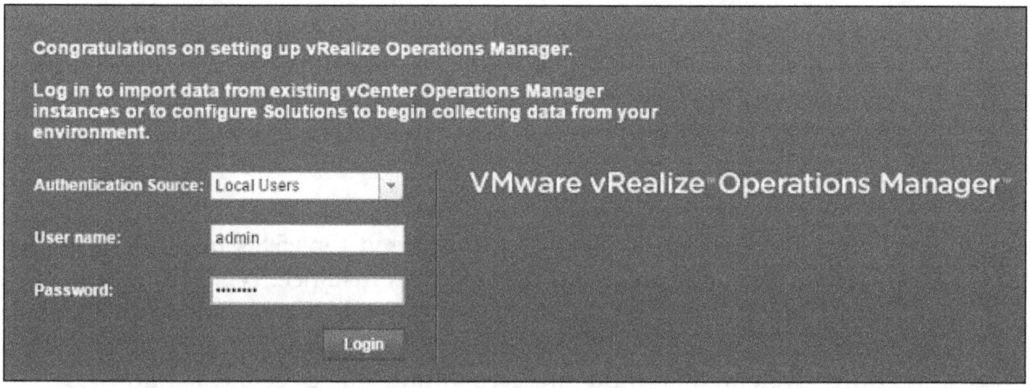

4. Once successfully logged in, we are presented with a new window asking whether this is a new installation or we are importing an existing environment. In this case, as we want to import to vROps 6.0, select the import option as shown in the following screenshot:

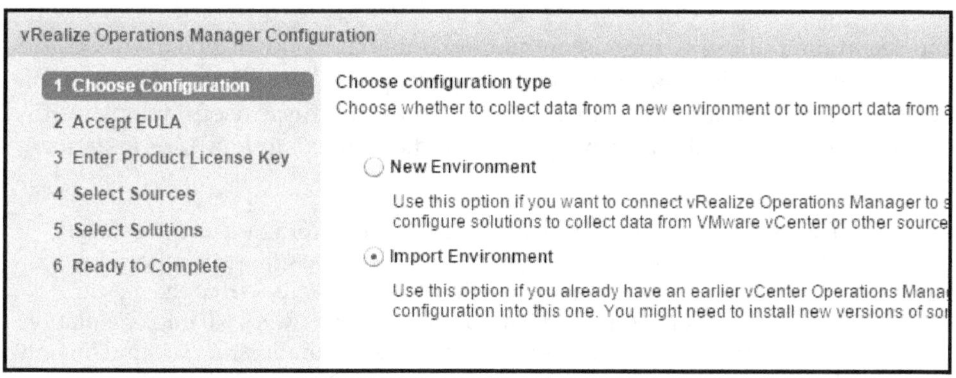

5. After selecting **Import Environment**, click on **Next** and you will then be presented with the normal EULA. Check the accept box and move on to the licensing section. Enter the vROps 6.0 license key; if you are licensed for vCloud Suite, use that key. Another option is to use the trial and enter a permanent license later.

> Earlier, vCOps 5.x used vCenter for its license management; this has now been removed and vROps 6.0 manages its own licenses to allow it to maintain independence from the other VMware product lines.

6. Once the license is entered and validated, click on **Next**. The sources section is where all of the existing vCOps 5.8.x sources can be entered for migration. In this case, we only have a single vCOps 5.8.x source; most environments generally will only have a single vCOps 5.8.x instance deployed, however, vROps 6.0 can import multiple vCOps 5.8.x deployments into a single vROps 6.0 instance if required.
7. Enter the IP address or FQDN of the existing vCOps 5.8.x instance followed by the admin account password for that 5.8.x instance. When **Add Source** is clicked, and if the connection is successful, two pop-up windows will be presented. The first window says that an agent needs to be installed on the source system; this could take five minutes. The second window is a certificate prompt asking you to accept the certificate of the vCOps 5.8.x host that we just added.

Once the migration agent is installed, we can see that the imported vCOps 5.8.x instance has 166 resources, 42,455 metrics, and needs 12.58 GB of space, as shown in the next screenshot.

We can see at the bottom of the screen that we only have one vROps 6.0 node and depending on the configuration and data being imported, how much of the vCPU and memory allocated to that node is estimated to be used. This is useful to ensure that you have sized your new cluster appropriately based on an existing vCOps instance.

> The import process will pull across everything from the source instance. This includes dashboards, super metrics, policies, groups, applications, authentication sources, and even the vCenter details so that the metric collection continues after the import on the new vROps 6.0 implementation. The migration mode can be changed to a configuration that will pull in only the configuration settings of the existing environment. This can be done by clicking on the **Migration mode** dropdown.
>
> A good cleanup prior to migration is highly recommended.

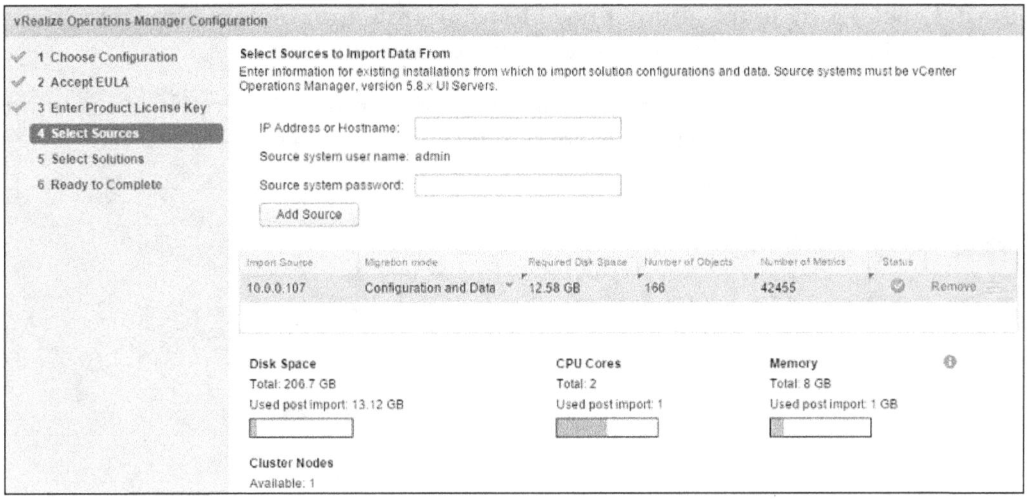

When all the import sources have been added, click on **Next** and move on to the **Select Solutions** section.

In this section, we will see all the previous adapters or management packs installed on the existing vCOps 5.8.x instance. They are now called solutions in vROps 6.0.

At this point, the wizard will provide information on which adapters were used in the previous environment and how the instance of the previous environment differs from the new 6.0 instance. The two built-in solutions, that is the **Http Post** adapter and **vCenter Adapter** will not need to be upgraded but all other adapters will need to be reinstalled on the new instance. If a solution needs upgrading or installing, it will have a **Missing** status, as we can see in the following screenshot:

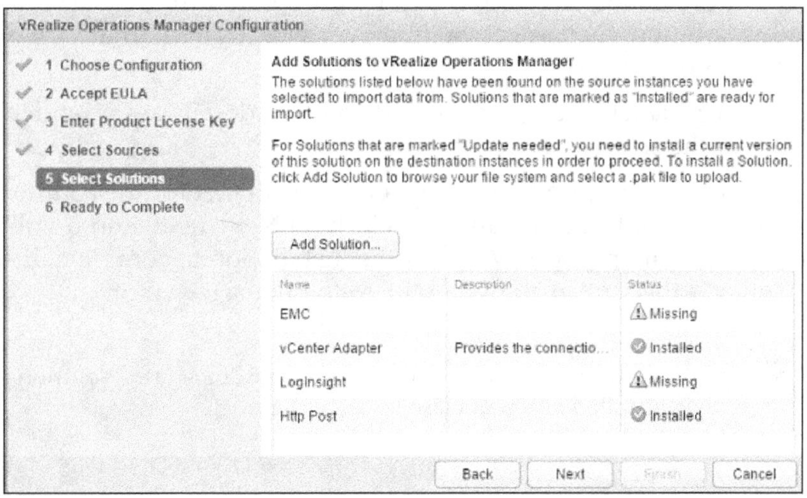

If the data belonging to the adapter need to be migrated, the solution must be installed at this point. To do this, perform the following steps:

1. Click on the **Add Solution** button. We will then be taken to the add solution dialog box similar to the one shown in the following screenshot:

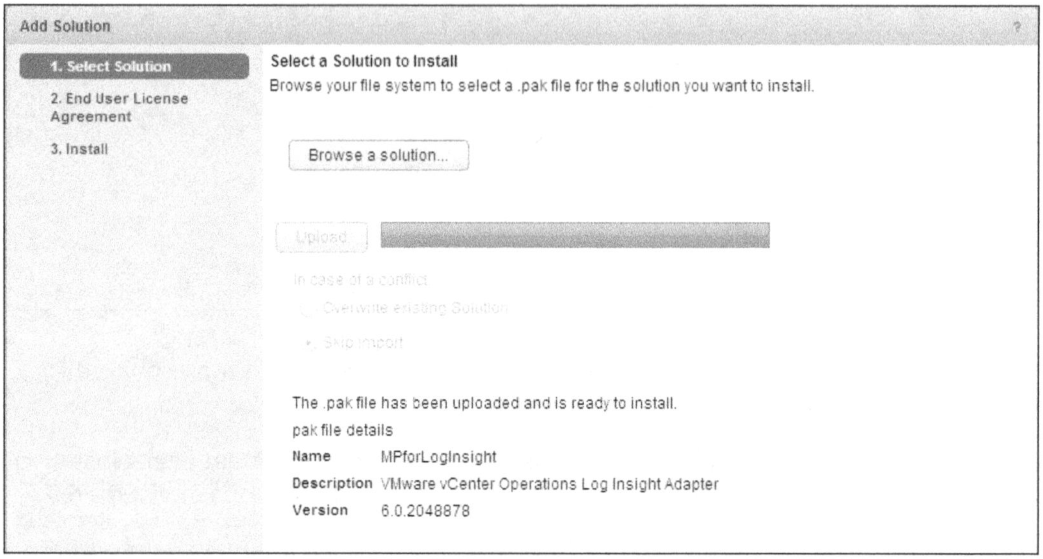

2. Ensure that the latest version of the solution has been downloaded from VMware or third-party providers. Click on the **Browse a solution** button, which will open an explorer window where we choose the `.pak` file.
3. Once selected, click on **OK** and choose the **In case of conflict** action. The **Skip import** is the safest option but if you really want to overwrite an existing solution, then select the first overwrite option. In this case, we are selecting **Skip import**.
4. Click on **Upload**. Once uploaded, the solution details are provided at the bottom of the screen.
5. Click on the **Next** button and move on to the EULA for the solution, accept that and move into the installation. Click on **Next** again and it will initiate the installation straight away. Wait for the installation to complete. If successful, you will see the output shown in the following screenshot:

> If multiple nodes exist in the vROps 6.0 cluster, the solution is installed automatically on all of them.

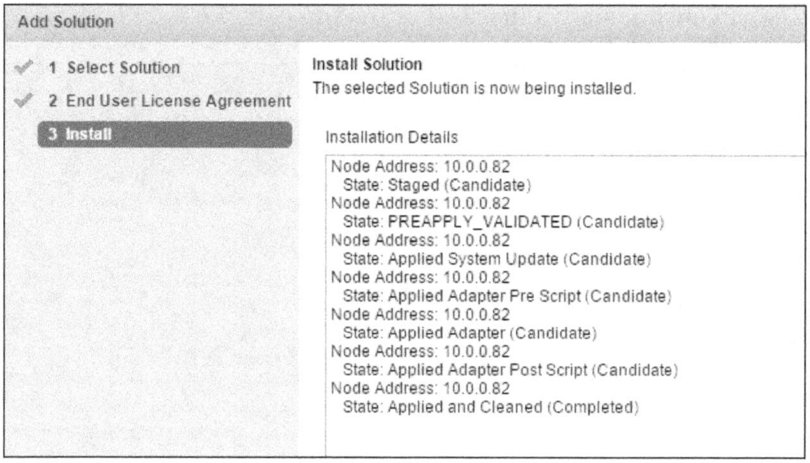

6. Click on the **Finish** button and it will take you back to the solutions section. Repeat this for all the adapters or solutions that need to be installed. Then click on the **Next** button to move on to the import data section.

> You do not need to install or upgrade adapters; if you decide not to install, a prompt will be displayed asking your confirmation to proceed and the data for that adapter will not be imported.

7. Section 6, **Ready to Complete**, is the final step in the wizard, which will just display our selected choices. Click on **Finish** when you are ready to move on to importing the data.

   After **Finish** has been clicked, the web page will redirect to the administration section of the vROps 6.0 Product UI. Here, we can see the status of the data being imported, as shown in the next screenshot.

The import process can take a significant amount of time. A small amount of data in this demo environment took 1 hour and 26 minutes to import. So for a large environment, it will take quite a few hours. Keep in mind that the original instance of vCOps continues to collect metrics, and as such, no significant amount of data will be lost during the import.

> Time taken for the import process will depend on many infrastructure factors such as SAN storage and network speed.

The following screenshot shows the start of the import:

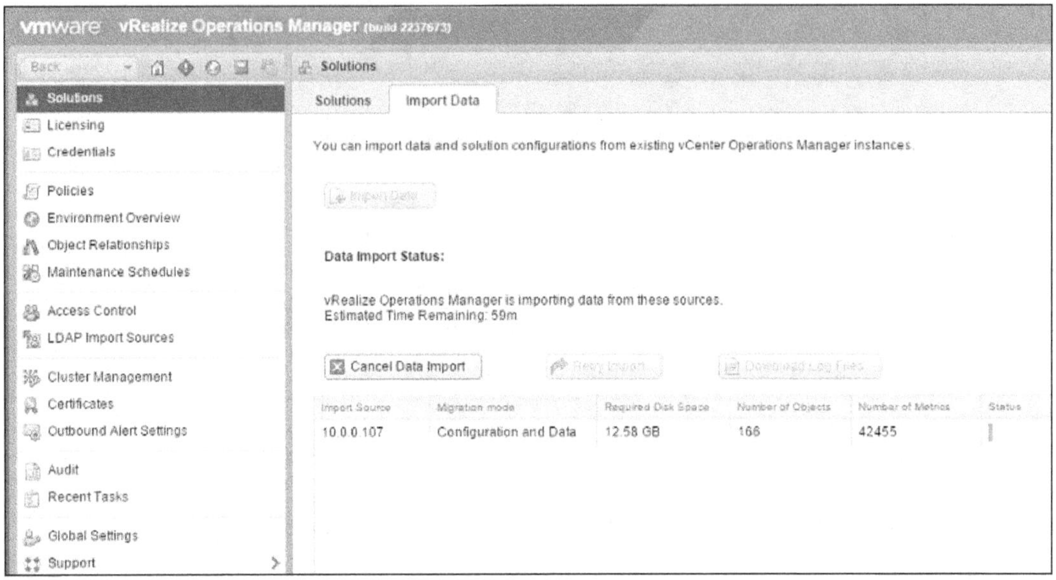

Once the data has been imported, click on the **Solutions** tab next to the **Import Data** tab currently being displayed.

In here, we can see that the vCenter adapter has been included, which was imported over with the credentials. We can see in the next screenshot that data is set for collection and reception. All the metrics of the old vCOps 5.8.x are now being collected on this new vROps 6.0 instance. We can also see the **LogInsight** solution we installed previously.

> Depending on the number of vCenters your 5.8.x vCOps implementation was monitoring, the number of vCenter adapters to be be shown will be decided. For example, the following screenshot only shows one vCenter as that was all that the vCOps 5.8 instance was monitoring, but if the vCOps 5.8.x instance was collecting metrics from four vCenter servers, all four vCenters would be displayed.

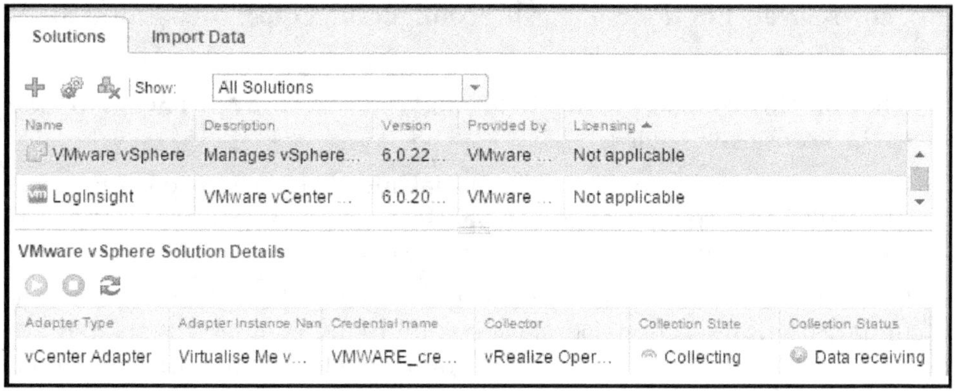

We have now successfully migrated to vROps 6.0.

Fresh installation

A fresh installation has almost the same steps shown in the *Configuring a new vROps instance* section, but there is one difference. After the installation, when we log in to the system for the first time as the admin user, we choose **New Environment**, as shown in the following screenshot, whereas previously we had chosen the **Import Environment** option:

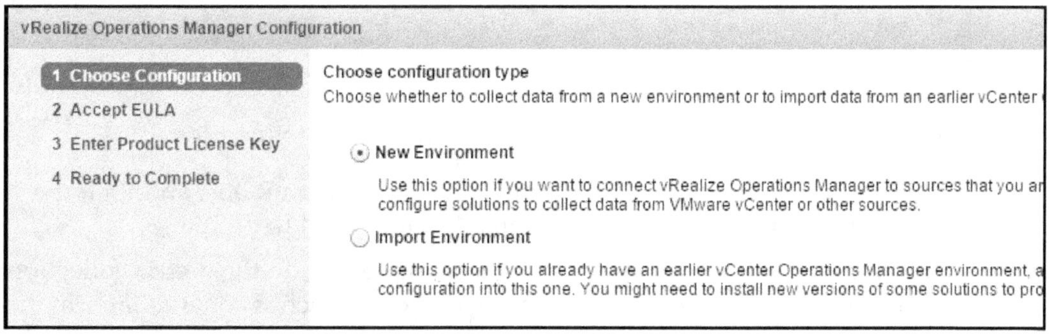

Once we choose **New Environment** as the configuration type, we perform the following steps:

1. Click on **Next** and accept the EULA and then click on **Next** again to move on to the license key section.
2. Enter the license key or leave it as a trial and click on **Next** one more time. This will bring up the **Ready to Complete** section, which shows the steps we have taken and what is to be done next.
3. Click on **Finish** and the webpage is redirected to the vROps 6.0 user interface in the **Solutions** section. Here, we configure the vCenter servers that vROps has to monitor. Select a vCenter solution and click on the configure icon as shown in the following screenshot:

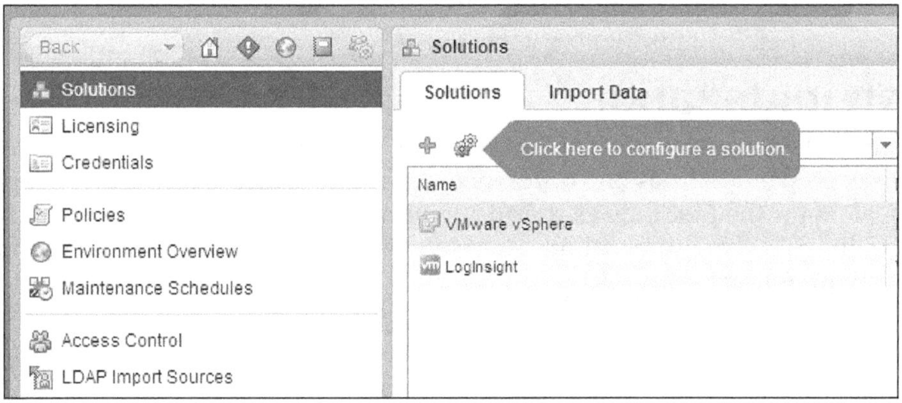

This is where we configure the vCenters that vROps 6.0 has to monitor.

1. Enter the name that the vCenter will be referred to in vROps, and then the description. The description is optional but it is good to fill it in.
2. The collector determines which vROps 6.0 node will do the metric collection; this is only the case if multiple data nodes exist, which is covered later in this chapter. It is recommended that you select the **Automatically select collector** option, as shown in the next screenshot. This will allow vROps 6.0 to allocate the collector intelligently where it would best fit.

[As discussed in the previous chapter, if a vROps data node instance were to fail, the adapter instance will automatically be migrated to another data (or master) node. However, this is not the case for adapters registered against remote collectors.]

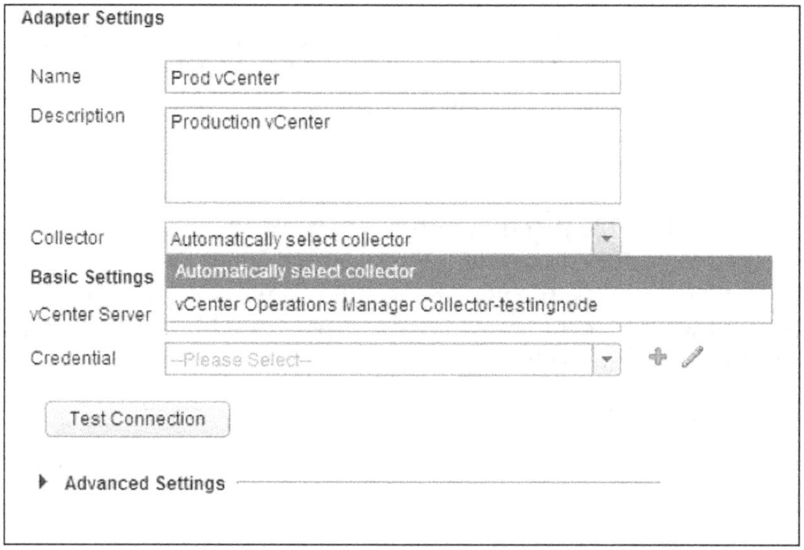

3. Enter the FQDN or IP of the vCenter vROps to be monitored. Create a credential that will be used to connect to vCenter. Click on the little green plus icon and you will then be prompted with the window shown in the following screenshot.
4. Enter the account that has the correct access that vROps requires, which at a minimum is read only so it can collect the data, register extensions if you would like vROps to provide health badges, and so on in the web client.
5. Click on **OK** and you will return to the previous window.

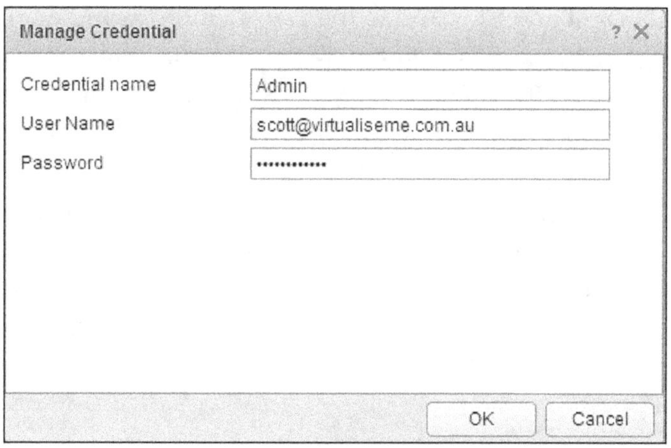

The credentials entered can be reused later when connecting additional vCenters. If possible, use a service account that can be used across all the vCenters you want to monitor.

It's now time to test the connection:

1. Click on the **Test Connection** button to check whether vROps 6.0 is able to connect to the entered vCenter. If successful, we will be prompted with two windows, first will be the vCenter certificate we need to accept, which shown in the following screenshot. The second popup will inform you that the connection was successful.

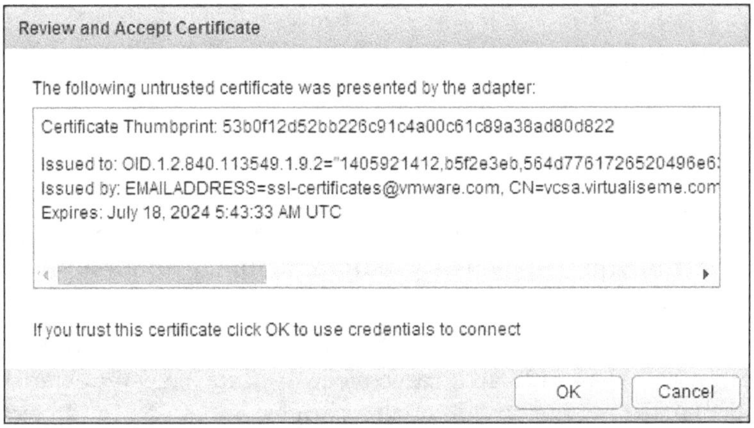

2. Once all the vCenter servers have been added, click on the **Next** button on the bottom right and move on to the **Define monitoring goals** section.

   This section is a way to quickly define a policy for the environment. Policies are used for capacity management, alerting, and recommendations, and are covered in *Chapter 5, Policies in vRealize Operations Manager 6.0*.

3. If the environment that has been added cannot fit under a single policy, skip this section and apply policies later. Alternately, selecting some of the options will lead to vROps 6.0 making a policy based on the selections made. In the following screenshot, we have selected some settings to allow the policy creation.

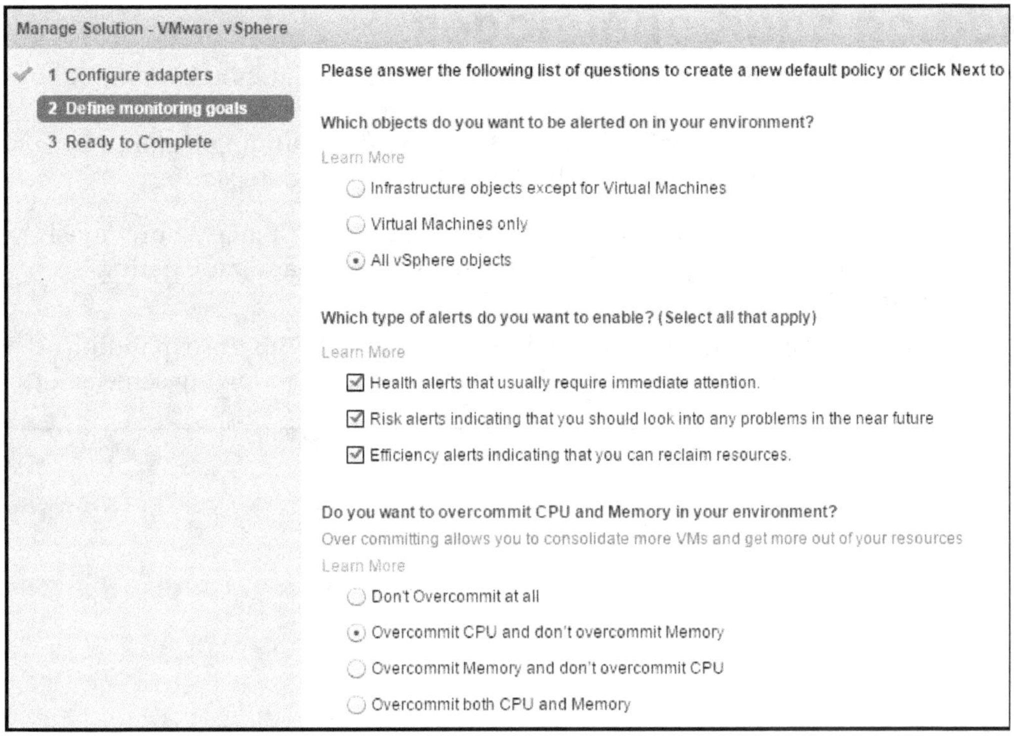

4. Once done, click on **Finish**.

We will then return to the solutions page and will now be able to see the vCenter(s) that has been added; the data should be in a collecting state, as shown in the following screenshot:

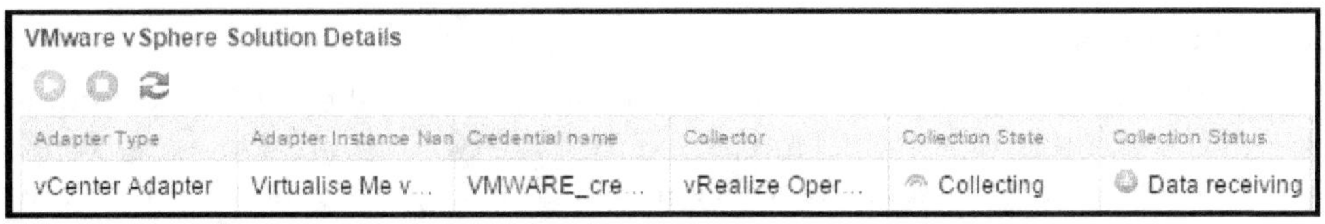

That's it, vROps 6.0 has been installed and we have added the vCenter servers for data collection. Continue through this book to fully configure every aspect of the installation.

Adding additional nodes

Adding additional nodes is easy with the new installer and architecture in vROps 6.0. It is recommended that all the nodes be added before the cluster is started. Though in this instance, we will add a node to an existing running instance as this is also supported and works well, as shown in the following steps:

1. Deploy another vROps 6.0 node with the same OVA file used previously. When at the **Getting Started** screen, choose the **Expand an Existing Installation** option.

   When this option is selected, we will be presented with the expanding existing installation wizard popup, as shown in the following screenshot.

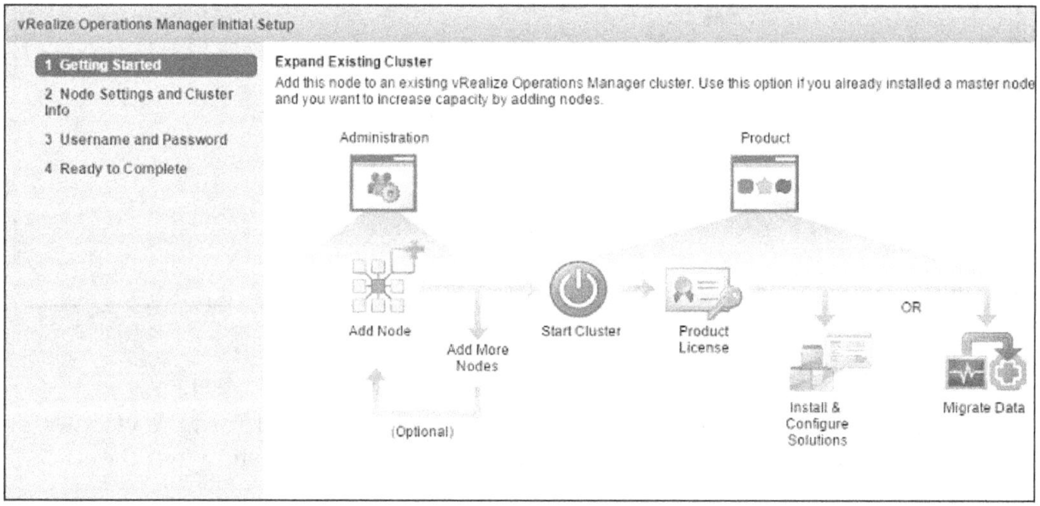

2. Click on **Next** to move to the node setting and cluster info section.
3. In the **Node Settings and Cluster Info** section, give the new node a name and select the node type. Here, we only have two options **Data** and **Remote Collector**. Select **Data** as **Node type**, which will give us the option to use an HA cluster as a data node that can be made into a replica node or added into an HA cluster.
4. Enter the FQDN and IP address of the first node of the cluster, as shown in the following screenshot. Click on **Next** to proceed to the next section.

> A remote data collector is recommended for use at remote sites. If a site's link was to fail, the remote collector will continue collecting data and send it back to the data nodes when the link is re-established, assuming that the remote collector did not exhaust all its memory if the time window was too large.

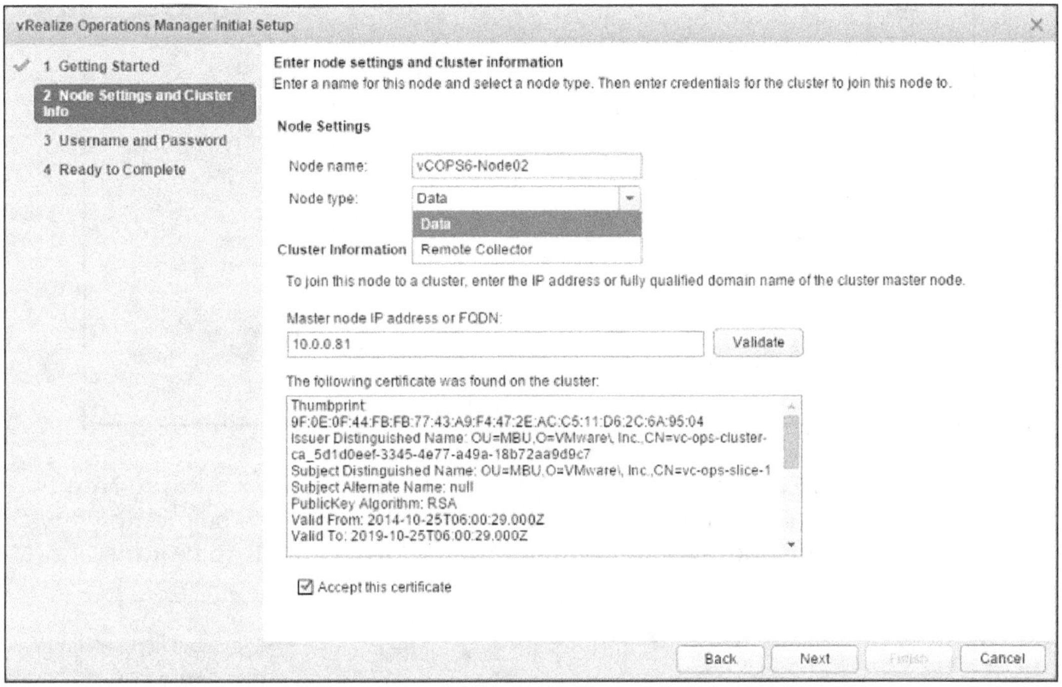

5. The next section is where we enter the password of the admin account of the first node deployed. Alternately, we use the shared pass-phrase if one was generated. In this instance, we will just use the password of the admin account.

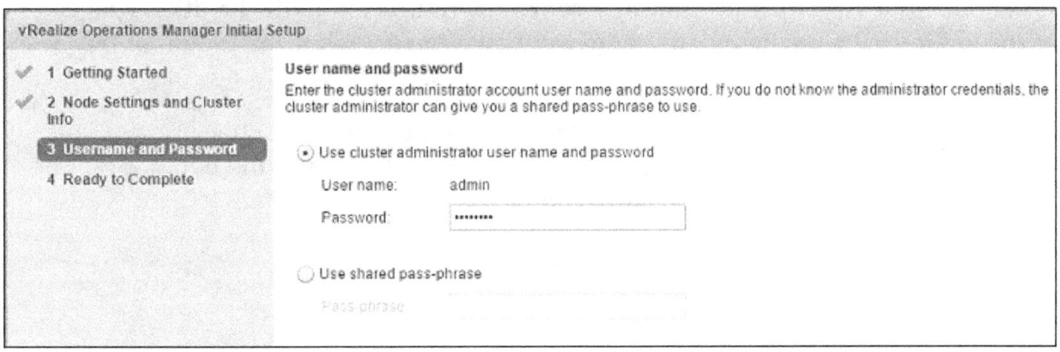

6. Once on the **Ready to Complete** section, click on **Finish** and you will then be redirected to the admin interface. Here, we can see the original vROps 6.0 node and the newly added data node, which will be in an offline state, as shown in the following screenshot:

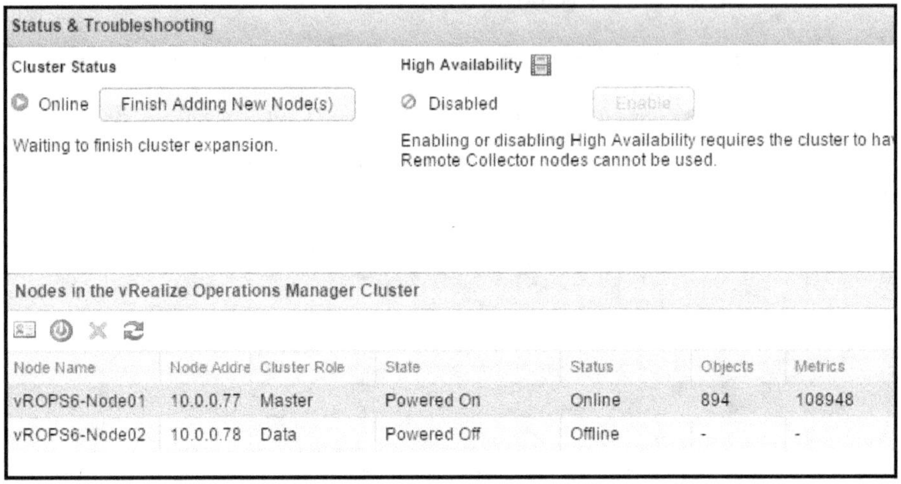

7. Once finished adding additional nodes, click on the **Finish Adding New Node(s)** button just under the cluster status. You will then be prompted with the following window. Click on **OK** and wait for the node to be added.

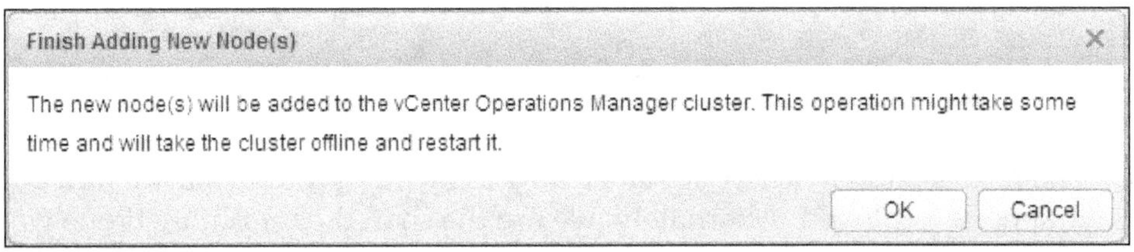

When the nodes are up and running, we will be redirected to the solutions page of the vROps 6.0 UI, where both nodes are now seen as online, as shown in the following images.

You may have noticed that while a cluster has been created, the cluster is not yet highly available. However, this has split the resource load over the two nodes. The master is the only node that will store configuration data though.

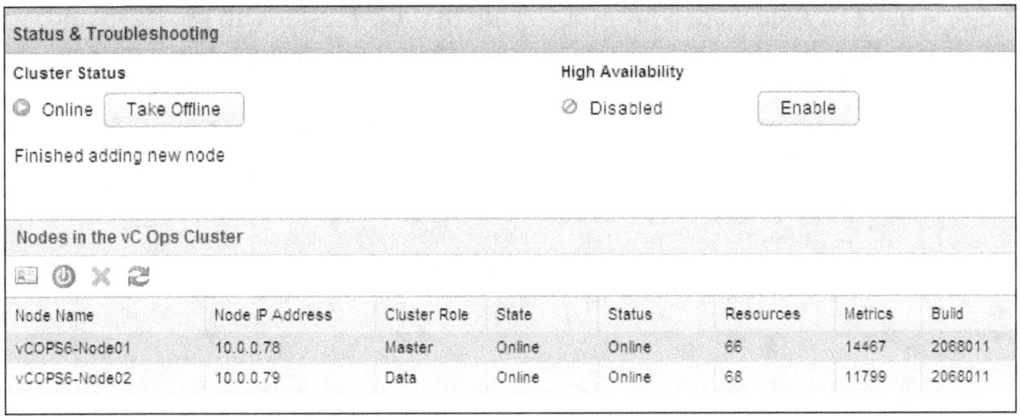

To form an HA cluster, we require at least the master and one data node and both the nodes need to be on or off to enable the cluster. To do this, perform the following steps:

1. Navigate to the admin interface at `https://<vROPS FQDN or IP>/admin` and log in.
2. Click on the **Enable** button under **High Availability** at the top of the screen. We are now prompted with a new window to determine which data node to make a replica node of the HA cluster. In this case, we only have one other node available to be selected, as shown in the following screenshot:

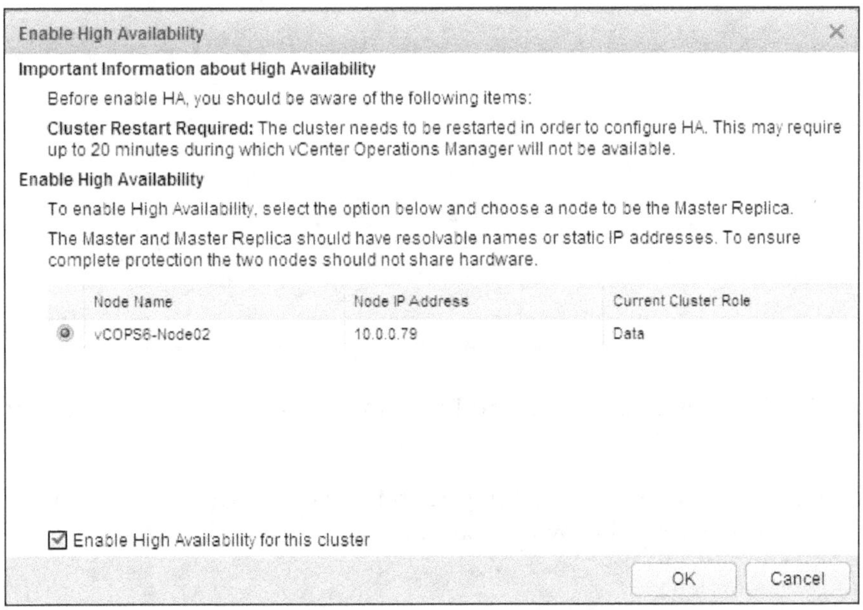

3. When **OK** is clicked, a prompt saying that the cluster will go down and may take 20 minutes to create the HA cluster will pop up. Click on **Yes** to continue.

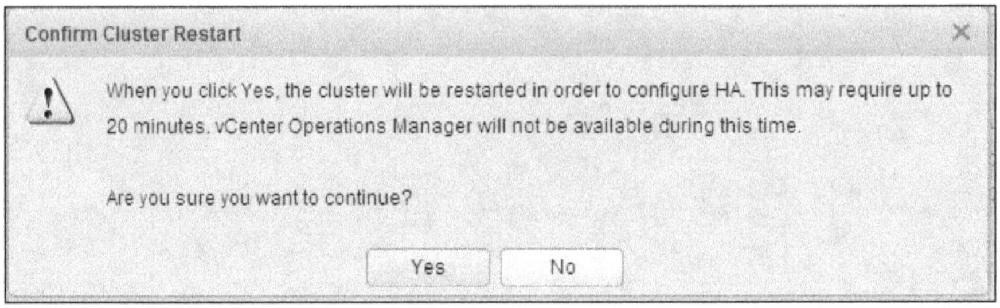

When the cluster is backed up, the previous data node becomes a master replica node and the **High Availability** option is shown as enabled.

A high availability cluster is now up and running. Data is being sharded across the two nodes, and a copy of the configuration data is also replicated.

Additionally, a load balancer can be placed in front of the two nodes and can balance the web UI traffic between the two of them.

> It is recommended that at a minimum of four nodes be used in a high availability cluster. This is because once HA is enabled, the compute, storage space, and IOPS generated are essentially doubled.

Scaling and high availability

Although one of the great new features of vROps 6.0 is the scale-out architecture, it drives obvious questions such as how many nodes should I deploy and what size should these nodes be?

Performance and redundancy are the two main reasons to scale out a vROps 6.0 cluster. Due to vROps 6.0's new architecture where every node is the same, we can add nodes to the cluster to scale and meet the requirement for large number of objects and sustain failure of a vROps cluster node, or both.

When architecting vROps 6.0 solution, one of the first tasks is to look at the number of objects that will have metrics being collected and using the following table, work out a solution that will fit best.

The vROps sizing guidelines will evolve over time as VMware continues to tune and test vROps 6.x in different environments. The following sizing is based on vROps 6.0.1; however, it is recommended that you check the VMware knowledge base site prior to deployment to get the latest information.

Characteristics/Node size	Extra small	Small	Medium	Large
vCPU	2	4	8	16
Single-Node Maximum Objects	250	2,400	7,000	12,000
Single-Node Maximum Collected Metrics	70,000	800,000	2,000,000	3,500,000
Multi-Node Maximum Objects Per Node	NA	2,000	5,000	10,000
Multi-Node Maximum Collected Metrics Per Node	NA	700,000	1,500,000	2,500,000
Maximum Objects for 8-Node Maximum	NA	NA	40,000	75,000
Maximum Metrics for 8-Node Configuration	NA	NA	12,000,000	20,000,000

Source: VMware KB 2109312

Eight nodes is the current cluster limit in vROps 6.0 and if HA is required, which will give you data redundancy, the rule of thumb is that you have to double the nodes to enable HA. Going with the preceding table, if the environment only has 2,000 objects and deployed a small node, it will require two nodes when using HA. If at a later date, the environment grows and is required to expand, we will have to add another two nodes to HA. Adding just one more will work perfectly fine but performance problems may occur.

While each vROps 6.0 data node including the master and replica can be accessed directly and provide the same web frontend and data, it is recommended to use a load balancer between the data nodes.

There are two main reasons why this should be done. The first is that it gives a central connection for all administrators to connect to a node that will operationally be simpler to manage, and if a node was to go down, everyone will be redirected to another node automatically.

The second reason is for custom data importing, which is covered in *Chapter 11, Expanding vROps with Solutions*. When making REST calls to the load balancer IP, we will distribute the load between all the data nodes instead of only hitting one server; this will also ensure that if a node goes down, the custom data collection continues to function.

When configuring the load balancer, it is recommended to not use the standard HTTPS monitoring but to implement a custom send and receive string. Here are the two strings that can be used:

```
Send String: GET  /vcops-web-ent/login.action HTTP/1.0\r\n\r\n
Receive String: HTTP/1.[01][23]0[0-6]
```

> All nodes of a cluster should be co-located within the same site. The cluster requires LAN-like speeds and latencies and is not guaranteed to work effectively across sites. This is where the remote data collectors can come into play.

Summary

In this chapter, you learned how to migrate existing data and upgrade from vCOps 5.x. We covered how to expand the cluster with a data node and make it a highly available cluster. We also touched on the sizing and load balancing options available for vROps 6.0.

In next chapter, we will cover the iconic vCOps badge systems in vROps 6.0 and how they have improved from the previous version of the product.

3

vRealize Operations Manager Badges

This chapter discusses in detail the critical concept of Operations Manager 6.0 badges and how they assist in effectively managing your vSphere and non-vSphere environments. You will discover the differences between badges in Operations Manager 5.x and 6.0 as well as the details of how the badges are calculated and tuned to best suit your own environment.

What are vRealize Operations Manager badges?

An Operations Manager badge is a graphical representation of the state of the current environment or object. A badge can range from using a few metrics to millions of metrics. It provides a summarized piece of useful information that would sometimes take an administrator hours or even days to collocate manually in the vSphere Performance Overview tab or a similar monitoring system.

Badges are seen as an important source of information rather than just data. If at anytime an administrator wishes to understand more about a certain badge state or score, they can review the metrics or events that are behind the badge to get a more in-depth understanding of the environment.

One of the most unique and powerful aspects of badges is that they allow an administrator to view the same important information from the VM or datastore level all the way up to the vCenter (or even higher) level. This is because all objects can have the same set of badges applied to them; it is just that they may slightly differ in the way they are calculated. As all objects can have the same set of badges, it enables badges to be rolled up to higher levels by leveraging parent child relationships. For example, the workload badge of an ESXi host includes all the workload of its children virtual machines in its score. Similarly, the workload badge of a vSphere cluster includes all the workloads of its children ESXi hosts and virtual machines.

The badges in vROps 6.0 can be split into two distinct categories: major or minor. The major badges are Health, Risk, and Efficiency. These badges are represented by a color from red to amber to yellow and finally to green (red indicating an issue or alert). Unlike the minor badges, the major badges do not contain a score (we will touch on this in the next section).

Each major badge also has a set of associated minor badges that are part of the same discipline. The relationship of the major and minor badges is as follows:

- Health:
    - Workload
    - Anomalies
    - Faults
- Risk:
    - Time Remaining
    - Capacity Remaining
    - Stress
- Efficiency:
    - Reclaimable Capacity
    - Density

The following screenshot depicts the major and minor badges:

Changes in badges of vROps 6.0

Badges are not a concept that is new to vROps 6.0; however, they have changed a little over time from vCOps 1.x to 5.x. vROps 6.0 continues to leverage these useful snapshots of information and at the same time, badges have undergone some major improvements. These improvements include applying badges to non-vSphere objects and how major badges are calculated.

Badges for non-vSphere objects

Although badges were originally introduced in Operations Manager 1.0, they were limited to the vSphere UI and therefore to vSphere objects. There were a few exceptions such as the Health badge for certain objects; however, in general, principal badges were used for vSphere only.

One of the major aspects of Operations Manager 6.0 is that all objects are treated as first class citizens or in other words, all solutions and adapters are treated and respected equally. This concept of equal weighting for all solutions is one of the driving factors behind the merged UI. This has allowed all objects to support the badges, allowing a consistent reporting and troubleshooting experience no matter what the source of the data is.

The ability of non-vSphere objects to provide data to the full badge set will vary depending on the maturity level of the associated solution (adapter). In most cases, this will allow administrators to create dashboards that display common badge dashboards no matter the context of the object.

Major badges are now set by definitions

One of the most important changes in badges from Operations Manager 5.x to 6.0 is how the major badges are calculated and presented to the administrator. The most common initial observation is the absence of the score on all the major badges. This is not a mistake, but more of a change in the way the major badges work. This comparison is demonstrated in the following figure:

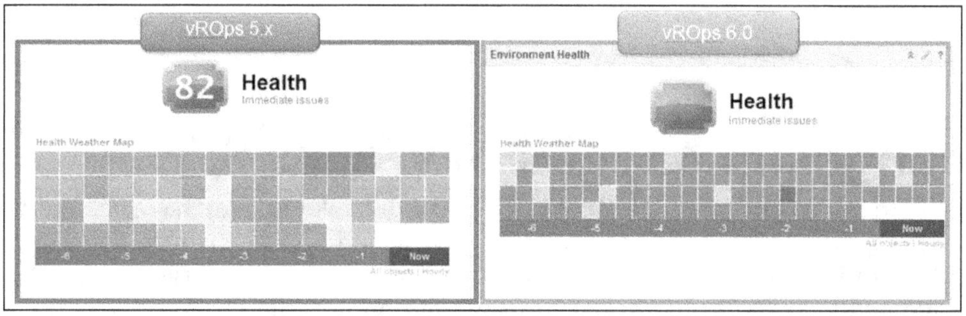

In Operations Manager 5.x, the major badges were derived from the minor badges based on a particular formula weighting. The major Health badge score for a particular vSphere object was determined by looking at its relevant Workload, Anomalies, and Faults score with a weighting applied to them. This weighting, for example, would be heavily applied to faults (after ensuring that faults have a large impact on the score). At the same time, workload would have a relatively low rating on the overall health score. Let's look at an example.

The following is a screenshot from Operations Manager 5.8 that looks at the Analytics VM itself. Although the current workload score is **51** (or 51 percent), as it has zero current faults and its anomalies are below the noise threshold, it has a high health score of **94**.

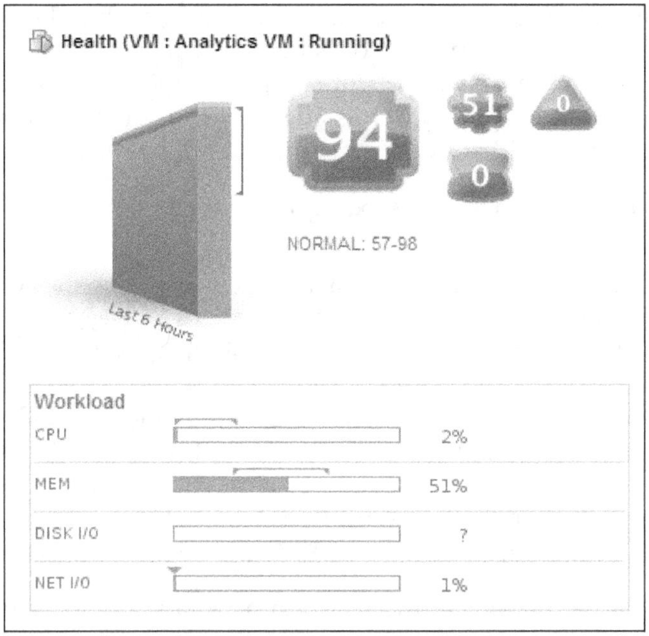

Conversely, if we look at a particular datastore that has a relatively high workload score of **72** and a high Anomalies score of **73**, we can see that the end result is an overall low health score of **27**. This low score would generate an immediate alert, which would be appropriate in this case, as high workload with a high number of anomalies would usually warrant further investigation.

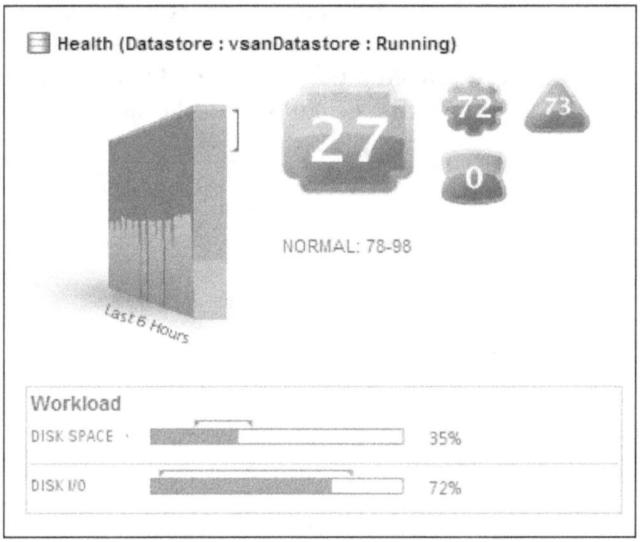

Although this method for calculating a major indicator, such as health, works well for an object that is working very hard or is behaving in an unusual way, it can lead to a high number of false positives unless it is properly tuned for a particular workload. It also has the capability of missing very important changes to key metrics that in a service sense should heavily affect the overall heath score.

We will look at a network packet loss example in just a moment.

> The major badge scores that are calculated using the vCOps 5.x formulas are still available in Operations Manager 6.0. They are available under the badges metric group as legacy health.

In vROps 6.0, the major badges Health, Risk, and Efficiency *are no longer directly derived from their associated minor badges*. Instead, alerts and symptom definitions define the state of a badge for a particular object type. This in turn allows more intelligent alerting based on the key symptoms that can be observed from multiple sources providing an informed recommendation to administrators.

This symptom-based approach allows solution pack creators to define a series of alerts on particular observed metrics, messages, faults, and so on and then allows them to link to an overall single alert and possibly even an automated remediation action to resolve the issue.

Looking at the example shown in the following screenshot, we can see that the symptom **Port is experiencing dropped packets** is observed on a particular port group. This is a key piece of information that an administrator would want to know. If this were Operations Manager 5.x with Health primarily used only to observe workload and anomalies, this issue could easily be ignored. Operations Manager 5.x did support setting threshold alerts as part of attribute packages in the Custom UI; however, these had to be manually created by administrators and required expert knowledge of what the individual thresholds should be set to.

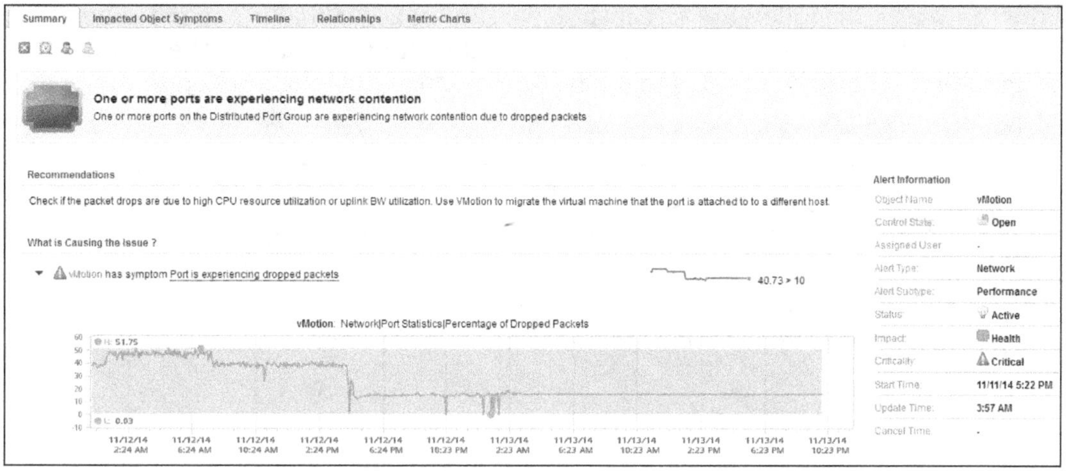

We will discuss major badges and their associated definitions later in the book in *Chapter 13, Alerting, Actions, and Recommendations.*

Understanding the Health badge

The Health badge is the first high-level indicator of the overall status of your environment. This is the first badge that should be looked at by an administrator and acted upon as soon as possible. The Health badge shows how your environment or object is *right now*. This helps in identifying issues that need immediate attention.

As previously mentioned, all major badges in Operations Manager 6.0 are now based on alerts and symptom definitions that determine the overall badge state. This does not imply that the major badges no longer have any relation to their existing minor badges.

For example, in the following screenshot, we can see a VM that is experiencing critically high CPU demand as well as a high number of anomalies. These minor badge alerts are also symptoms that have lead to an alert being applied to the major Health badge.

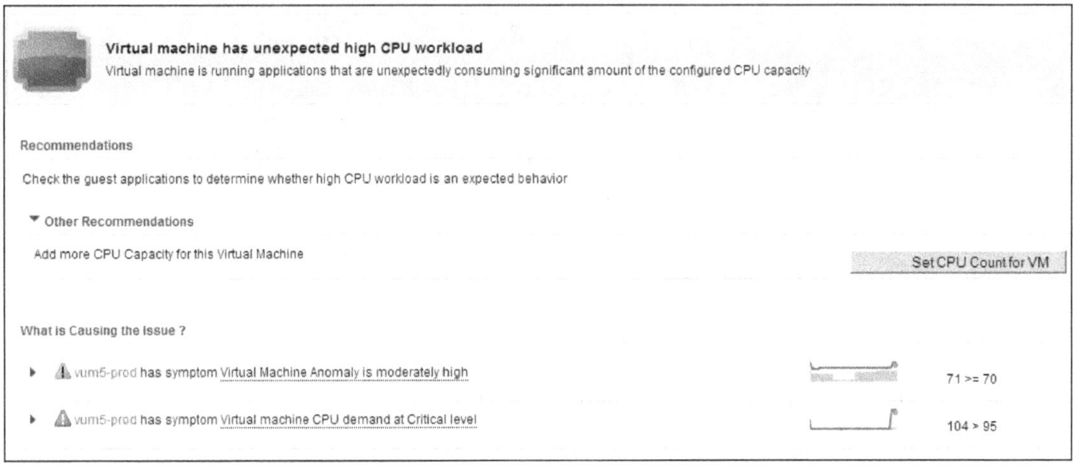

The Workload badge

The Workload badge indicates how hard an object is working. The score for the Workload badge ranges from 0 being good to 100 being bad.

Workload is most commonly measured against CPU, RAM, disk I/O, and network I/O for a particular object with the Workload score based on the most constraining resource. There are exceptions, such as datastores, as well as other vSphere objects that may have different factors that contribute to the workload.

Workload is calculated by taking the demand of a resource and dividing it by the effective capacity of that resource. If workload is just below, at, or above 100 percent, then the object has a high likelihood of having performance problems.

> Workload can be greater than 100 percent, as demand can be greater than 100 percent of its currently assigned capacity.

Host, virtual machine, and datastore objects will have their workload calculated directly from their own raw metrics, while cluster and data center objects will be derived from an average of all the children that are both vSphere hosts and virtual machines.

The Anomalies badge

The Anomalies badge is a measurement of how abnormally an object is behaving. The score for the Anomalies badge ranges from 0 being good and 100 being bad.

Anomalies are based on the most powerful feature of Operations Manager, Analytics. Analytics allow Operations Manager to understand the normal behavior of any performance metric no matter the resource or metric type. It is incredibly useful to generate alerts without the need to hard-set static thresholds and assist in the discovery of hidden metric relationships. Anomalies use *dynamic thresholds* to create an upper and lower boundary for a metric in a particular time period. If a metric leaves this dynamic threshold, it is considered as an active anomaly.

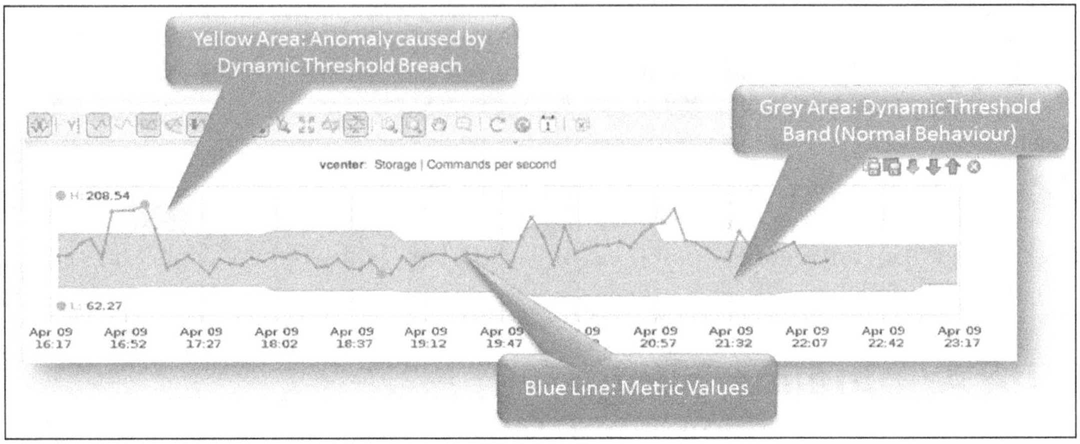

Anomalies will not be available as a metric or alerting source until Operations Manager monitors the resource for four weeks. This is the amount of time that it takes to learn the normal behavior of the resource. The object's dynamic threshold is calculated and is visible in the UI after one week (or one cycle) of data collection. It then takes further three cycles for Operations Manager analytics to learn the normal behavior of the resource. During this time, the dynamic thresholds become more refined to more accurately reflect the normal operating range of the metrics.

The Anomalies badge itself is based on a noise line or problem threshold. The noise line is required as some level of noise (abnormality) in the data center is always found in normal conditions. Once the amount of anomalies is greater than the noise line, the score starts to increase. This is shown in the following analogy in the figure:

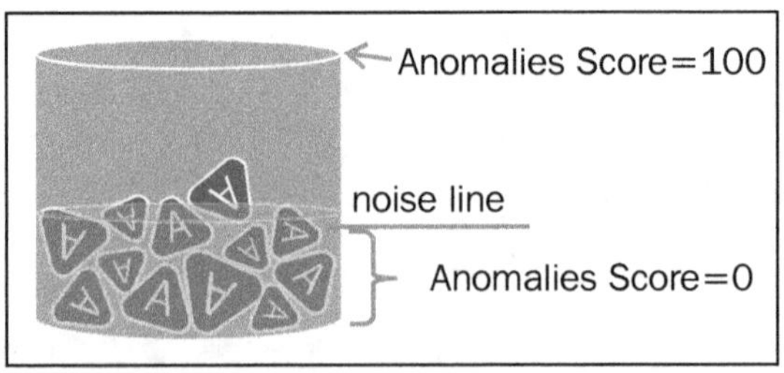

The Fault badge

The Fault badge is a measure of immediate problems that the object has. The score for the Fault badge ranges from 0 being good and 100 being bad.

The Fault badge is mapped against events of the object. This could be loss of a storage path event from the vCenter server, or CPU temperature warning, or memory DIMM failure retrieved from the ESXi host's CIM providers. The Fault badge usually highlights issues that require immediate action. The Fault badge is also the only badge that is solely event-driven and is not derived from any metrics.

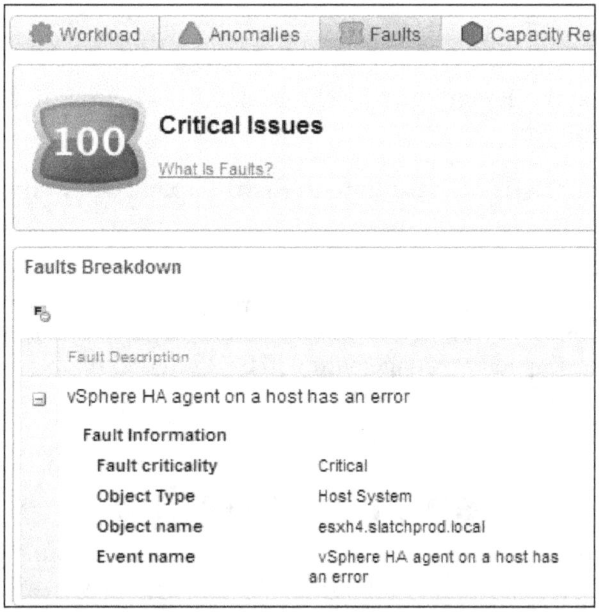

The Health badge summary

In summary, the Health minor badges can be defined as:

- **Workload**: This determines how *hard* your object is working
- **Anomalies**: They determine how *normal* your object is right now
- **Faults**: They determine what's *wrong* with your object right now

Understanding the Risk badge

Since the Health badge is about looking at the current issues in the environment, the Risk badge is looking at the future issues and health of the environment or object. If there are no immediate issues to address from the Health badge, Risk should be looked at next.

As was the case with the Health badge, the Risk badge is now derived from alerts and symptom definitions.

There are three minor badges that relate to Risk: Capacity Remaining, Time Remaining, and Stress.

> The accuracy of Risk, Capacity Remaining, and Time Remaining for your environment is heavily affected by what policies are in effect. Capacity management will be discussed in detail in *Chapter 6, Capacity Management Made Easy.*

The Capacity Remaining badge

The Capacity Remaining badge shows the percent of usable capacity not consumed. Therefore, an object with a score of 100 has all of its capacity available for use, and an object with a score of 0 would indicate that there is no capacity available at that moment.

In Operations Manager 5.x, Capacity Remaining was based on the number of virtual machines as the unit of capacity. In Operations Manager 6.0, the unit of capacity varies depending on the object type. This is primarily due to the fact that capacity management has been opened up to non-vSphere objects.

It is important to note that Capacity Remaining is based on the resource that is *most constrained*. For example, in the screenshot that follows, we can see that a vSphere cluster with CPU, memory, disk space, and vSphere configuration limit are selected as resources that are included in capacity management, which is the currently applied policy.

Looking at the four selected resources, memory is the most constrained at 30.19 percent, remaining after buffers are taken into account. Therefore, this is where the Capacity Remaining score is derived from for this object.

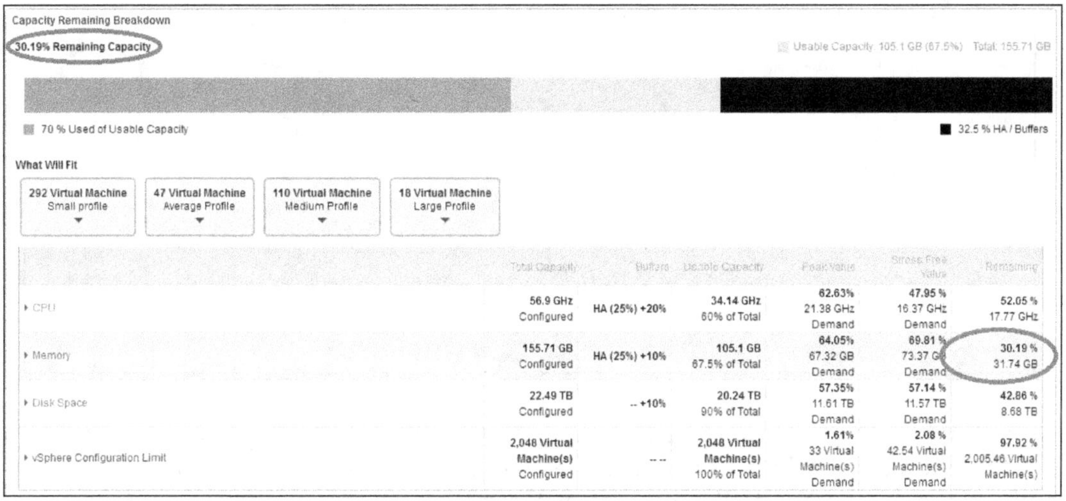

> Another major improvement with vROps 6.0 is that the capacity manager data is now provided with 5 minutes of granular samples. The original 1 hour samples are now only used for Time Remaining calculations.

The Time Remaining badge

The Time Remaining badge is the amount of time before an object runs out of capacity. The Time Remaining score is based on the number of days minus your provisioning time buffer based on the current rate of consumption or forecast.

The score for the Time Remaining badge ranges from 0 being bad and 100 being good. The most restrictive computing resource will be the one that makes an impact on the badge score. The following figures show a graphical example of Time Remaining:

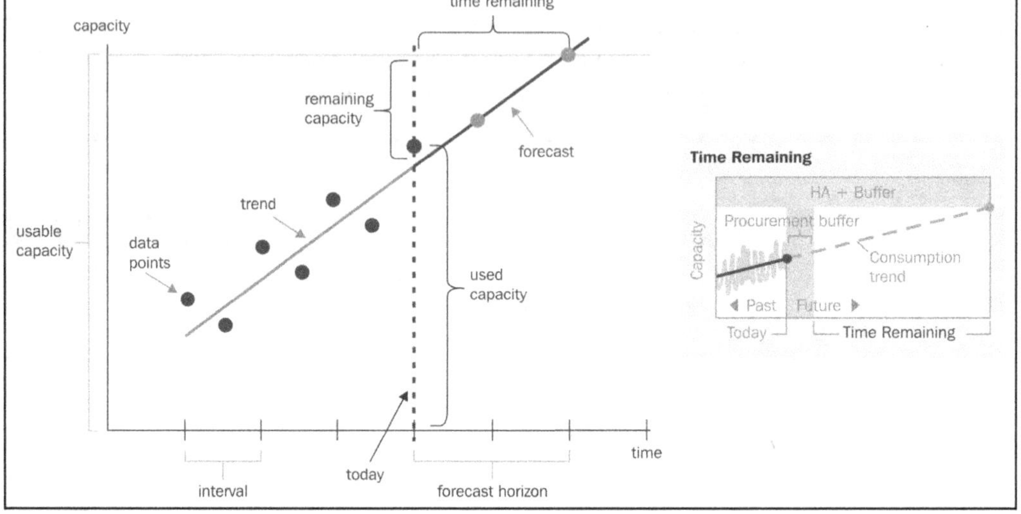

As is shown in the preceding figure, data points collected over a period of time are used to build a trend line. This line is then used to forecast capacity into the future, both for the demand and allocation of each relevant resource, for example CPU, memory, disk space, and so on.

The first component of the forecast is the provisioning buffer that is set in the associated policy. This buffer (30 days by default) is used as a value that administrators set to reflect how long it will take to add an additional capacity to the object. If the object is a vSphere cluster, for example, this setting should reflect how long it would take to provision another ESXi host that may even include the procurement time.

The time left after the provisioning buffer is exhausted, as shown in the preceding figure, is used to provide the score to the Time Remaining badge. If the estimated Time Remaining value is equal to or less than that of the provisioning buffer, the Time Remaining score will be 0. Each passing day, after the provisioning buffer is exhausted, will add to the Time Remaining scale with a maximum score of 100.

> The Time Remaining badge is only calculated once a day with the overnight batch processing. In vCOps 5.x, this was done at 1 A.M. and now with vROps 6.0, this process occurs at 10 P.M. Keep in mind that although changes to policies for capacity management will take effect straight away in terms of breakdowns and trending, the badge itself will only update overnight. One small exception to this rule is as soon as the project is committed, the Time Remaining badge will be updated soon afterwards.

The Stress badge

The Stress badge is an early warning view of the upcoming provisioning needs. An object that is experiences stress also experiences high usage of a resource over a period of time.

The Stress score accumulates when Workload exceeds the stress line. The Stress score is the percent of the stress zone area, shown with a dark color in the following figure. By default, the stress zone is above 70 percent and is observed in any 60-minute peak period. This is a change from Operations Manager 5.x, where the default was when demand exceeded 70 percent over the entire range.

> The entire range option is still available in vROps 6.0 and uses the date range set under **Policy** | **Time**. We recommend that you use peak periods over the entire range as it more accurately accounts for spikes in both undersized objects and capacity planning.

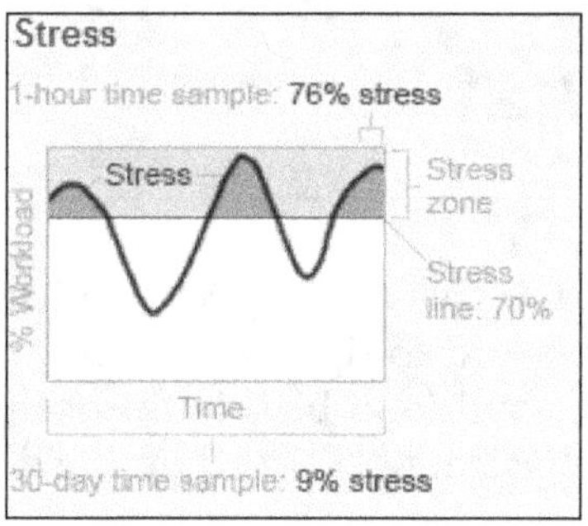

The Risk badge summary

The easiest way to look at the minor badges that are related to Risk are as follows:

- **Capacity Remaining**: This determines *what percentage of capacity* you have left on this object
- **Time Remaining**: This determines *how long* you have until you are out of resources
- **Stress**: This determines *how much pressure* a given object is under, whether it demands most or more of its currently assigned resources

Understanding the Efficiency badge

The Efficiency badge is the last major badge and it shows us how efficient we are with our resources in terms of rightsizing and target density ratios.

Issues related to efficiency are rarely issues that you would need to be alert of; however, they are useful to report and ensure that you are getting the most out of your infrastructure.

The Reclaimable Capacity badge

The Reclaimable Capacity badge is a graphical representation of the amount of unused computing resources currently assigned to your virtual machines.

In vSphere, Reclaimable Capacity is only applied to virtual machines, as it is seen that VMs are fairly straightforward to rightsize as requirements keep on changing in the environment. The same could not be said for hosts, for example, adding or removing resources from a physical host based on the demand would not be seen as a common task.

Although Reclaimable Capacity only applies to virtual machines, objects such as clusters, hosts, datastores, and other containers still have a badge (and associated score) due to the relationship of child VMs.

Reclaimable Capacity has four specific items that impact the score. These are:

- Oversized virtual machines
- Idle virtual machines
- Powered-off virtual machines
- Unused file capacity

The Reclaimable Capacity score is based on the resource that has the highest percentage of Reclaimable Capacity divided by its total capacity. This score ranges from 0 (good) to 100 (bad) and for virtual machines, this score filters up to the object's parent containers.

Idle VMs

Idle virtual machines are exactly as the name suggests, the number of virtual machines in your environment that are idle. How is a virtual machine considered idle? The idle calculation is directly related to the threshold settings that are set in policy for virtual machines under Reclaimable Capacity. Idle virtual machines are virtual machines with a computational usage less than the configured threshold. The settings that you would change are shown as follows:

By default, a virtual machine must spend 90 percent of its time consuming less than:

- 100 MHz CPU
- 20 I/O operations of disk
- 1 KBps of network I/O (both VM and host)

Take a look at the following figure showing idle and non-idle times of a virtual machine in normal conditions:

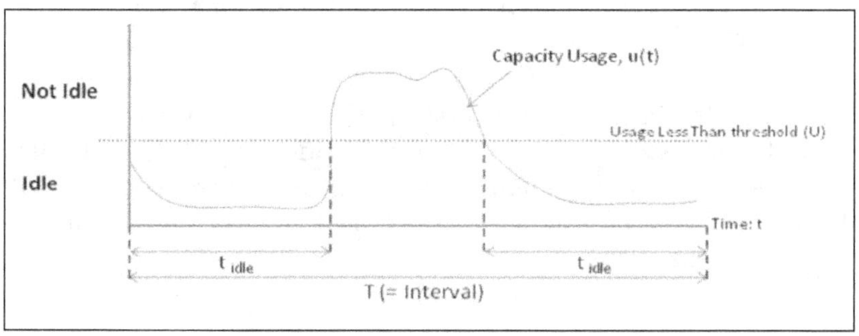

As per the preceding figure, the time interval (**T**) is the same value as was used for stress and other non-trended analytics.

> Some resource containers may need to be excluded from analysis to accurately detect idle VMs. Consider the scheduled activities, such as antivirus scans and possibly disabling disk I/O analysis to compensate for the inaccuracy.

Powered-off virtual machines

This is the simplest part of Reclaimable Capacity. By default, if a virtual machine is powered off for 90 percent of the time, then it is considered powered off and included in the Reclaimable Capacity. The percentage can be changed in the settings. This will include CPU, RAM, and disk capacity from the powered-off virtual machines.

> If you are using the default data range (time) of 30 days or longer, it is recommended that you adjust this value to 100 percent. This will ensure that VMs that are flagged as reclaimable due to being powered off are not used in the given time period.

Oversized virtual machines

Oversized VMs will generally be the bulk of the Reclaimable Capacity in your environment.

By default, a virtual machine is flagged oversized when the amount of CPU, memory, or disk space demand is below 50 percent for the selected data range (time period).

> For a production environment, it is recommended that the stress that accounts for the spikes and peaks setting is checked. This will ensure that VM peaks are taken into account to determine whether a VM is oversized.

A common question that arises with oversized VMs is what is the right-sizing value based on the data shown in the VM optimization report. The rightsizing recommendations are calculated using *demand + HA + buffers*. Therefore, it is important to consider which buffers are appropriate for your environment to ensure accuracy in these reports.

The Density badge

The Density badge score is the ratio of current density to calculated ideal density. Ideal Density is calculated using demand that is generated, the amount of virtual capacity that is provisioned, and the amount of actual, physically usable capacity deployed.

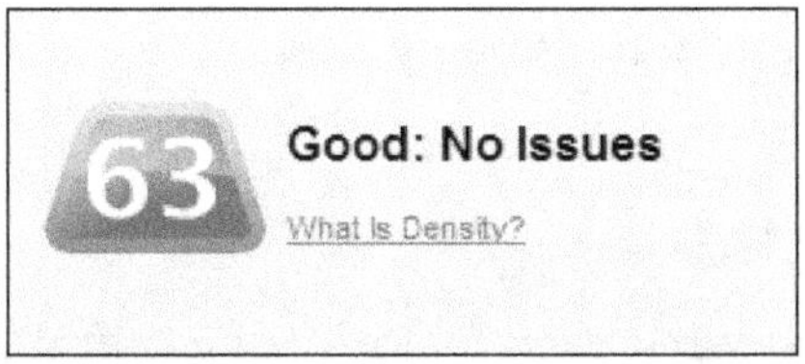

The goal of Density is to calculate the amount of resources that can be provisioned with minimal contention, and therefore, you can maximize the **return of investment (ROI)** you can receive from your infrastructure. There are three parts to density that are calculated. These are:

- VM to host
- vCPU to pCPU
- vMem to pMem

The Density score ranges from 0 (bad) to 100 (good) and the resource type with the highest Density score is taken as the badge score.

Child Population Breakdown

Ratio	Average	Optimal	Density Score
▸ Virtual Machine:Host System	6.32 : 1	10.06 : 1	62.82
▸ CPU	3.67 : 1	9.56 : 1	38.36
▸ Memory	0.56 : 1	0.89 : 1	62.82

Density is a badge that is useful to understand your workloads at a macro level in terms of what ratios your environment is actually achieving. It is also important that as the Density score of a host or cluster increases over time, its Capacity Remaining score will decrease.

The Efficiency badge summary

The best way to sum up the minor badges of the Efficiency badge is as follows:

- **Reclaimable Capacity**: This determines which *resources* you have assigned that are not being used at all or used very little
- **Density**: This determines how close you are to an "*ideal*" *density* based on all your resources and what's being used

Summary

In this chapter, you learned what each major badge is and how it relates to your environment. We also covered the differences between badges in Operations Manager 5.x and 6.0. We then dived into each badge (major and minor) and looked at how they are calculated to give you a better idea of how the resultant numbers are generated and how to interpret them in your own environment.

4
The Merged UI

If you are familiar with vCOps 5.8.x Advanced or Enterprise, you will be familiar with how to use two different user interfaces—the vSphere user interface and the Custom user interface. Now, in vRealize Operations Manager 6.0, it has all changed.

Not only has the general look of the user interface (UI) changed, the vSphere and Custom UIs have been merged into what is the shiny new interface of vROps 6.0, called the Product UI (or just the UI for short).

In this chapter, we will look at the following topics:

- Overview of the new UI
- Different components that make up the UI
- Primary vROps sections overview

What has changed in the new UI?

vCOps has gone to see a Hollywood makeup artist and had a complete face-lift. Since vCOps 1.x, multiple user interfaces have been required to leverage vSphere data versus data from other adapter sources.

The vSphere UI only allowed us to view vSphere objects and (with the exception of policies) could not be customized at all. It also had a similar look and feel to the vSphere Web Client.

The vSphere UI has become rather iconic to vCOps and at the same time, it is very simple to navigate and can be used to find the information you are looking for. An example of the vCOps 5.x UI is shown in the following screenshot:

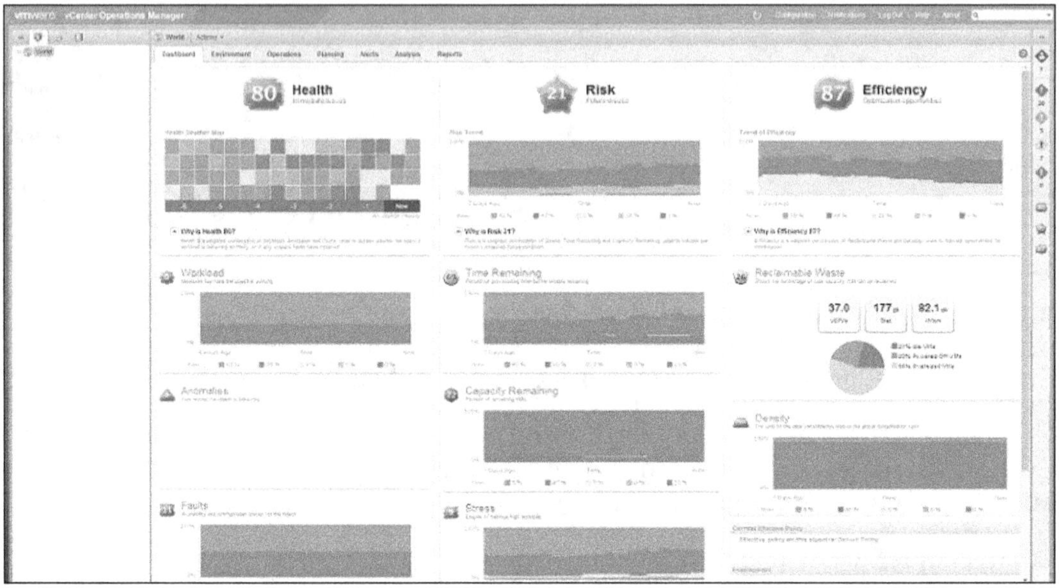

Then, there is the Custom UI. This is where you can find "other" objects from third-party adapters or management packs. In this UI, you can manipulate data and display it all in what are called custom dashboards. An example of this interface is shown in the following screenshot:

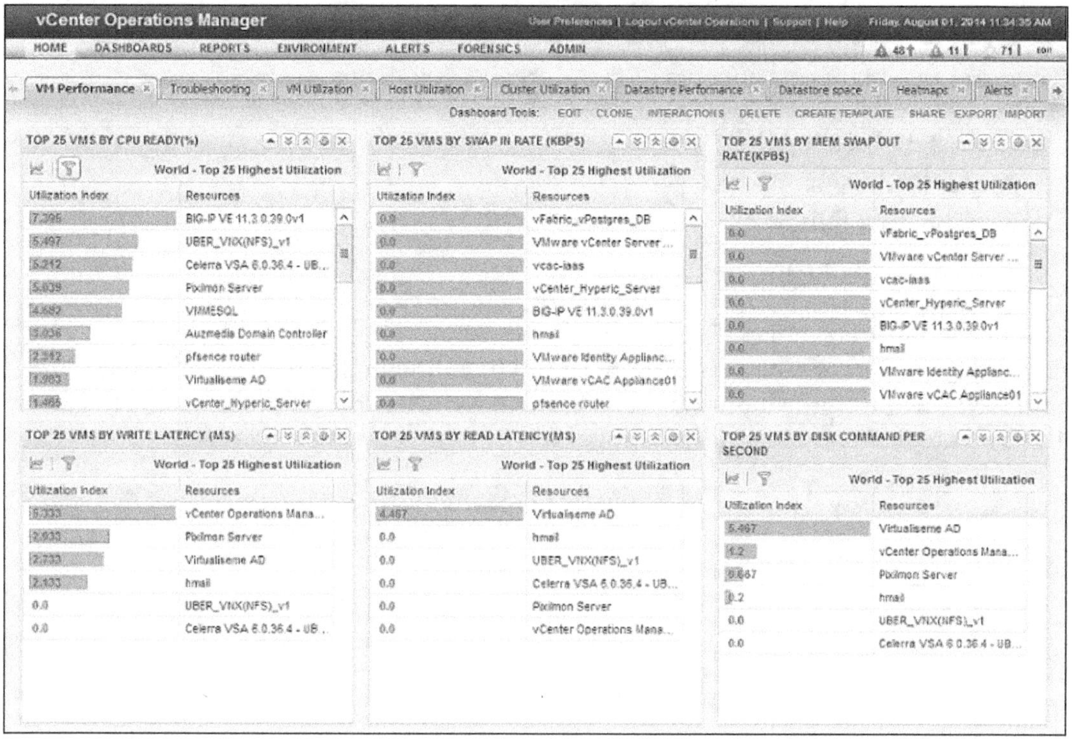

Now, what do we get if we merge these UIs together? We get one really functional and customizable dashboard that has everything in a single location. This is what is called the Product UI or what many administrators refer to as the Merged UI; an example of this is shown in the following screenshot:

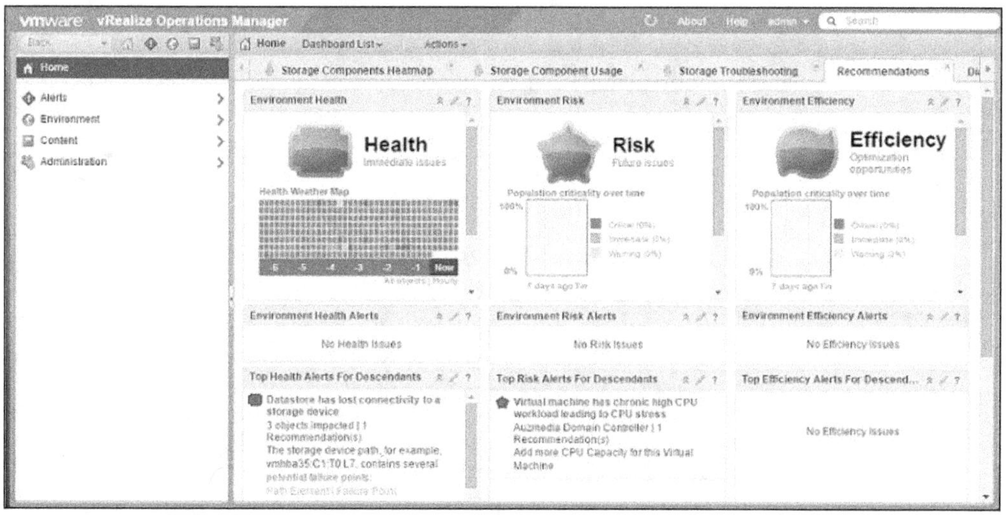

Components that make up the Merged UI

There are five main components of the Merged UI, which are:

- The navigation pane
- Quick links
- The back button
- The content pane
- Tabs

The navigation pane is the pane to the left, which houses the navigation tree to find and navigate through all our objects on which we are collecting metrics as well as the user-created content. This is highlighted in the following screenshot:

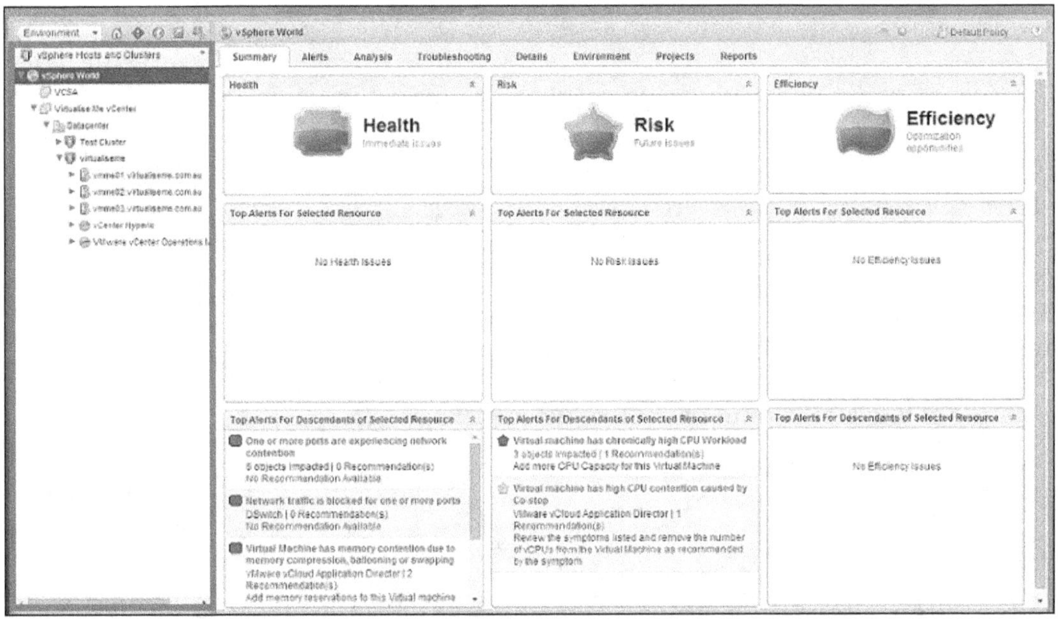

Next, we will look at the quick links; these are located just above the navigation pane as little icons. As the name suggests, they are quick links to different options of vROps 6.0. You can see the quick link section in the following screenshot:

The five icons highlighted in the preceding screenshot are for the following purposes:

- The house icon: This is the quick link to **Home** and is similar to the "world" view of the old vCOps 5.x vSphere UI.
- The warning icon: This is a quick link to the **Alerts** section of vROps 6.0.
- The globe icon: This is a quick link to the **Environment** section that takes us to the environment overview where we can pick from hosts, storage, networking, and so on; basically, everything in the environment that we can collect data from.
- The book icon: This is the quick link to the **Content** section that will take you to an area that has content such as dashboards, alert definitions, and super metrics; basically, anything that has been created by the users of vROps as well as provided out of the box by various installed solutions.
- The cogwheel icon: This is the quick link to the **Administration** section. This link takes you to the admin section where we can create users, modify global settings, and manage the vROps 6.0 cluster nodes, such as rebalancing. This is similar to browsing directly to the Admin UI on a vROps node at `https://<NodeIP>/admin`.

Next we see, to the left of quick links, is the back button, something that we will become very familiar with. When the button is clicked, it will take you back to the last page visited. The writing on the button is where we will be taken to if it is clicked. So, with the example shown in the following screenshot, if we click the button, we will be navigated back to the **Environment** section:

The **Content** section is next on the list. This is where all the content is displayed, and this is a large pane to the right, which displays the information based on what is selected in the navigation pane, as shown in the following screenshot. As was the case with vCOps 5.x, the content pane shows the previously selected objects in the navigation pane. Keep in mind that the values or badges are alike and always in context of the selected object.

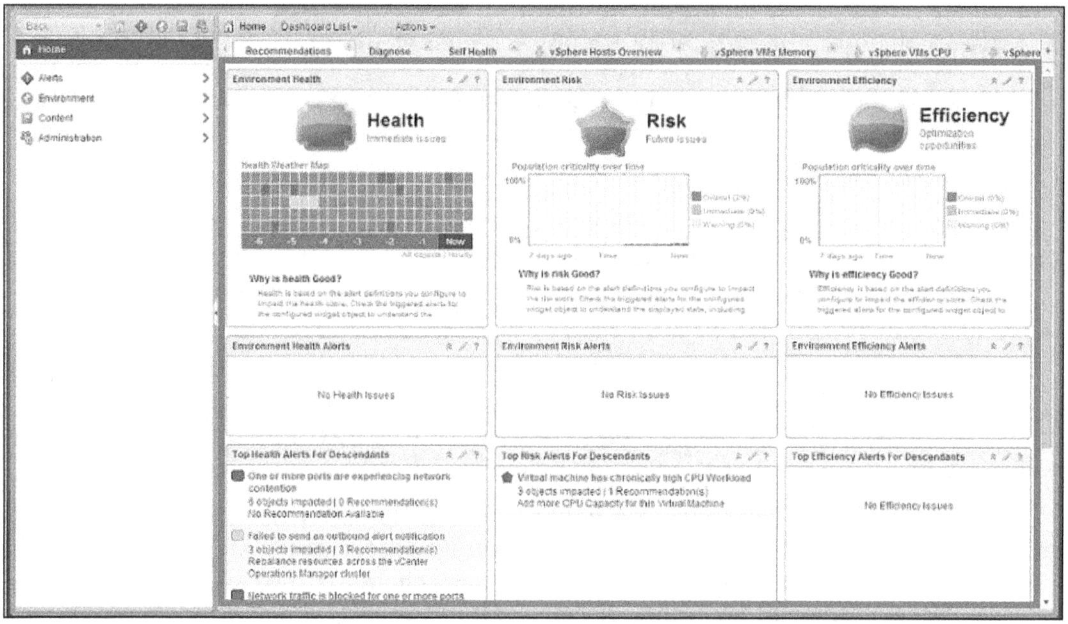

Last but not least are the tabs. The tabs are located directly above the content pane and some would say are a part of the content pane. They have been separated out as they also change what is displayed in the main part of the content pane, which can be different for different users as this is where the custom dashboards will sit. Some such tabs are shown in the following screenshot:

The primary vROps sections overview

Now, it is time to dive into the different areas of the Product UI. The first section we will cover is the **Home** screen.

This screen is where all the custom dashboards you have access to will be displayed. For those of you who are familiar with the vCOps 5.x world screen, this will look similar. The default dashboard is similar to the old vSphere UI home screen in vCOps 5.x.

The navigation pane houses:

- **Alerts**
- **Environment**
- **Content**
- **Administration**

These match the quick links at the top-left next to the **Back** button, as shown earlier. When you click on these links, they will navigate you to the corresponding sections.

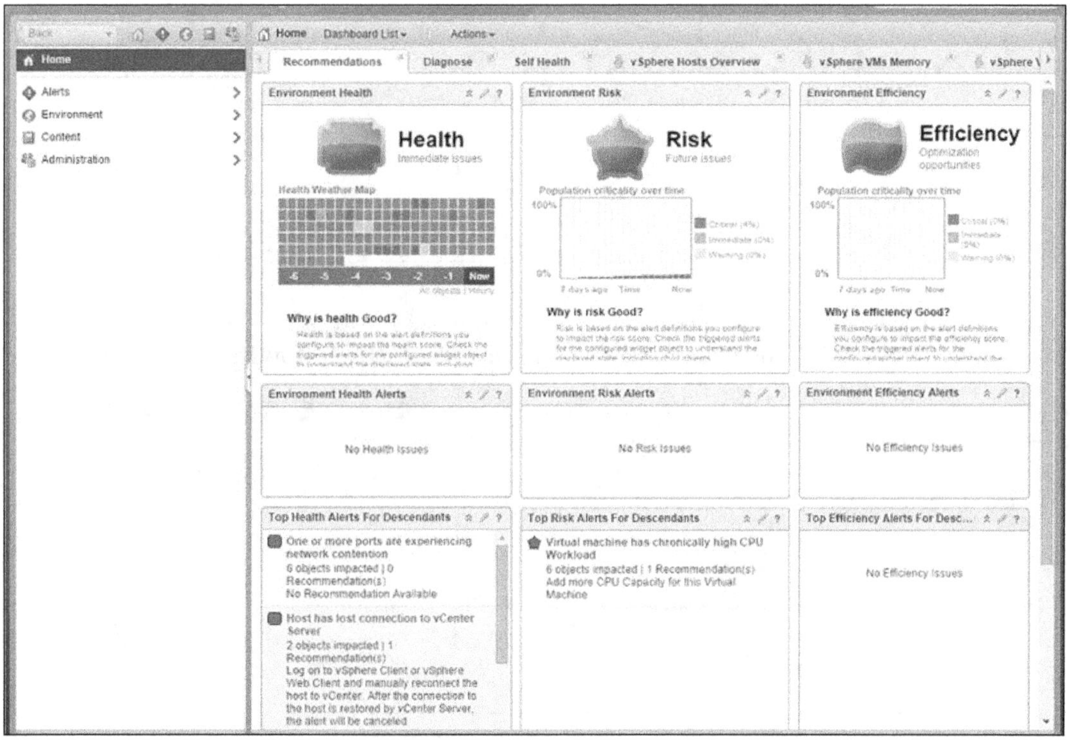

Alerts

The **Alerts** section is exactly as the name suggests and it shows by default all the active alerts. This can be changed with the filter options that are on the top of the content pane. The following is an example screenshot of the **Alert** section:

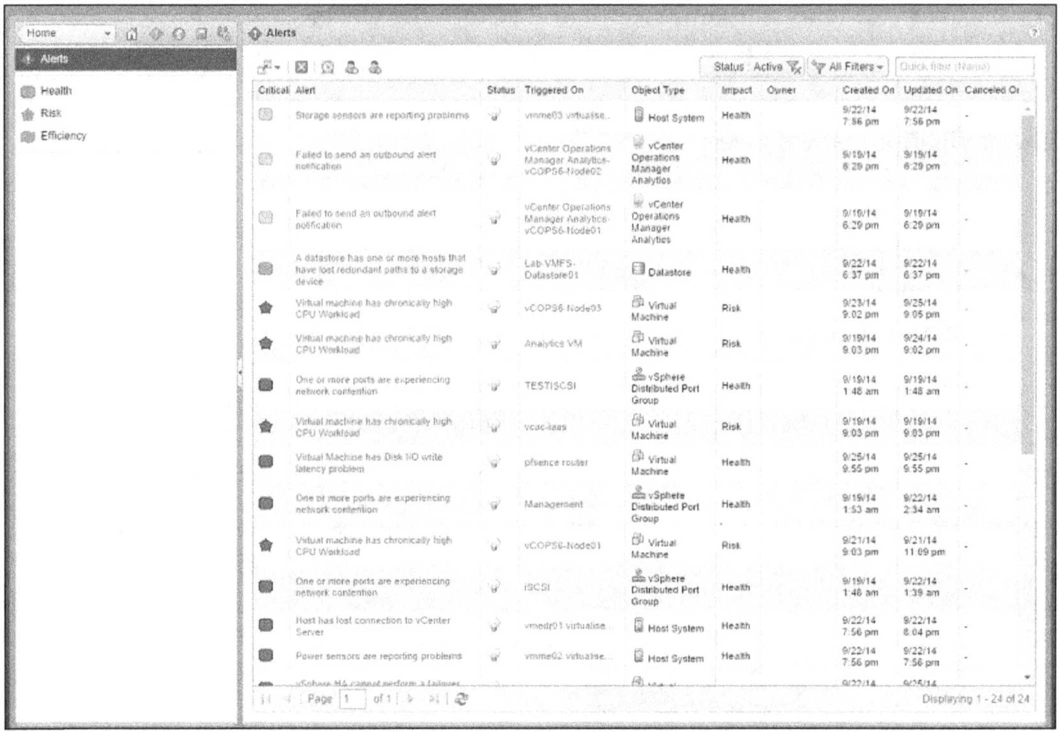

The **Health**, **Risk**, and **Efficiency** options in the navigation pane when selected, will filter the alerts by the selected badge, as shown in the following screenshot:

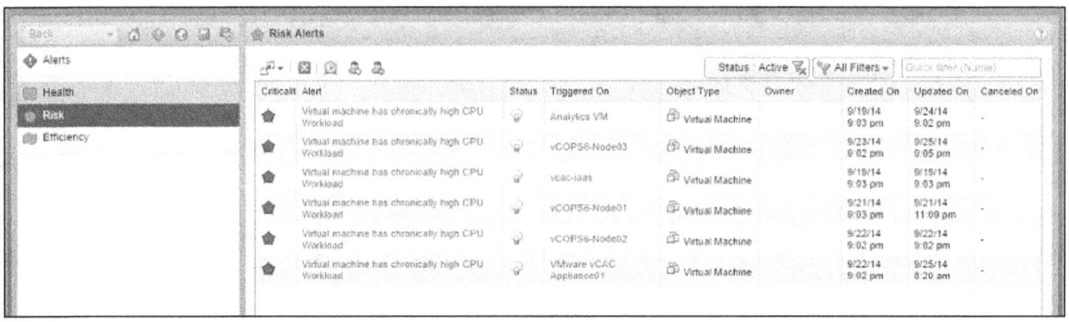

Environment

The **Environment** section is where you can find all the objects that vROps 6.0 grabs information of. This is the place to go when you want to look at the metrics or details of objects, such as, VMs, hosts, datastores, and so on.

At the top of the navigation pane is the environment overview, which allows you to see all the groups, applications, and the inventory of all objects in vROps 6.0 via the tabs in the content pane to the right.

Under the **Environment Overview** section, there are two different types of selectable menu items in the navigation pane. These are **Groups** and **Applications**, and **Inventory Trees**. This is shown in the following screenshot:

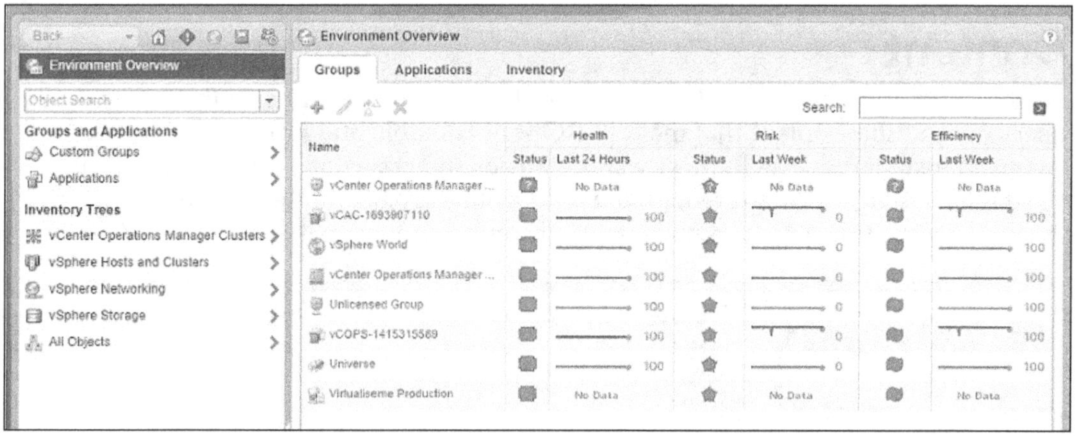

The navigation pane of the **Environment** section will vary depending on which solutions have been installed. By default, it will have the following options:

- **Custom Groups**: This is the first option in the environment navigation pane that displays the custom groups information. These groups are the same as in the previous versions of vCOps 5.x. These are groups of objects that are created by users, imported by solutions, or are built-in.
- **Applications**: This option takes us to the section where you'll see all the applications that have been defined by you or using VMware Infrastructure Navigator to import applications that have been mapped out. An application can have one virtual machine, five virtual machines, or more. vROps 6.0 will monitor the application as a whole, taking into account the health and metrics of all the virtual machines or other objects that are part of it.
- **vCenter Operation Manager Clusters**: This navigation option just takes us to the nodes that make up the vROps 6.0 cluster we are currently logged in to.

- **vSphere Hosts and Clusters**: This option provides access to the vSphere navigation tree where all the details and metrics of all the vCenter objects, such as clusters, hosts, and virtual machines can be seen. It has a similar tree structure to what we saw in the vSphere Web Client.
- **vSphere Networking**: This option is similar to the preceding option of hosts and clusters, but this option will only show all of the virtual switches and port groups.
- **vSphere Storage**: This option is similar to the preceding option and the networking option, but shows the datastore objects.
- **All objects**: As the name suggests, this option will show all the objects that vROps 6.0 collects metrics for and are listed by solutions.

Content

As the following screenshot shows, the **Content** section contains all the user-configurable content that makes vROps 6.0 flexible and powerful. Because this is a fresh installation, it will mostly show out-of-the-box configuration items, but if the environment was migrated, all the data from the 5.8.x implementation, such as custom dashboards, super metrics, and groups would be visible too.

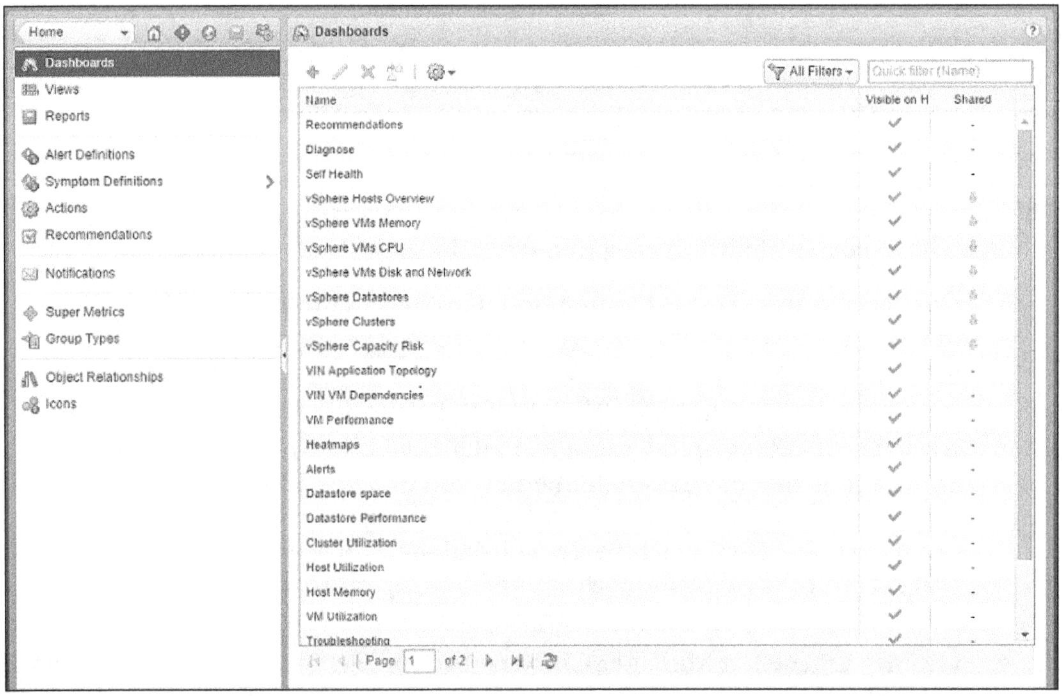

The content navigation pane contains the following sections:

- **Dashboards**: This section shows all the dashboards within the content pane that come preinstalled, installed from solutions (adapters), or are user-created dashboards. In the content pane, select which dashboards should be visible, which ones should be shared, or whether to create new or delete old dashboards.
- **Views**: This section is similar to the **Dashboards** option and will show all the views that come preinstalled, installed from solutions, or the views that are created by users. Views prior to vROps 6.0 could not be added or changed. Views will be covered in *Chapter 8, Reporting and Views*.
- **Reports**: Reports are basically a collection of views wrapped in a cover sheet. This section is similar to both views and dashboards. We can create and edit reports within the content pane. Reports will also be covered in *Chapter 8, Reporting and Views*.
- **Alert Definitions**: This section shows all the definitions that make up alarms. This section allows the creation of new alarms or allows us to edit the existing alarms. It is recommended that you do not change the prebuilt alarms, but you can copy and create new alarms.
- **Symptom Definitions**: This section is similar to **Alert Definitions**. Symptom definitions is where you can create new symptoms to be associated with alarms. These definitions will be covered in more detail in *Chapter 13, Alerting, Actions, and Recommendations*.
- **Actions**: This section shows all the actions that have come prebuilt in vROps 6.0. Actions can be used to fix symptoms. Creating custom actions is possible, but there is no way to build these through the UI currently.
- **Recommendations**: This section shows all the prebuilt recommendations where we are allowed to create custom recommendations. Recommendations are attached to alerts to show how to remediate the cause of alerts. We will also discuss this in *Chapter 13, Alerting, Actions, and Recommendations*.
- **Notifications**: This section is where notifications can be created. Based on alerts that have been configured, notifications can be e-mailed or sent via the REST API.
- **Super Metrics**: By default, there will be no super metrics in the content pane if it is a fresh installation. If you've migrated from an existing vCOps 5.8.x environment, all the previous super metrics should be visible. In this section, super metrics can be created and edited.

- **Group Types**: In this section, all the default group types in the content pane will be visible. You can also create or delete group types from this page. Group types are folders or headings to add groups, for example, adding Finance group as a Department type.
- **Object Relationships**: This section shows the most important part of the **Content** section where we can select an object and see its child and parent resources. Moreover, we can add and create custom relationships between objects.
- **Icons**: This section is where we can assign icons to objects or adapter kinds. We can also upload and add in custom icons if the built-in icons are not suited to our use.

Administration

The **Administration** section is where the vROps 6.0 instance is administered from. In the following screenshot, you can see everything that a vROps admin would need, such as, licensing, access, policies, and more:

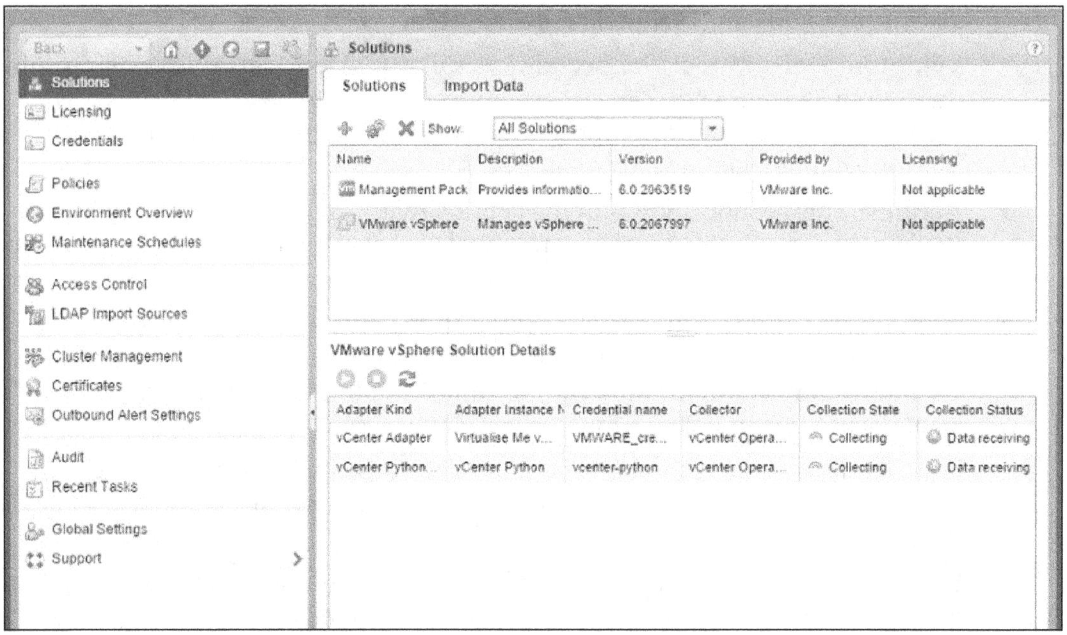

The following links are located in the administration navigation pane:

- **Solutions**: This is where adapters are configured; in vROps 6.0, these are now referred to as solutions.
- **Licensing**: This is where you can apply for licenses of vROps 6.0 and solutions.
- **Credentials**: This is where we can add, modify, or delete credentials that are used to connect to solutions, including vCenter.
- **Policies**: We can create, edit, or delete policies in this section.
- **Environment Overview**: This section is exactly as it sounds, an overview of the entire environment. It gives an overview of every object that the vROps 6.0 instance collects data on and its collection status.
- **Maintenance Schedules**: In this section, we can create or edit maintenance schedules. By default, there will be nothing in here unless a schedule is created. Maintenance schedules are used for patching cycles or anything that would see alerts raised due to outages.
- **Access Control**: This is where users and groups are granted access to vROps 6.0. Moreover, roles are defined and password policies are configured in this section.
- **LDAP Import Sources**: This is where the LDAP authentication sources are configured. This configuration is used to authenticate users of vROps.
- **Cluster Management**: This is where the vROps 6.0 cluster can be managed, nodes can be shut down, and clusters can be rebalanced.
- **Certificates**: This is where all the certificates of all the endpoints that vROps 6.0 is connected to are shown. So, all vCenters that vROps 6.0 monitors would be in here.
- **Outbound Alert Settings**: This is where the outbound alert instances are configured.
- **Audit**: This is where all the user activity on the system is shown.
- **Recent Tasks**: This is where all the recent tasks that have taken place on the system are listed.
- **Global Settings**: This is where all the changes to the global vROps 6.0 settings are made. These settings persist across all the users.
- **Support**: In this section, we can see the logs on all the nodes, generate support bundles, and can start or stop dynamic threshold calculations.

Summary

In this chapter, we had a quick overview of the new vROps 6.0 UI. We learned what each section is for and which components make up the UI.

In the next chapter, we will learn about policies and how they can be created and used to get the most out of vROps.

5

Policies in vRealize Operations Manager 6.0

In the previous chapter, you learned about the Product UI and the components that it comprises of. It is time now to look at policies and what role policies play in vROps 6.0 over its previous versions; this will give us an insight into how ingrained policies are in day-to-day use of vROps 6.0. In this chapter, we will cover the following:

- What are policies?
- How to create and modify policies
- How to create modular policies to allow the reuse of small policies across the environment

What are policies?

In vCOps 5.8.x or its earlier versions, policies were primarily focused on capacity management and to what extent badges changed alert levels. vCOps gave the ability to change allocation ratios, including stress level, adding buffers, and all the usual virtualization capacity management settings we would like. Policies could also affect badge thresholds and alerts, but only their basic in functionalities, and in many environments settings for policies was left as default.

However, in vROps 6.0, policies have become the core of what drives vROps. All alerts, metric collections, notifications, badge scores, and capacity management values are driven by the new policy engine and can be applied to a single object or the entire environment. The following bullets shed some more light on the different areas that policies now drive:

- **Policies for any solution or adapter**: With the merged UI and the shift of focus towards treating all solutions and adapters equally, polices are no longer limited to the vSphere adapter.
- **Capacity management**: This is similar to the earlier versions of Operations Manager. Capacity management allows us to configure allocation ratios, undersized and oversized machine thresholds, and capacity buffers.
- **Badge thresholds and scores**: We can configure all the minor badge thresholds by setting various threshold levels and scores, which range from 0 to 100.
- **Disabling or enabling metric collection**: Policies give us the ability to control which metrics get collected and which ones don't. This is a big improvement over previous releases that only allowed two collection types that could only be applied at the adapter level. Now, we can specify the object-level collection.
- **Enabling or disabling alerts**: This was one of the big issues with the previous releases of Operations Manager from an operations standpoint. We could disable alerts, but it was applied to the entire object type. For example, you could not easily disable capacity alerts for datastores while keeping fault issues still active. Now, we can specify which alerts are disabled or enabled.
- **Enabling or disabling symptoms**: Similar to the preceding alerts, we can enable and disable specific symptoms. Symptoms are new to vROps 6.0 and are used to configure alert triggers as well as highlight issues in the environment.

While the policies have overall been greatly improved in vROps 6.0 over vCOps 5.x, two of the best new features introduced in vROps 6 are inheriting policies and overriding policies. For the administrators new to the environment, this reduces the amount of work needed to create policies to match the environment.

The base policy is an important part of how inheritance works. While creating a new policy, a base policy is selected. This can be any policy that's been created or that is out of the box. While selecting this base policy, all the policy settings and configurations are automatically set in the new policy.

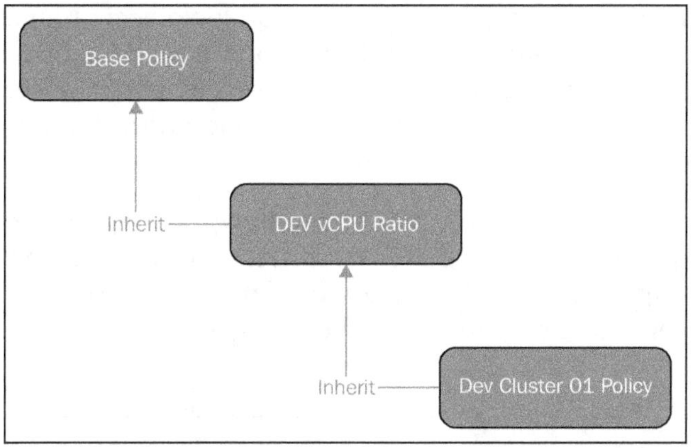

If a change was to be made to a policy and that policy is used as a base policy, then any policies using it as the base policy will automatically receive those changes. Unless what is changed is specifically set within the policy, the inheritance settings are overwritten.

While creating a policy, an override policy can be used, which is very similar to a base policy. The difference, given that any policy can be used as an override policy, is that multiple override policies can be used. If a change is made to a policy that was used as an override policy, the policy that used it as an override would *not* receive those changes. Editing a policy and reapplying the override policy would implement any changes made.

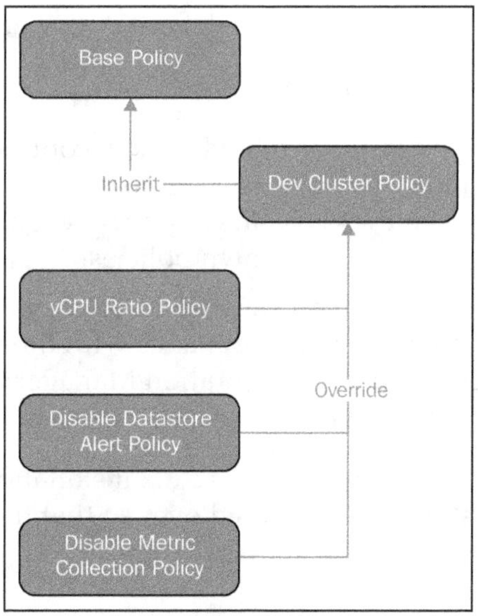

Policies are assigned to a group, which can be a single object or an entire collection of objects. An example of a group is the built-in vSphere world group that encompasses everything that is vCenter-related. So what happens when an object belongs to two or more groups? What will happen if each group has a different policy? Which one would take effect?

In vROps, the policy in effect is based on the policy priority; whichever policy has the higher priority will win when there is a conflict, priority 1 being higher than priority 5, for example. The priority is shown on the active policy tab, as shown in the following screenshot. The policies can be dragged and dropped in the priority that is desired.

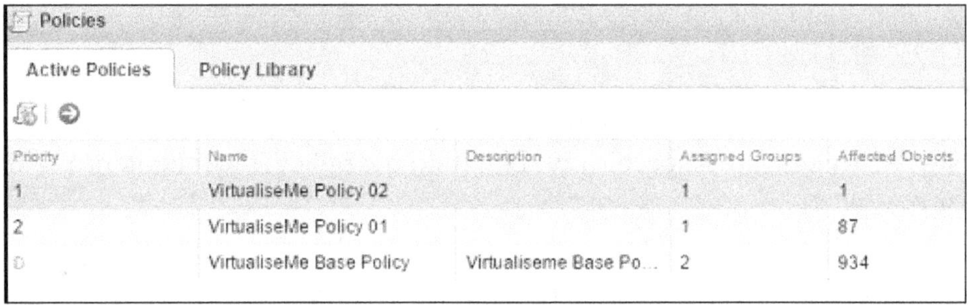

Creating policies

To create policies, navigate to the policy section. This is located under the Administration section of the UI. If this is a fresh installation and we don't choose the policy creation option, we will only see the default policy and other built-in policies.

Two of the built-in policies worth mentioning are:

- **Base settings**: These cannot be edited as they contain all the policy configuration settings available in vROps 6.0. These base settings are designed to be the vendor's baseline of policy recommendations that can then be copied and modified for your own policies.
- **The vSphere 5.5 hardening guide**: This is a policy that is configured to check whether the environment is in compliance with the vSphere 5.5 hardening guide. Note that if vCenter Configuration Manager is being used, this policy will be overwritten and will no longer be shown in the compliance tab.

If we have migrated from an existing vCOps 5.8.x installation that had profiles already configured, they should be migrated over so that they are visible, as shown in the following screenshot:

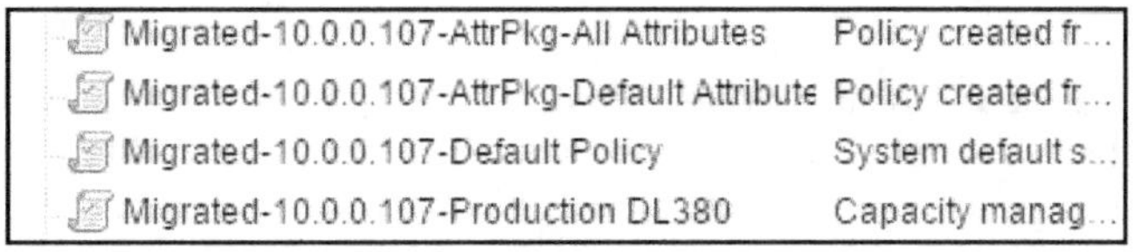

Let's now go through the motions of creating a policy. It's a good idea to create a new standard environment policy for an environment that would be used as the environment's "default" policy, rather than using the out-of-the-box default policy.

The new standard policy doesn't have to cover every little detail but just the common settings that are likely to be the same across the entire environment. These could be capacity buffer amounts, alerts, or metric collections that would be the same across all the clusters or hosts in the environment. This can then be used as the base policy for all future policies to reduce the amount of time required to configure these policies.

The settings used in the following demo are just examples and are simply used for demonstration purposes. The changes made are purely to show what can be configured and then a set of processes is undertaken to configure them, as follows:

1. To start off, click on the green plus symbol. This will bring up the policy creation dialog window.
2. In this window, enter the name and a description. Since this is the new default policy, it is best to name it accordingly.
3. Under **Start with**, select what will be the base policy for this policy. Because we are creating a new default policy, it is recommended that you select **Base Settings**. This is shown in the following screenshot:

> Base settings cannot be edited by the users of vROps. They only change when new solutions are installed, which will generally add policy settings for objects related to the solution installed.

4. Once you are happy with the name, description, and the selected base policy, move on to the next part, which is base policies. To access this, click on the option that is labeled as **Select Base Policies**. We will then be presented with a bunch of settings, which are similar to what is shown in the following screenshot:

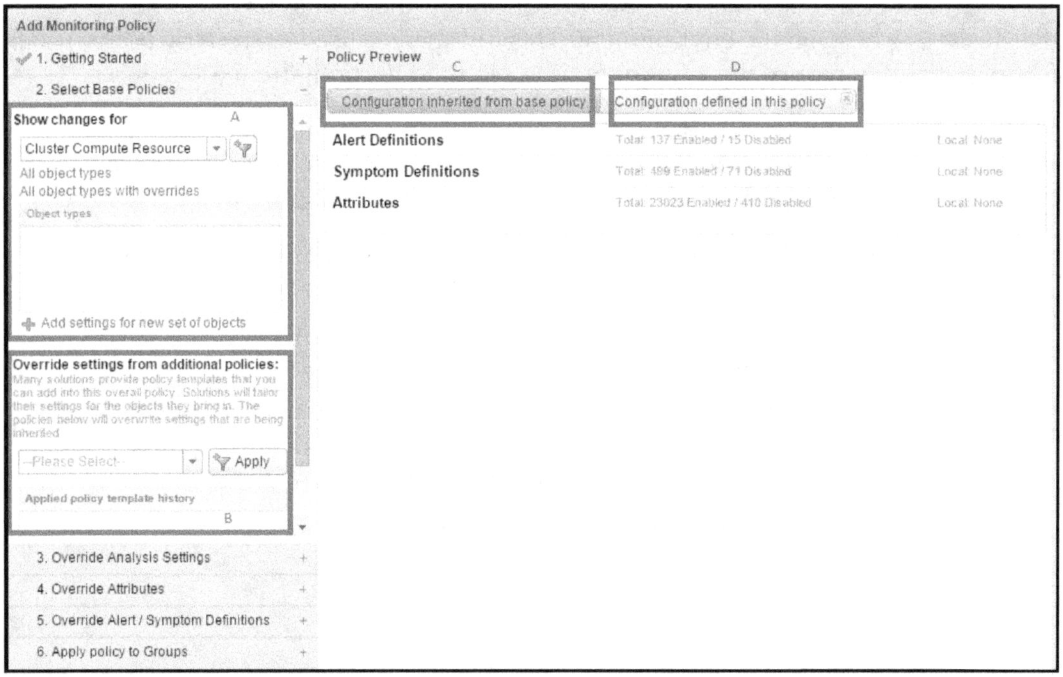

The following is a breakdown of what we are seeing here in the preceding screenshot:

- **Show changes for**: This section allows us to display any modifications that the override section would apply.
- **Override section from additional policies**: This section is where policies can be added and the settings of those policies get added to the current policy. This will be covered later on in this chapter.

- ° **Configuration inherited from base policy**: This defines what configuration is being inherited from the base policy. In this case, the policy base settings. For example, cluster CPU usage is being collected in the base policy would mean cluster CPU usage will also be configured in the new policy.
- ° **Configuration defined in this policy**: This is the configuration that has been set locally in this policy. Initially this will be blank when first creating a policy, until we make changes or apply override policies.

5. To show which policy settings are available here, select the **All object types** link under **Show changes for**, so that we can see what is available and what settings can be changed. When this link is clicked, we should see something similar to what is shown in the following screenshot:

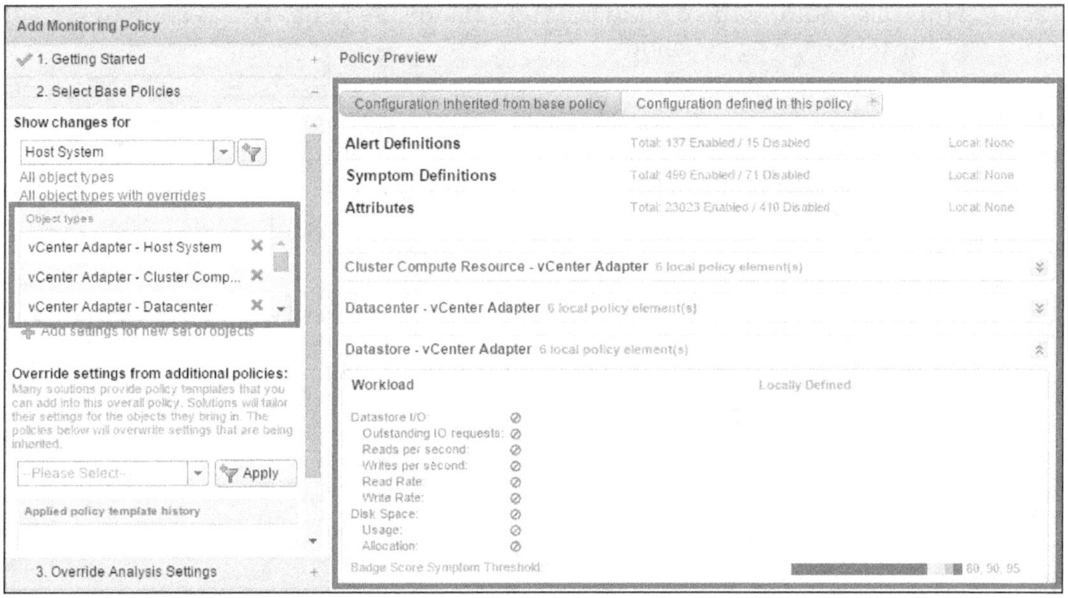

You will notice that on the left, the **Object types** section, which was previously empty now contains all the available configuration sections that have little red crosses next to them. If you click on them, vROps will remove that object from both the right and the left frame.

On the right side pane, all the objects are color coded for the adapter type. These are all the different objects on which we can make configuration changes.

While we have selected to show all, if for example, this policy was only targeted at virtual machines, then from the drop-down list, virtual machines could be selected specifically and only virtual machine policies settings will be shown.

For this initial configuration, we can see that there are zero local policy changes. Click on the down arrows on each of the objects and see the detail of the current configuration as inherited by the base policy and/or overwritten by another policy, which is not used in this case.

1. For now, there is nothing that we actually need to do in the base policy section, as purely informational content is shown on this screen. Now, we will click on the **Override Analysis Settings** option to the left.
2. This section is where badge-related and capacity-related changes can be made. Under the **Show changes for** section, click on the **All object types** link. This will add all the available object types in the object type's box while also adding them all to the right-hand side pane. This is shown in the following screenshot:

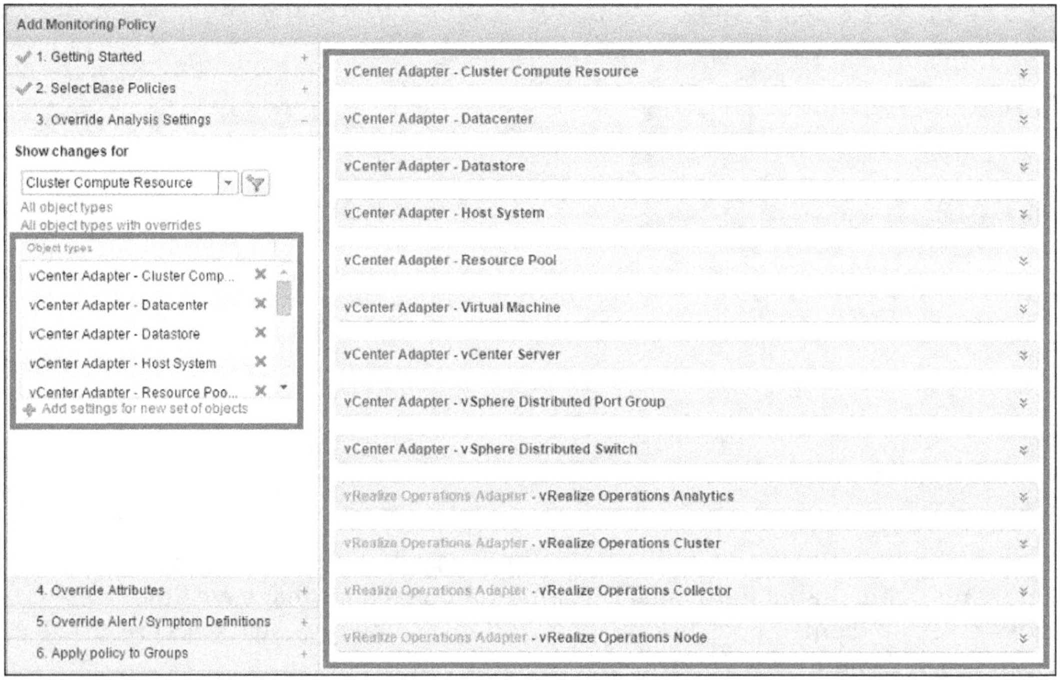

3. The pane on the right is where the changes are made in each of the object type's row and there is a small double arrow to the very right for each object type. Click on this arrow to expand the object type so that it reveals the configuration settings for that object, which can be changed.

   In this example, changes will be made to **Cluster Compute Resource** and **Virtual Machine resource**.

4. Click on the **Cluster Compute Resource** type to expand it. You should now see something similar to what is shown in the following screenshot:

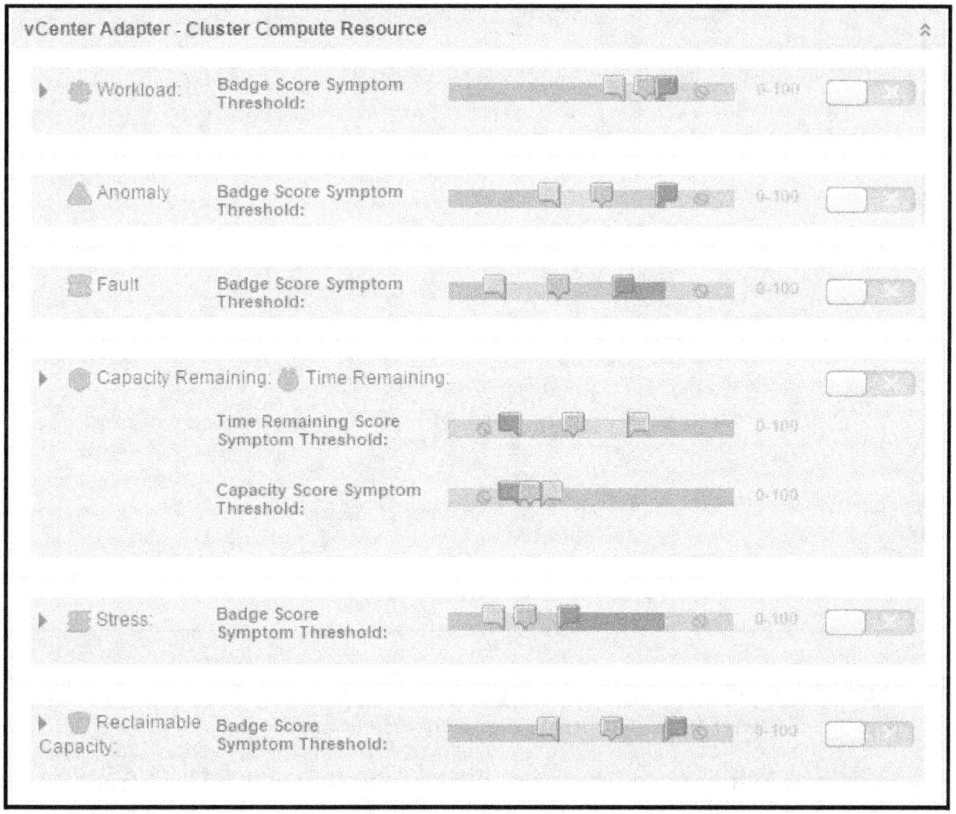

5. You will see all the options available that are currently grayed out. They are grayed out because they are inherited settings. If changes are to be made, click and drag the switch-like icon to the on state.

6. In the cluster compute resource object, we only want to make changes to a couple of items for this demo, of which one is the **Capacity Remaining** and **Time Remaining** option. Switch it on.

7. Once this is done, click on the little black arrow to the left of the screen. It will now be expanded to show all the properties, as shown in the following screenshot:

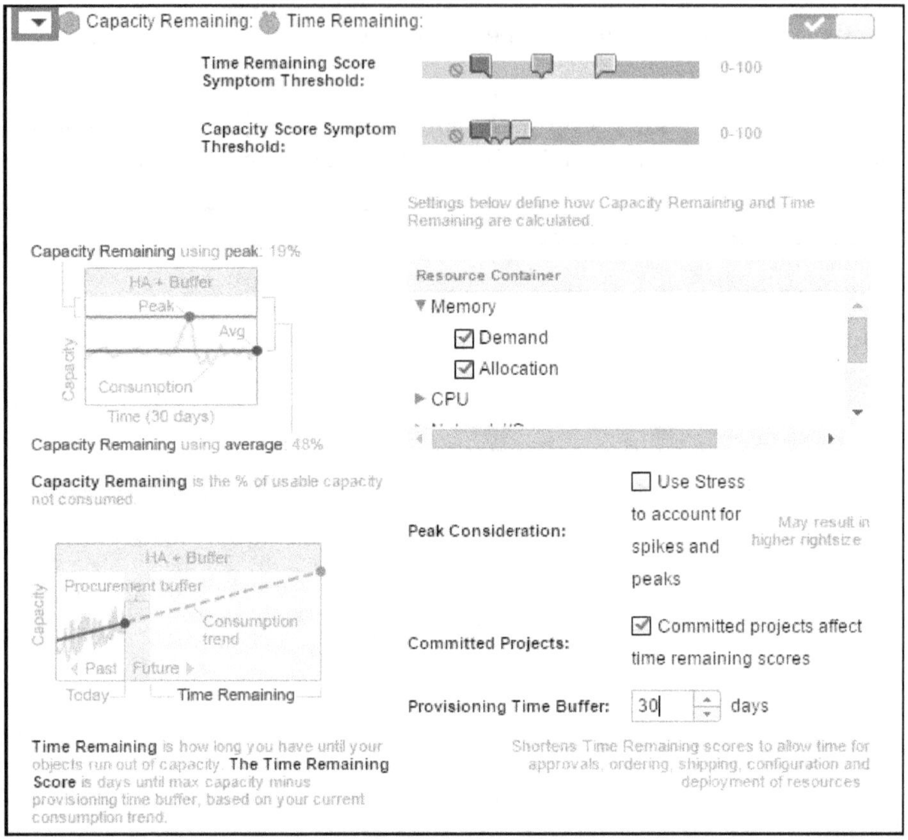

The options that are seen and chosen in the next steps are explained in detail in *Chapter 6, Capacity Management Made Easy*.

8. As shown in the preceding screenshot, we will uncheck **Use Stress to account for spikes and peaks** for our demo, and select **Allocation** as well as **Demand** for the **Memory** resources.
9. The next item to be changed is **Usable Capacity**. Again, unlock it and expand. In this area, we will remove all capacity buffers from all resources by unchecking them. Also, change the allocation overcommit to **50** percent, as shown in the following screenshot.

So why did we make these changes? This is going to be our environment's default policy. We may want to leave buffers to particular clusters and situations. Also, at the very least, we would like to have 50 percent memory overcommit across all clusters in this environment, as shown in the following screenshot. Use of large pages would be disabled so that we could get this overcommit.

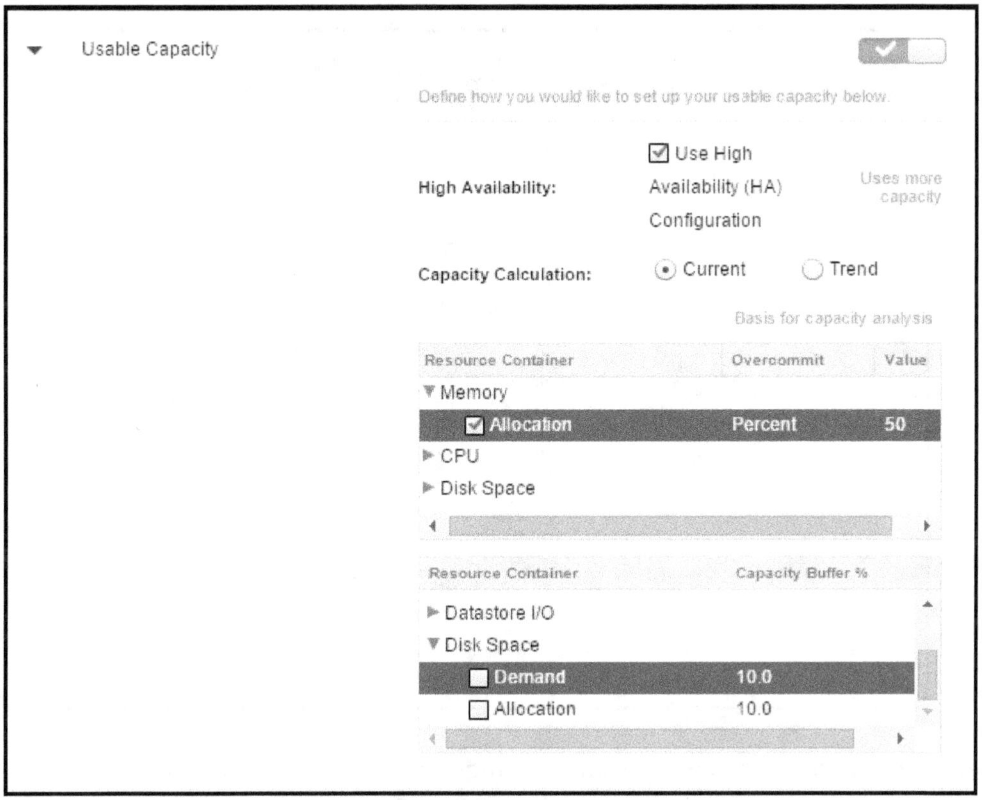

Now, we will move on to the Virtual Machine object.

1. Enable and expand **Reclaimable Capacity**. Here, we will change the number of days a snapshot to be retained when not in use from **180** to **30**. It is generally a good idea to reduce this number as snapshots should not be kept for long periods of time.

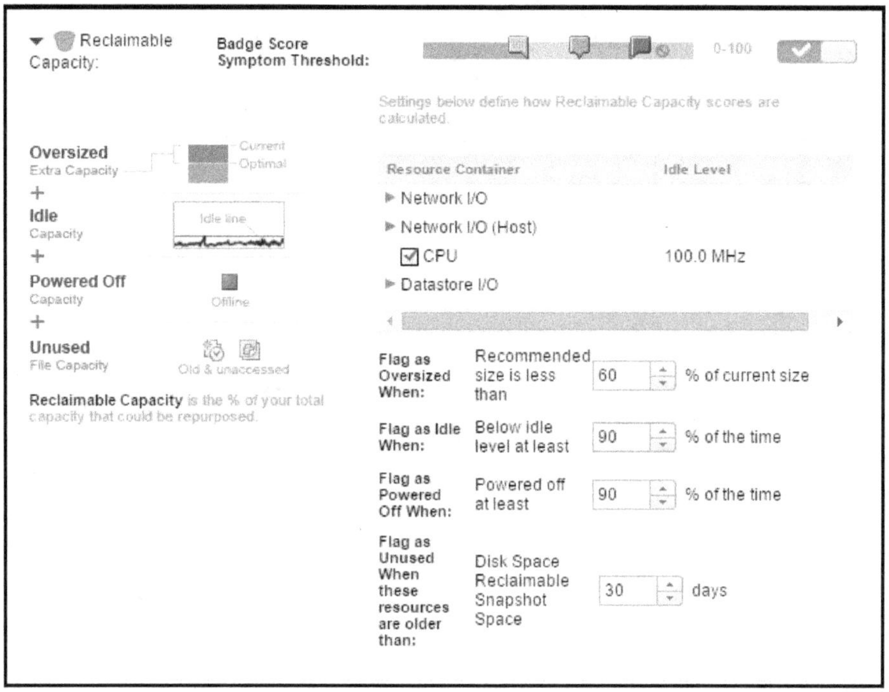

2. These are all the configuration changes that we will make for this new default policy. Now, click on the **Override Attributes** section. This is where the metric collection can be disabled or enabled. By default, there are 1,010 plus pages of attributes, so make use of the drop-down menu and search button to find specific attributes.
3. While showing all 1,010 pages would make for some stimulating reading, for example, we will just show how to disable a metric from being collected. We will disable **CPU | Total Wait (ms)**, as shown in the following screenshot:

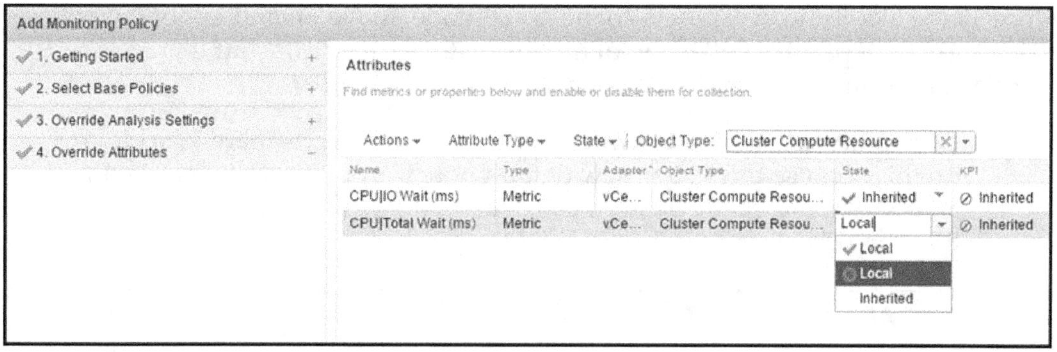

> While it is a time-consuming task, disabling metrics that you know are of no use in your environment is recommended, as it will reduce load and cut down the space used.

The next option is **Override Alert/Symptom Definitions**; click on it to bring up the alerts and symptom definitions page.

In this section, we can disable or enable alerts and symptoms. For symptoms, we can actually change the condition or modify the threshold from the default settings. In this profile, disable the datastore space warning and immediate symptoms. The storage in this environment is fixed with a strict 10 percent threshold to limit the alerts and warnings on datastore capacity. This is represented in the following screenshot:

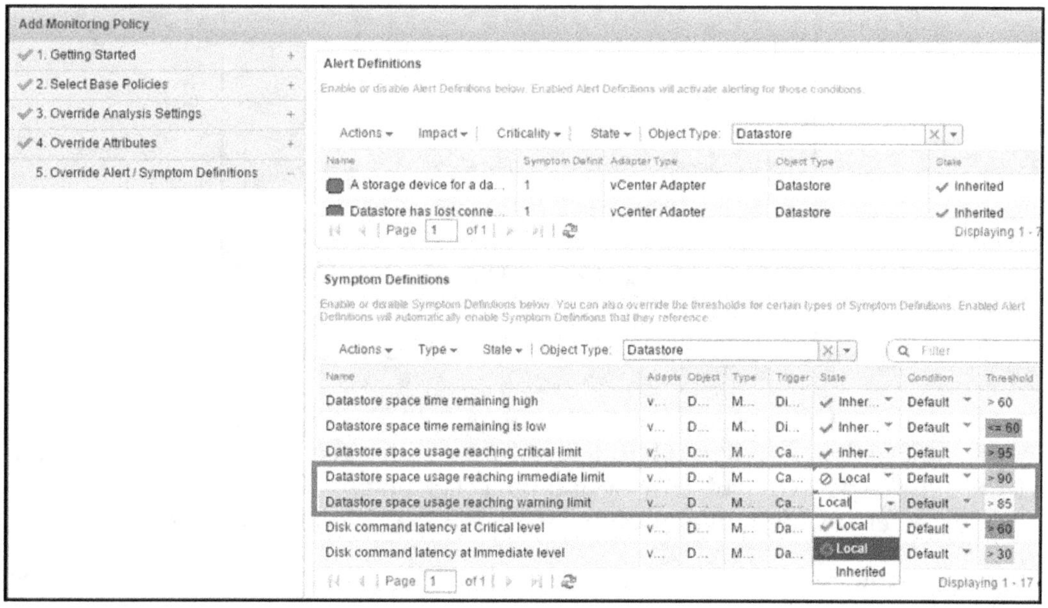

Once all the alerts and symptoms changes are made, move on and apply the policy to a group. Groups are a collection of objects that we can create, but there are a couple of built-in groups as well.

1. Click on **Apply policy to Groups** and then click on **vSphere World**. We do this because this is our new default policy and we want it applied to all vSphere objects by default. Once this is done, we will see something like the following:

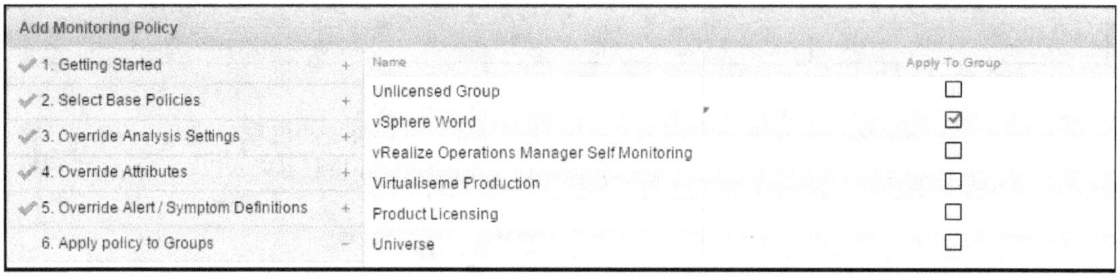

2. Click on the **Save** button to save the new default policy. We can now see the new policy linked underneath the built-in base policy.

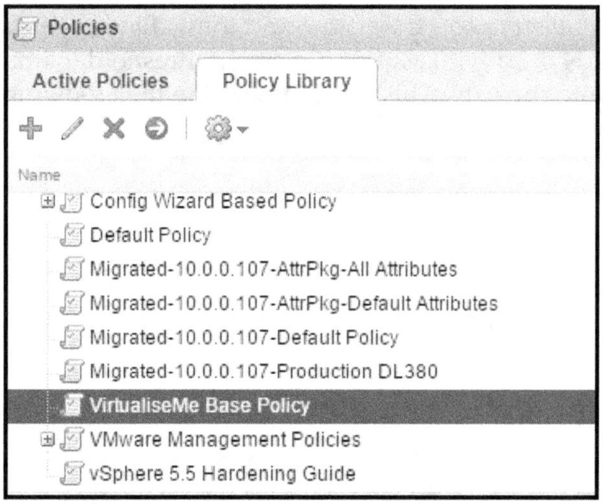

3. The last step needed is to take this base policy and actually turn it into the official default policy. Highlight the new policy just created and click on the blue circle with white arrow and then click on **OK**. This base policy is now the default and will apply to every object that gets added to vROps.

Done, that's the process of creating a policy. Next, we will look at how to use policies in a modular fashion.

Modular policies

One of the great new features of vROps 6.0 is being able to make policies modular. This means giving us the ability to make smaller, specific policies and then combining them together to make a single policy.

As an example, create a development vCPU ratio policy, an alarm policy canceling all critical alarms, and a policy to collect fewer metrics. Combine these together to create a policy for a development environment. However, since these policies can be very generic, they can then be reused to create another policy quickly for a new cluster and this allows you to leverage the work done previously.

We will now have a quick look at how this can be done. We will create a policy that only changes the allocation ratios for a specific environment and hardware type:

1. First, create a new policy and give it a name and description.
2. Then, under **Start with**, select the base policy we created previously. This is similar to what is shown in the following screenshot:

3. Skip the **Select Base Policies** section and move on to the **Override Analysis Settings** section. Here, we will change the settings of two objects: **Cluster Component** and **Host System**.

4. Select the two objects from the drop-down list one at a time. First, change the usable capacity. In this policy, set the memory at 200 percent overcommit and vCPU ratio at 8 to 1, as shown in the following screenshot. This is just an example setting that we can use on a development cluster.

Do exactly the same settings for the host object. Select the defaults for all the rest of the sections and save the profile. You should now see the new ratio profile in the policy library, as shown in the following screenshot:

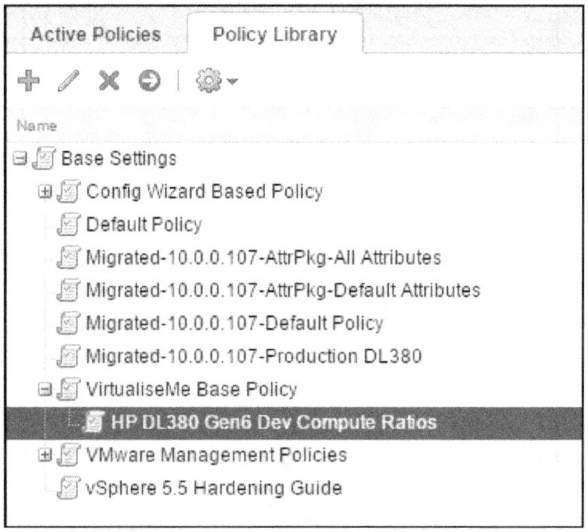

Now, it's time to use this policy to change another policy. So, the next policy created will be for a development cluster, and we will use the base policy and the policy we just made.

1. Create a new policy and give it an appropriate name and description, start with the default policy we created earlier.

2. Move on to the **Select Base Policies** section. For the first time, we will choose a policy in **Override settings from additional policies**. From the drop-down menu, select the development ratios policy created previously.

   What this will do is inject the ratio's policy settings in this policy. This policy will use the default policy and the ratios policy to make this new cluster policy. This is shown in the following screenshot:

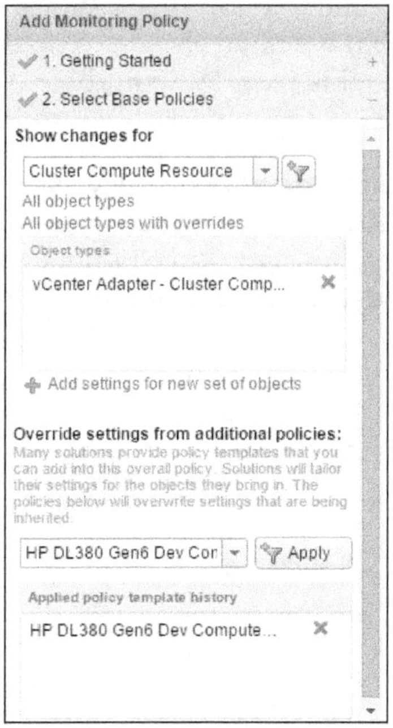

3. Click on **Save** and now you will have a policy for the development cluster. This policy can now be assigned to a group that was configured for the development cluster. We should now see the policy in the policy library, as shown in the following screenshot:

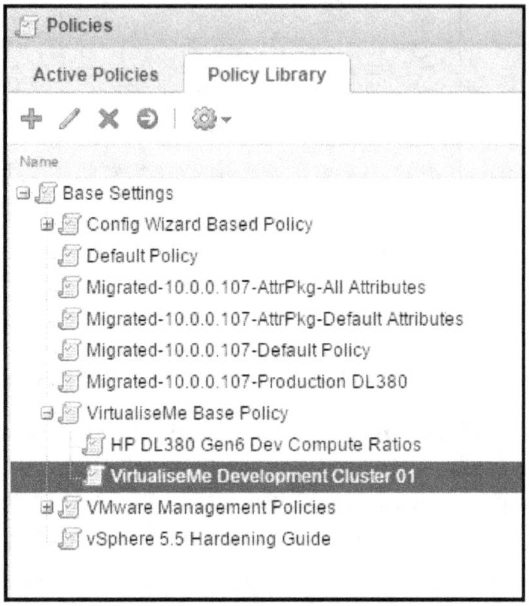

We could have achieved the same thing in this instance if we had chosen the ratios policy as the starting policy, but we have chosen to do it this way because we can add multiple different policies this way. We could have had a policy for just the CPU ratio and another for memory overcommit and we could have applied both.

In the previous example, we only added one policy as an override, but think about the different possible ways in which this can be used as we have lots of smaller policies for different vCPU ratios, memory ratios, resource buffers, metric collections, and alarms or badge settings. These can be reused to make multiple different, larger policies.

Summary

In this chapter, we talked about what policies can now do and the improvements made in vCOps 5.x. We then stepped through the process of creating a new base policy for an example environment.

We learned how to put policies together and what can be changed in a policy and how we can use multiple policies in a modular fashion to create a single policy. In the next chapter, we will look at how vROps 6.0 can make capacity of virtual environments easy to manage.

6

Capacity Management Made Easy

The capacity management components of vRealize Operations Manager are a vital tool that should be in every administrator's tool shed. In Operations Manager 5.x, these features allowed administrators to easily report on critical capacity management metrics, such as the number of VMs remaining and time remaining, based on historical data. What traditionally has let some administrators down in Operations Manager 5.x is that capacity management concepts and policies were not well understood or implemented. This poor understanding of capacity management lead to capacity remaining values or reports that did not seem realistic and were hence ignored.

In this chapter, we will dive into the detail around Operations Manager's capacity management, including the major improvements made in Version 6.0. We will also cover the capacity management policies in detail and understand how they need to be tuned to your environment to ensure that the recommendations are of the highest quality. In addition, we will also cover the following topics:

- The initial policy creation wizard
- Resource containers
- Demand versus allocation
- Setting overcommitment
- Accounting for peaks
- High availability and buffers
- Projects

An Introduction to capacity management for Operations Manager policies

The first and most important aspect to cover with capacity management in Operations Manager is policies, which are the kings. The calculations and recommendations for all areas of capacity management are directly related to what policy options are configured and currently active on the selected resource.

It is highly improbable that one policy is suitable for all workload types such as server, VDI, production, dev/test, and so on. It is important to understand when defining policies that the configuration is usually a trade-off of performance versus utilization. An example of this is shown in the following figure:

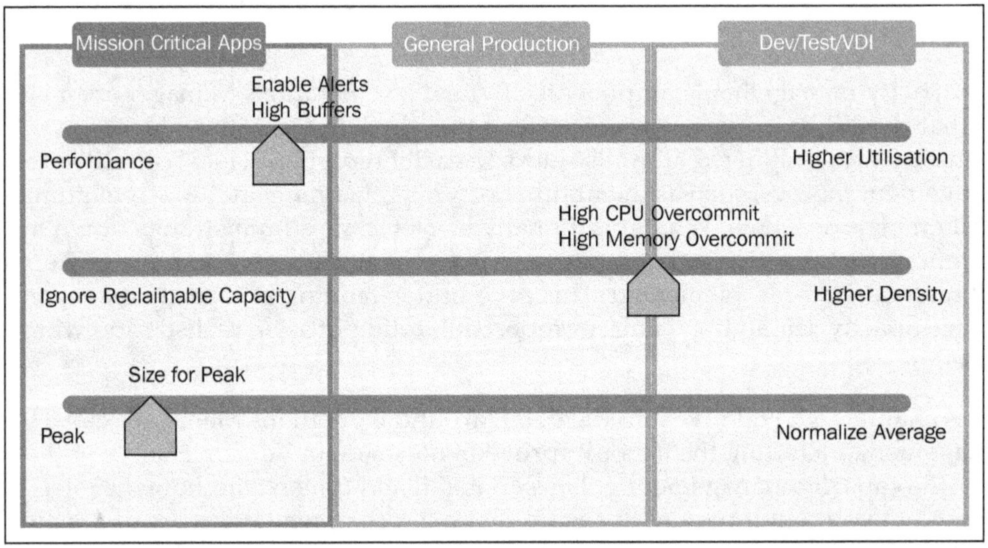

The initial policy configuration wizard

A handy new feature with vROps 6.0 is the initial policy configuration wizard, which allows administrators to quickly set some of the major policy decisions when adding their first vSphere environment. The wizard helps configure some of the major policy decisions that often vary based on the target environment or organizational policies.

The initial policy creation wizard is only shown when the first vSphere environment is added; an extract from this wizard is shown in the following screenshot. If you have imported an existing vCOps 5.x deployment, the new 6.0 polices will be based on the original vCOps 5.x instance policies. In this case, it is highly recommended that you review your existing capacity management polices based on the recommendations in this chapter.

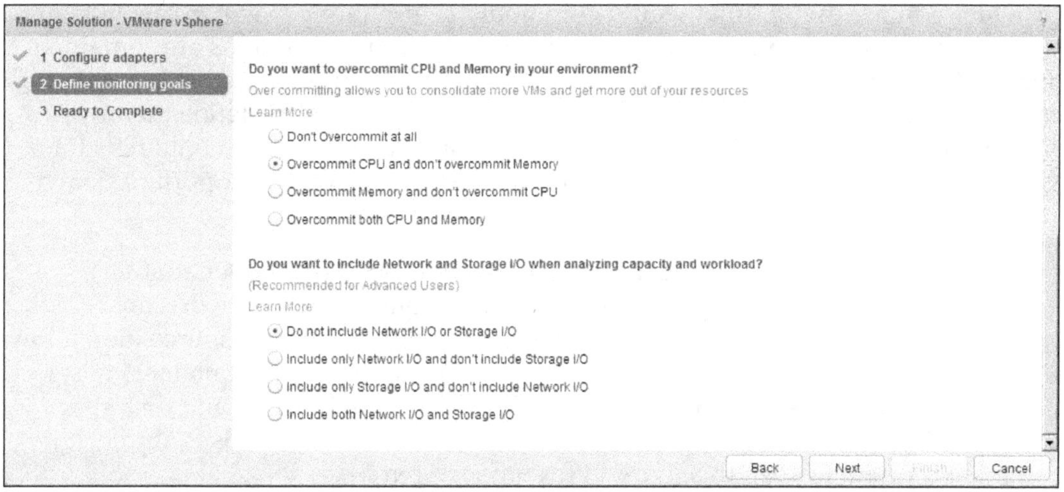

Defining the correct capacity management policies for your environment

As just discussed, the accuracy and value of the capacity management views and reports relies on an administrator's ability to correctly translate his/her environmental requirements into policies. Although it is important to understand that capacity management in vROps is no longer limited to vSphere instances, for the purposes of this chapter, vSphere will be the primary focus. The ability of capacity management to extend to non-vSphere components is based on the associated solution (aka management pack), and as such will not be covered in detail in this chapter. It is important to note, however, that many of the concepts in this chapter relate to capacity management in general, and as such may also be useful for non-vSphere solutions.

Resource containers

One of the first decisions that needs to be made in relation to capacity management is what resource containers are going to be selected. A resource container is a set of metrics of an object type that gives capacity data for one particular aspect of an object. The resource containers for a resource are usually quite predictable and are defined in the capacity/time remaining section of a vROps policy. The solution provider will use metrics that would commonly be used for capacity management within that field. In vSphere, for example, the most common options are containers such as CPU, memory, network I/O, disk space, and so on. Although administrators cannot define which metrics are used for resource containers, or define their own resource containers, they can select which of the available resource containers for a given resource kind are used to calculate capacity. There are two important points to take away from this:

- Even within the same adapter type (for example, the vCenter adapter), different object types will have different resource containers that are available to choose from. For example, a vSphere cluster resource kind allows memory, CPU, network I/O, disk I/O, and disk space as containers to select from, whereas a vSphere datastore only supports disk I/O and disk space. Although it may be quite obvious why this is the case in this example, it is important to keep this in mind for other resources.
- Only select the resource containers that you believe should contribute to capacity management for the selected environment. By default, most adapters have all available resource containers enabled.

The second point also leads to a very important design decision when creating your capacity policies. vROps will always calculate the remaining capacity of an object based on the *most constrained resource*. Although this seems very practical in most use cases, it requires the administrators to be aware of how each container is calculated and if they really want to use that container type for everyday capacity management.

Let's go through a few quick scenarios to explain these points. Both these scenarios will be based on the commonly used vSphere cluster as the object type. To keep things simple, we will just use total capacity, used capacity, and the remaining capacity for calculations.

vROps also allows us to apply virtual machine profiles to the remaining capacity, to give us an idea of how many more VMs we could provision using the remaining capacity. These profiles reflect common sizings as well as your environment's average VM profile. For this example, an average VM profile has been provided, as shown in the following table:

Scenario 1: CPU and memory enabled only

Container	Used	Average VM usage	Total capacity	Used capacity	Remaining capacity
CPU	Yes	3.0 Ghz	560.0 Ghz	300.0 Ghz	260.0 Ghz (46.4 percent)
Memory	Yes	7.0 GB	800 GB	700 GB	100 GB (12.5 percent)
Disk I/O	No	2.6 MBps	760 MBps	260 MBps	500 MBps (65.7 percent)
Network I/O	No	3 Mbps	20,000 Mbps	300 Mbps	19,700 Mbps (98.5 percent)
Disk space	No	195 GB	20.0 TB	19.5 TB	500 GB (2.5 percent)

Looking at Scenario 1, we can see that as only the CPU and memory containers are enabled, the most constraining resource is memory with a remaining capacity of 12.5 percent. This would then result in an overall capacity remaining value or score of 12.5 percent. As per our average VM profile, only another 14 VMs could fit (assuming we were filling up 100 percent) based on their memory usage. However, hypothetically, another 86 VMs could fit based on CPU alone, but this fact is largely irrelevant, as you can't provision VMs with one or more CPU and zero memory.

Scenario 2: CPU, memory, disk I/O, and disk space enabled only

Container	Used	Average VM Usage	Total Capacity	Used Capacity	Remaining Capacity
CPU	Yes	3.0 Ghz	560.0 Ghz	300.0 Ghz	260.0 Ghz (46.4 percent)
Memory	Yes	7.0 GB	800 GB	700 GB	100 GB (12.5 percent)
Disk I/O	No	2.6 MBps	760 MBps	260 MBps	500 MBps (65.7 percent)
Network I/O	No	3 Mbps	20,000 Mbps	300 Mbps	19,700 Mbps (98.5 percent)
Disk Space	Yes	195 GB	20.0 TB	19.5 TB	500 GB (2.5 percent)

Looking at Scenario 2, we are using exactly the same figures; however, we have now also selected the datastore's disk space to be included as a container for capacity management. This has had quite a dramatic effect on the capacity remaining score as we are now down to 2.5 percent remaining capacity (or two VMs based on disk space).

Now, initially your immediate thought might be "Well this container should be enabled or else we are excluding important data from the capacity calculations." However, this all varies based on the target environment and what principles are in place.

In most environments, unless you are provisioning all your SAN storage to your vSphere clusters upfront, the total capacity value for disk space is misleading as your storage administrators provision new **logical unit numbers** (**LUNs**) as required. This is because what is total capacity to a vSphere administrator is actually used/allocated capacity to a SAN administrator, and in most cases, vROps has no actual visibility of how much unallocated storage remains on the physical array.

Now there are exceptions to this example, as was just mentioned, such as pre-allocating all your storage to vSphere clusters or using a technology such as VSAN where one large pool of storage is simply created at creation time. However, generally, you will need to rely on a partner solution pack such as EMC Analytics to provide the capacity data metrics required to properly analyze the storage array. As such, you would disable the disk space container at the vCenter adapter layer and enable Free FAST VP Pool capacity at the EMC Analytics adapter layer.

> As vROps will always calculate the remaining capacity based on the most constrained resource container of an object, ensure only the required containers are selected in the applied policy.

Observed versus configured metrics

Another important factor to consider when choosing what resource containers should be used is where the data supporting the resource container originates, and how it is calculated. With vSphere data, each container's total capacity is either configured or observed, as shown in the following screenshot:

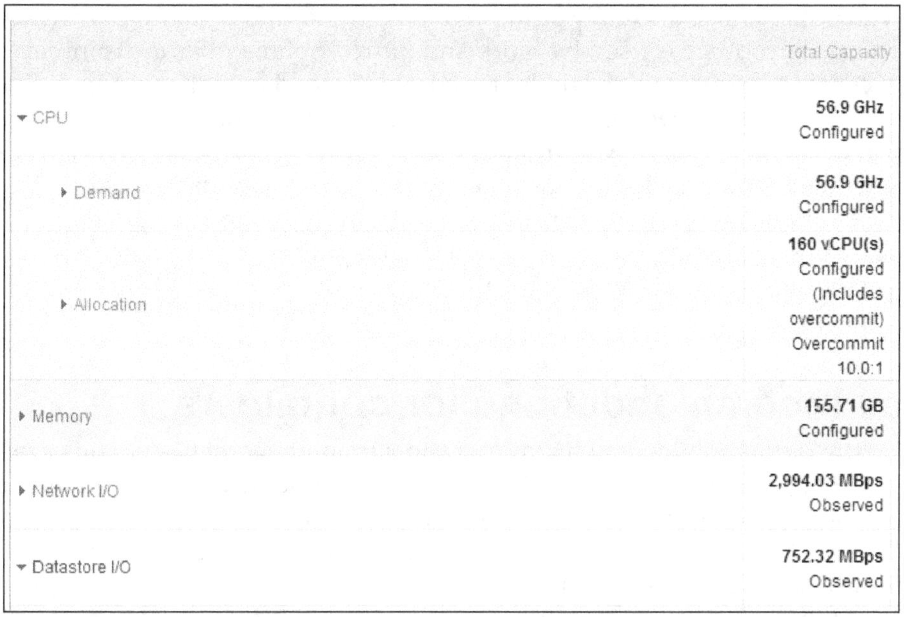

Configured total capacity is a hard factual piece of data that vROps has access to or is able to directly derive from other data. A good example of this is host or cluster CPU and memory capacity. Through vCenter, vROps knows exactly how much GHz and GB of memory an ESXi host has.

Conversely, observed total capacity is a value that vROps has to estimate based on historical maximums observed. Although this is not necessarily ideal, it is necessary for certain data sources. For example, datastore I/O capacity can be a useful capacity management metric; however, there is no way for vROps to know exactly what the maximum I/O of a datastore is when little is known about the underlying storage. Even if vROps did have a detailed understanding of underlying disk pools and RAID groups, there are just too many variables in the equation to give a definitive maximum.

Observed containers also usually suffer from the trade-offs of using infrastructure. When a shared resource is used by more and more vSphere objects, its initial total capacity estimate becomes less and less accurate. A good example of this is if a new array is commissioned and one LUN is presented as a datastore to vSphere for performance testing. vROps will observe the I/O during the performance testing and determine whether a very high total capacity is available on that datastore. However, as more LUNs and datastores are provisioned from the same array/disk pool/RAID group, they are all sharing the same backend total pool of performance and, as such, the original observed total capacity for the original datastore will be too high for normal operation.

Policy recommendations for containers

Selecting the right containers to include in capacity management depends greatly on the adapter (source of the data), the target environment, and any organizational policies. Continuing on from the current focus on a vSphere compute cluster, as it is the most common object on which administrators would be required to perform capacity management reporting, we will quickly cover some common recommendations for which containers we should enable our generic production vSphere cluster policy.

CPU (enabled)

CPU should generally be enabled when assessing capacity for virtual machines, hosts, and clusters. CPU is a configured container and is probably the most accurate container used on vSphere objects. As a general rule, when administrators are sizing vSphere clusters or deciding what type of new hardware should be procured, CPU and memory are usually at the top of the list. This is because CPU and memory are the two most commonly constraining factors of capacity in virtualized environments.

Memory (enabled)

Similar to CPU, memory is usually always enabled and is generally a critical container for capacity management of virtualized environments. Memory is also a configured container; however, the accuracy of memory demand (soon to be discussed) does vary based on the workload and right-sizing. In most production server virtualization environments, memory is the constraining resource for capacity management. It is also often the most wasted resource and as such is critical for capacity management reporting.

Network I/O (disabled)

Due to some of the drawbacks of observed containers and the fact that most administrators will use a separate solution pack for network and storage, network containers are commonly disabled for capacity analysis in many environments. It is also rare that network I/O is a constraining factor in most environments since the common adoption of 10 GB Ethernet.

Datastore I/O (disabled)

Similar to network I/O, datastore I/O is commonly disabled due to the constraints of observed containers. However, unlike network I/O, datastore I/O and storage performance in general is a highly important area of capacity management for vitalized environments. As such, it is recommended that an administrator keeps an eye on the performance capacity of his/her storage (not just the storage capacity); however, this is commonly performed using a vendor-provided solution pack.

Disk space (situational)

The use of disk space as a capacity management container depends on your target environment and procedures. As a general rule, disk space can be extremely useful as a capacity management metric if your storage is pre-provisioned or you are using thin provisioning at the VMDK level. As such, the following are some situations in which you may or may not enable disk space.

It is recommended to enable disk space in the following scenarios:

- All storage from the physical array is pre-provisioned to the vSphere environment
- Using datastore level thin provisioning (thin VMDKs)
- Using VSAN or local storage

It is recommend to apply another solution in the following scenarios:

- Storage capacity is managed at the array level and LUNs (datastores) are provisioned on demand
- Array level thin provisioning is being used, such as FAST VP, and your environment has target over allocation ratios at the array level

As mentioned earlier, in the case where storage is being provisioned on demand or where array-based thin provisioning is being used with overcommitment, it is recommended that a vendor-provided solution pack be used to pull in capacity metrics from the array directly.

vSphere configuration limits (enabled)

The use of vSphere configuration limits as part of capacity management is a new feature of vROps 6.0. In most cases, it is unlikely that these will be a concern; however, they still provide useful information and it is recommended to leave them enabled. vSphere configuration limits for capacity management can be particularly useful when looking at the ESXi host level for example.

Demand versus allocation

Now that we have discussed the importance of containers, it is time to move onto an equally important discussion on demand versus allocation. Demand and allocation are different methods for calculating capacity on containers and are set in the same location as enabling the containers themselves, as shown in the following screenshot.

Before we dive into specific containers, you can simply think of a demand as how much of a resource is being used, where allocation is being made, how much resource has the object been configured with or given, and so on.

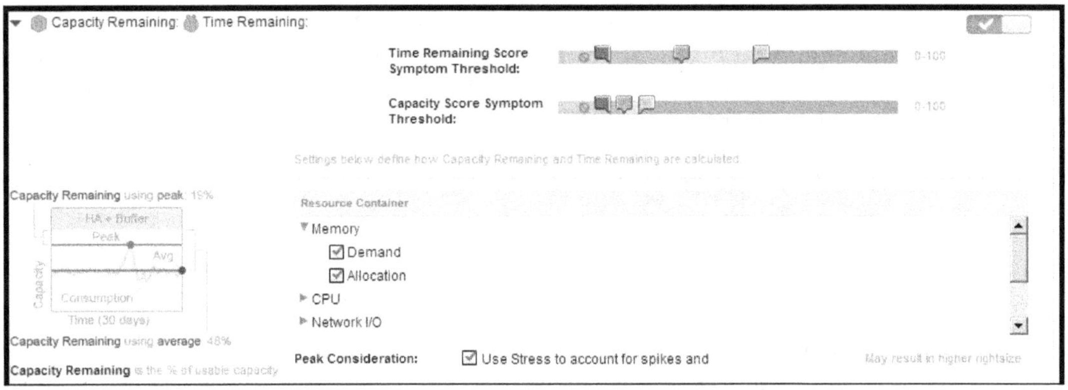

If both demand and allocation are enabled for a container, it results in two different calculations being performed on the resource, and just like an overall capacity, the most constraining result will be used. Therefore, it is important to understand where these calculations are derived from to ensure that the capacity estimates match your real-world environment.

Demand and allocation – calculations and recommendations

First let's see what a CPU demand and allocation means, where each come with their own recommendations.

CPU demand

CPU demand is a derived metric that is made up of multiple sub-metrics (such as CPU usage, CPU ready, and so on) that it is used to estimate the amount of CPU an object actually wants to consume. Although demand and usage are often identical, it is possible for demand to exceed usage, and this would indicate resource contention. Demand is a useful way to manage capacity with, as a virtual machine will rarely use all the CPU that it has been configured with, and this is the basic principle of overcommitment. You will also find that demand usually matches the usage percent metric that is observed inside the vCenter Web Client.

Recommendation

As CPU demand accurately reflects the amount of CPU that the workloads in your environment are requesting, regardless of what they have been allocated. We recommend enabling this container in nearly all situations.

CPU allocation

From a host or cluster perspective, CPU allocation is the ratio of virtual machine CPUs (vCPU) to physical ESXi host cores (pCPU). Ignoring buffers and overcommitment (as this will be discussed soon) allows an administrator to manage capacity simply based on this one to X mapping. Using CPU allocation as a capacity container is usually based on environment design or special use cases. For example, if an administrator had a cluster dedicated to mission critical applications, and there was an associated organizational policy that CPU overcommitment should not exceed 2:1 (2 vCPUs to every pCPU), the administrator could then use the allocation model in combination with overcommitment to ensure that this ratio was never breached.

Recommendation

As a general rule for generic production server clusters, it is recommended to either disable this container altogether or ensure that you have an overcommitment ratio high enough, so that this container does not unnecessarily become the most constraining resource.

Memory demand

Memory demand is often the least understood metric in vROps, and as such causes a great deal of confusion and often leads to incorrect capacity management data. Memory demand such as CPU demand is derived from a variety of metrics to easily show the administrator how much memory a virtual machine requires or is asking for.

The difference between CPU and memory demand is that the CPU demand is based on CPU usage, which is a very accurate metric that vSphere is easily able to record. Memory demand, on the other hand, is primarily based on the metric of active memory.

Active memory is defined as the "amount of memory that is actively used, as estimated by VMkernel based on recently touched memory pages." This concept is well described in a VMware vSphere blog called "Understanding vSphere Active Memory" by Mark Achtemichuk.

For the purposes of capacity planning, active memory is a counter that can help an administrator understand how aggressively memory is being used inside a virtual machine. The active memory counter is based on an estimate on how much memory has been accessed in a 20-second period (vCenter sampling period) and then averaged into a 5-minute value for vROps. Due to the nature of such a short sampling period, it often does not reflect the full memory requirement of an application. This is because there is no guarantee that the memory accessed within the sample periods is unique. This can especially be the case if another layer of memory management is involved above the OS such as Java Virtual Machine or database engines.

With the issues surrounding active memory as a capacity planning metric, it often begs the question of why vROps does not instead use memory consumed for capacity planning. This is because the memory consumed metric also has its shortcomings. With the introduction of large pages and Address Space Layout Randomization (ASLR), it is very common that a guest's consumed memory will match its configured memory shortly after boot. This, in turn, essentially results in the memory consumed matching to that of the allocation model.

It is important to consider that the memory demand model does have its advantages and should not always be quickly dismissed as irrelevant. Memory demand is very useful in determining undersized virtual machines as well as playing a vital role in making recommendations for VM right sizing. For the purposes of capacity planning, vROps is also analyzing memory demand over a long period of time (30 days by default), and periods of high usage are used as the baseline for demand, rather than the raw average over that period.

Further reading can be found at one of our blogs `www.definedbysoftware.com`— VM large pages, TPS, and ASLR.

Recommendation

As a general rule for generic production server clusters, it is recommended that the memory demand model be left enabled as a container, as although its accuracy can vary, it is often too aggressive rather than conservative. This, in turn, results in memory demand rarely being the constraining container when memory allocation is also used.

Memory allocation

Memory allocation is very straightforward and often well understood. It is simply how much memory each virtual machine is configured within vSphere. Although this allows for a simple metric to perform capacity analysis with, it suffers from the obvious weakness of over-sized workloads being used to judge the amount of remaining capacity. Simply because a VM is configured with 24 GB RAM, it does not imply that it actually requires this amount of resources. This, in turn, results in overly conservative capacity planning, unless right-sizing is regularly undertaken.

Recommendation

We recommend using memory allocation as an enabled container mostly due to the issues surrounding memory demand. Using memory allocation as a capacity metric will imply what resources a virtual machine is configured in terms of memory it requires. As such, workload right-sizing will not be automatically taken into account.

The primary purpose behind this recommendation is that due to the effects of large pages, as previously mentioned, VMs now generally consume all the memory they are configured with, regardless of their normal demand. Therefore, unless large pages are not being used (such as in a VDI environment), the memory allocation model most accurately reflects the memory that is consumed at the vSphere host level.

Setting overcommitment

Overcommitment is a basic principle and benefit of virtualization, and it plays an important role in capacity planning. As discussed for demand and allocation, overcommitment is only applicable to the Allocation model and allows either a percentage or ratio of overcommitment to be set for CPU, memory, and disk space. Overcommitment is set as part of the **Useable Capacity** section of a policy, as shown in the following screenshot:

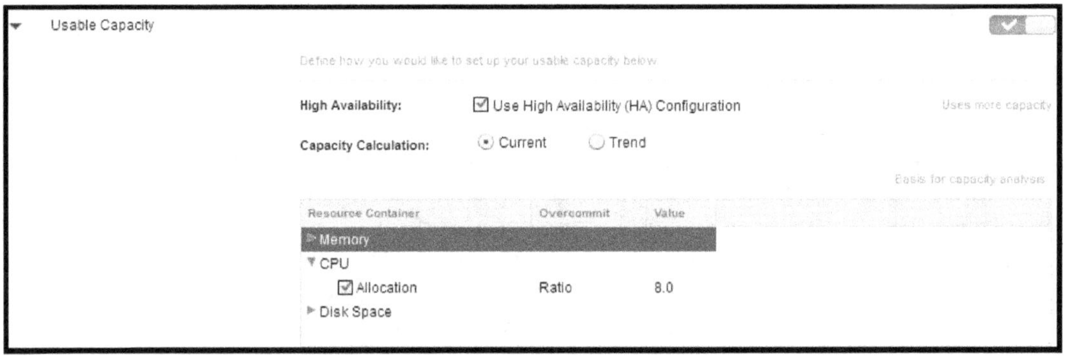

CPU overcommitment

As discussed in CPU allocation, CPU overcommitment allows a ratio or percentage of CPU overcommitment to be set, thus affecting the amount of total capacity. The following screenshot shows the effect that CPU overcommitment has on total capacity. The cluster shown here has 16 pCPUs configured. However, with an 8:1 overcommitment ratio in place, we now have a total cluster capacity of 128 vCPUs.

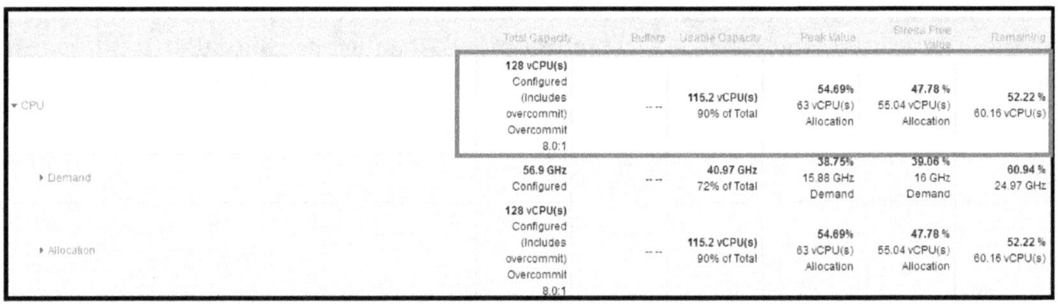

When using the CPU allocation model, it is generally the case that some level of CPU overcommitment should be set. If you do not have a specific level of CPU overcommitment in mind for an environment, then this can often be set at a fairly aggressive level such as 6:1 or 8:1.

Memory overcommitment

Memory overcommitment is relatively straightforward since the introduction of large pages and other factors that affect **Transparent Page Sharing** (**TPS**). Memory overcommitment is built on the age-old vSphere principle that due to VMs not requiring all the amount of memory they are configured with, as well as leveraging TPS to share common memory blocks, we can overcommit memory on a host or cluster relatively safely.

We have already touched on the introduction of large pages with 64-bit operating systems, and the hardware-assisted memory virtualization, which means that virtual machines now generally consume all the memory they are configured with. Also, combining this with a recent change to combat a rare security edge case, inter-virtual machine TPS is now disabled by default as per VMware KB 2080735.

Unless inter-VM TPS is re-enabled and large pages are disabled (which can be common for dev/test or VDI environments), memory overcommitment should generally be set to zero.

Disk space overcommitment

Disk space overcommitment is relevant if you are using vSphere thin provisioning (thin VMDKs) on VMFS datastores. This allows administrators to set a target overcommitment percentage on storage to benefit from thin provisioning. This percentage should be based on organizational policy and should be in line with the associated risks of overcommitting storage.

Accounting for peaks

With the big topics covered, it is time to move on to a relatively simpler, though just as important topic: that is, peak consideration.

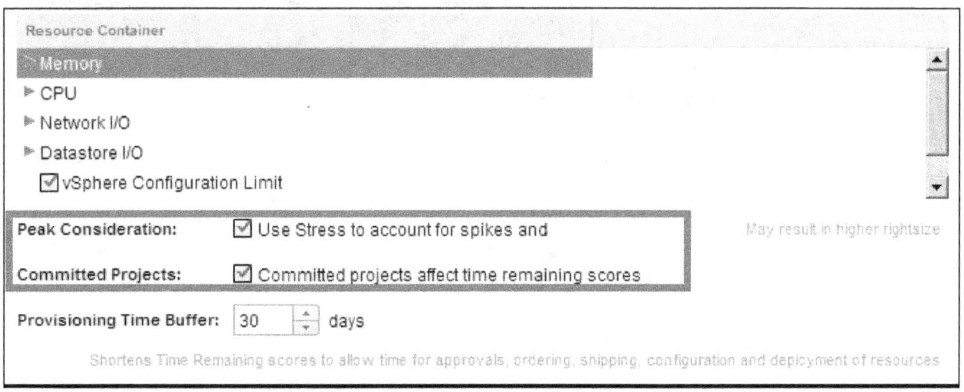

Peak consideration was originally introduced in vCOps 5.6 and it allows the stress metric to be used to account for capacity spikes and peaks. The use of this setting has two main effects:

- Virtual machine demand is now based on peak demand rather than average
- Right-sizing recommendations are based on peak demand rather than average

The first key takeaway is that this setting only affects demand, allocation is unaffected. Therefore, this setting is most relevant to CPU demand (as this is more often a constraining resource) and right-sizing recommendations for both CPU and memory.

The second key thing to takeaway is that it changes the way demand is calculated and therefore the remaining capacity calculation. Let's go through an example to see its effect. The following screenshot shows a vSphere cluster with peak consideration disabled. There is nothing much to note at the moment apart from the **Stress Free Value** (which is essentially used capacity) of **14.24** percent. You can also see in the following screenshot that the **Stress Free Value** of **5.83 Ghz** matches that of the average demand.

The cluster capacity with peak consideration is disabled here.

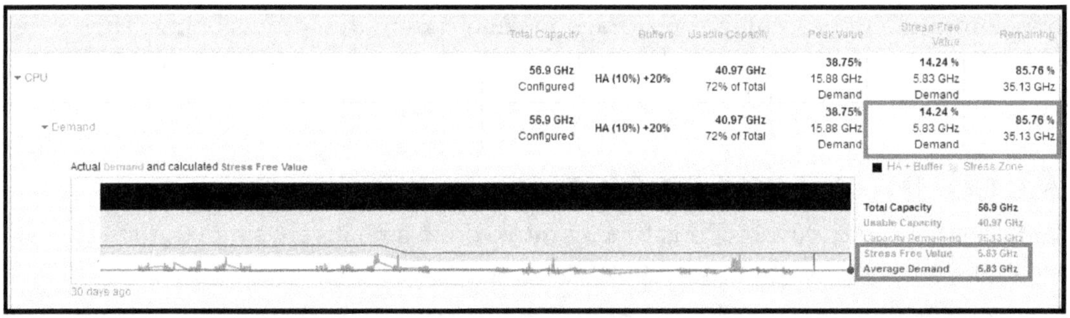

Now let's show the same cluster's capacity remaining with the peak consideration enabled, as shown in the following screenshot:

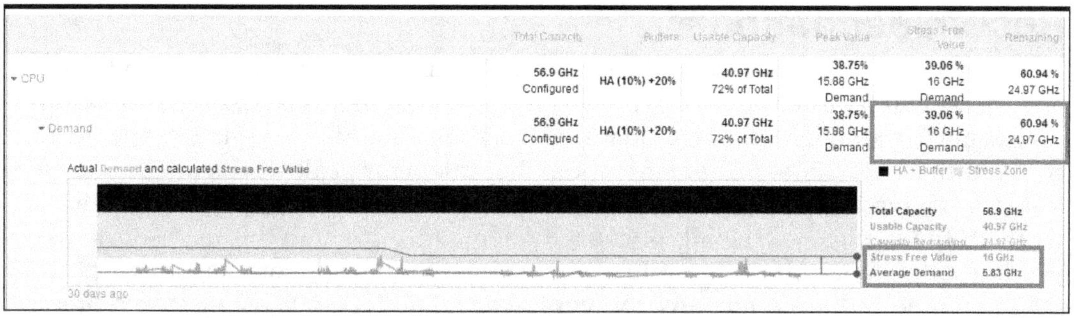

Probably the first and most important thing to notice is that the **Stress Free Value** (used capacity) has almost tripled from **14.24** percent to **39.06** percent. You can also see that the **Stress Free Value** and the **Average Demand** value in the bottom-right corner no longer match.

With peak considerations enabled, the stress free value is now showing the amount of used capacity based on the maximum observed in the time period.

The end result is a far more conservative estimate of used capacity, which is based more on peak than average.

As mentioned earlier, peak considerations also play a role in right-sizing recommendations. The effect is similar as the one seen at the cluster level; however, generally, the difference between the two options is less extreme. This is primarily due to the fact that the right-sizing recommendations are looking at an individual VM rather than the whole cluster level, and as such, a right-sizing recommendation is already taking workload peaks into account to some degree. This is based on the principle that few would have the need of a right-sizing report for virtual machines that only looked at average usage and could not cater for workload peaks.

Recommendations

At the end of the day, the use of the peak consideration option comes down to your environmental requirements as per the first screenshot in this chapter. For mission critical and production type workloads, this setting should be enabled to ensure a conservative capacity management model that caters for peak workload. For dev/test or VDI clusters, however, you may choose to disable this setting and simply work off the average workload for capacity demand. Although this may sound like you are setting yourself up for failure, remember that not all workloads peak at the same time and, in certain environments, consolidation and cost may be more important than guaranteed performance.

High availability and buffers – usable capacity

Now we reach the final component of capacity management policies: **high availability (HA)** and buffers. The concept of useable capacity is not new to vROps 6.0; however, there are some great improvements made, especially around virtual machines.

First and foremost, we need to discuss useable capacity versus actual capacity. In vCOps 5.x, it was possible to choose if your remaining capacity was based on useable capacity or actual capacity. Actual capacity is the raw capacity of an object based on its physical configuration. Useable capacity, on the other hand, is the physical capacity minus buffers to reflect a real-world environment.

The following screenshot shows the vCOps 5.x option:

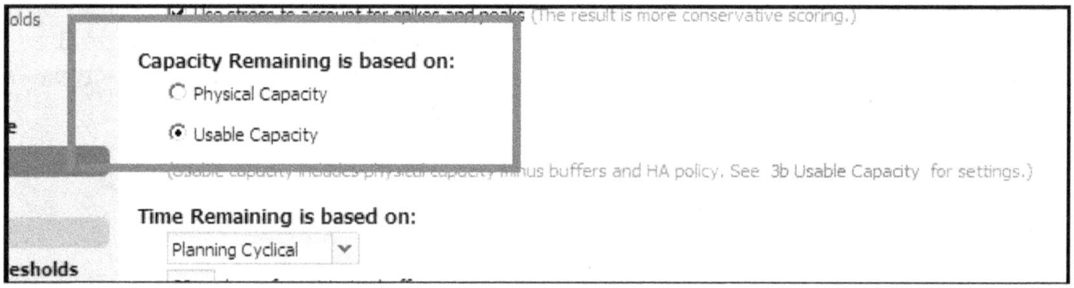

In vROps 6.0, you now no longer have the option to select actual capacity, only which buffers affect usable capacity. This is a far better outcome because I cannot think of one use case where an administrator would want capacity to be based on physical raw capacity. Even in an environment where HA was not required, without any CPU or memory buffer, you do not want your ESXi hosts filled up to 100 percent where swapping and unresponsiveness are occurring.

HA and buffers affect your capacity estimates by removing a percentage of total capacity, and therefore basing the capacity and time remaining badges using the smaller usable capacity value. This is a common practice that administrators would previously follow as running any hypervisor (or workload for that matter) at 100 percent usually encounters issues. An example of this is when memory becomes critically low on an ESXi host: the memory levels progress to the state where memory compression and hypervisor swapping are occurring.

The following figure is based on the vROps Time Remaining example diagram that shows the buffers' effect on capacity:

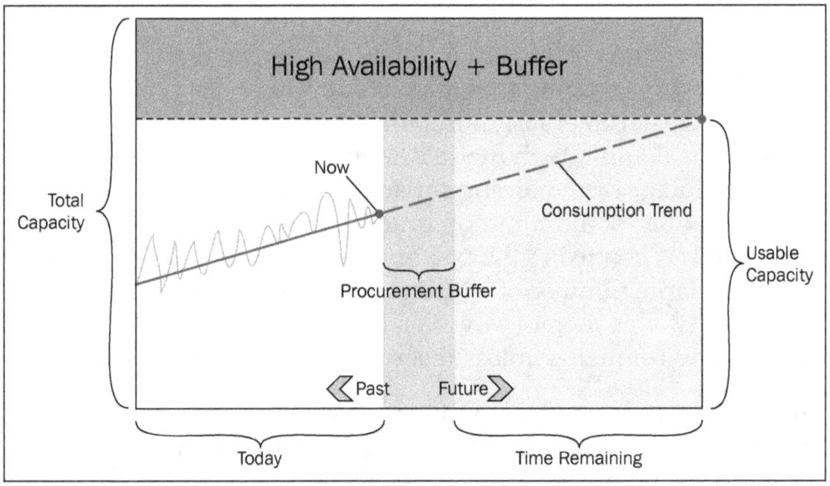

High availability

Asking vROps to take vSphere HA into account is as simple as enabling a checkbox. This is probably one of the best features of vROps capacity management as it is often something people forget to assess when judging cluster capacity, or are under the misbelief that HA admission control will do this for you.

> Although vROps does check what admission control policy is in effect and its value for each cluster, this inventory is only updated every 24 hours. Keep in mind that changes to HA (including enabling or disabling it completely) won't be reflected in usable capacity until the next day.

Without discussing vSphere HA in too much detail, I have a quote from the vSphere Availability Guide.

> *vCenter server uses admission control to ensure that sufficient resources are available in a cluster to provide failover protection and to ensure that virtual machine resource reservations are respected.*

What is important from this statement in relation to capacity management is that HA admission control is ensuring that machine resource reservations are respected. Although the "host cluster tolerates" and percentage models differ in how to calculate capacity, by default, both models are based on reservations to either determine the percentage or remaining capacity, or the slot size. Where this becomes an issue for administrators, the common practice of only using reservations where required is followed. When using the percentage of cluster resources model for example, as such, a large number of VMs are estimated at the default of memory size 32 Mhz and 0 MB plus memory overhead. This usually results in administrators overprovisioning environments unless reservations are used extensively.

vROps implements a much simpler model of accounting for vSphere HA, which, although is far more conservative, will save administrators the headache of commonly overprovisioning. vROps simply assesses which admission control is in effect and removes that total percentage of resources from the total capacity accordingly. For example, in the following screenshot, the percentage of cluster resources admission control policy is in effect with a 10 percent reservation on cluster CPU, and a 15 percent reservation on cluster memory:

	Total Capacity	Buffers	Usable Capacity	Peak Value	Stress Free Value	Remaining
▸ CPU	56.9 GHz Configured	HA (10%) +20%	40.97 GHz 72% of Total	38.75% 15.88 GHz Demand	39.06 % 16 GHz Demand	60.94 % 24.97 GHz
▸ Memory	155.71 GB Configured (Includes overcommit) Overcommit 0.0:1	HA (15%) +10%	119.12 GB 76.5% of Total	86.05% 102.5 GB Allocation	73.97 % 88.11 GB Allocation	26.03 % 31 GB

> vROps will only take HA buffers into consideration for usable capacity if admission control is active. If HA is enabled but admission control is disabled, vSphere HA will have no effect on usable capacity.

Buffers

Buffers like HA remove a percentage of total capacity to help define the usable capacity value that is used for analysis. An important point to be aware of is that buffers are applied to total capacity after the HA buffer is taken into account. This is why in the previous example for CPU capacity, where we have HA at 10 percent and other buffers at 20 percent, the total useable capacity is 72 percent rather than 70 percent.

Although most administrators would simply set both CPU and memory buffers at 10 percent, for example, it is important to understand that buffers need to be set according to your model (demand or allocation), and more importantly based on your workload types.

For example, when using the demand model, buffers become critical, thereby insuring sub-hour peaks can be handled that are too short to affect stress, and therefore the demand calculation. It is recommended that in conservative, mission critical, or production environments, large buffers be set to cater for sub-hour spikes in interactive server workloads or other workloads that are sensitive to user response time.

Projects

Projects are a new feature in vROps 6.0 that replace the old "what-if" functionality from vCOps 5.x. A project is an upcoming change to your environment that affects either the supply or the demand (or both) of capacity. Projects allow capacity modeling to help an administrator set up hypothetical scenarios such as adding or removing virtual machines and hosts from a cluster. These scenarios can then be used to determine how a pipeline of incoming organizational projects will affect the time remaining calculation. An example of the projects screen is shown as follows

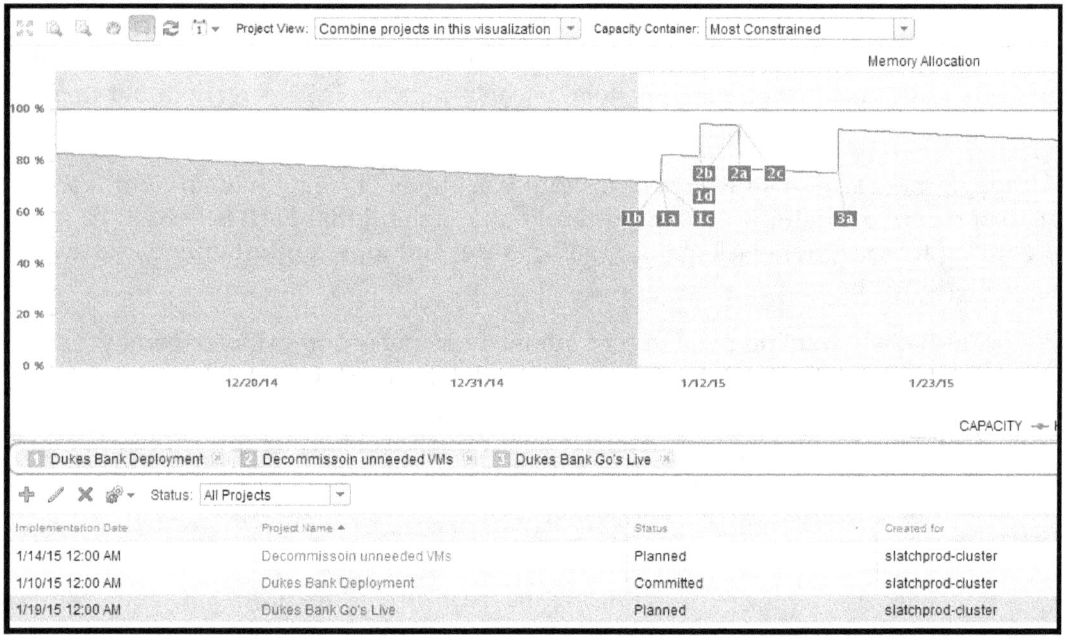

Although projects may be similar to the "what-if" scenarios, it is not just a small upgrade. Projects are a complete overhaul of the scenario modeling capability and their features and improvements include the following:

- Projects are persistent and can be saved, and as such they are no longer removed when you logout
- Projects can be shared among vROps' different users
- A project can be set to occur at a future date and time, not simply apply during the present
- Projects can be set to either planned or committed, and as such permanently affect time remaining

- A single project can have multiple scenarios that affect demand and capacity

Details on how to create projects can be found in the vRealize Operations Manager User Guide.

Improvements to demand or capacity trending

Previously, although vCOps did a good job reporting capacity remaining and forecasting time remaining, this was under the requirements that demand and/or supply were changing at a relatively steady and predictable rate. However, if sudden changes to supply or demand were encountered, vCOps would often readjust violently, throwing off the time remaining calculation completely for what could potentially be a one-off event.

An example of this would be the implementation of a large VM commissioning or migration project that may have added 100 VMs to a cluster in one day. vCOps would then adjust the trend line to compensate for the dramatic growth rather than analyzing if this growth was a common event.

In vROps 6.0, capacity trending has been greatly improved with new algorithms that can detect major changes in the environment. The first time vROps observes a major change in the environment, it will assume that this is part of a cycle and as such, the time remaining will not be affected. Once vROps determines, however, that this event was not a cyclical environment change, it will then be considered an offset and the time remaining will be accurately updated accordingly.

An example of this imported capacity trending can be seen in the following figure:

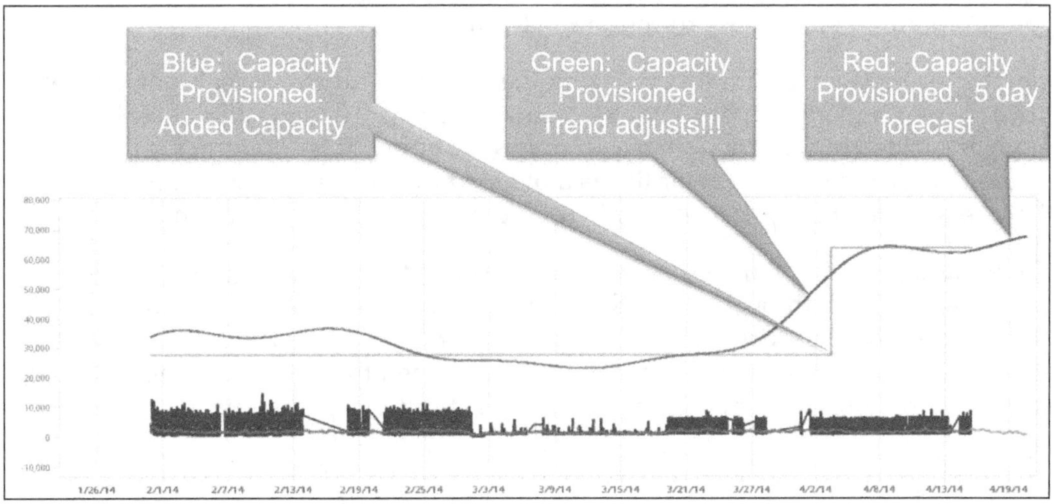

Pipeline management

One of the biggest reasons for the changes from "what-if" scenarios to projects is to allow administrators to have an increased focus on pipeline management and capacity forecasting. Previously, although the "what-if" scenarios were useful for determining the impact of an upcoming project or change without the ability to save them, they could not be used for pipeline management. As such, administrators often had to keep separate spreadsheets to keep track of how many incoming projects had been given capacity approval but were still to be deployed.

The projects' capability in vROps 6.0 allows administrators to not only see the impact of an upcoming project, but also keep track of all the projects that have been given approval and combine their result. This, combined with the fact that different implementation dates can be set on different projects, allows administrators to keep track of how much capacity they have committed to other teams, but have not actually delivered yet. By default, as per the image in the *Projects* section, vROps 6.0 combines all projects into one display that has been dragged into the active project bar. It also shows the most constraining resource; however, administrators can also select to view other resources or compare projects, rather than combine them.

Planned versus committed projects

Before we end this chapter, let's quickly discuss the difference between planned and committed projects. The major difference between planned and committed projects is that committed projects affect time remaining, assuming this policy option is enabled as per the recommendation in this chapter. The difference between the two project types also allows an administrator to see at a glance what projects are definitely going to occur versus what projects are in the maybe category.

Planned projects are useful for analyzing the impact of future projects or changes in your environment that have not yet been confirmed. They are also useful for modeling different scenarios such as changes to supply. It is common for most committed projects to start their life as a planned project. Once it is confirmed that the project will occur, an administrator can change it to committed.

Committed projects, on the other hand, are designed to reflect that a project is now confirmed and that the associated change to its capacity has been committed to external stakeholders. For example, a large upcoming project will require a number of machines in a week's time. The client has confirmed that the deployment is going ahead and requires that capacity to be available for the deployment.

Summary

In this chapter, we have covered the detailed yet important topic of capacity management in vROps 6.0. We have discussed how to set vROps 6.0 capacity management policies, and more importantly why a certain policy should be set over another based on your environment. In the next chapter, we will walk through the intricacy of dashboard design.

7
Dashboard Design

This chapter discusses what a custom dashboard is, and shows you how to create one. This will give you the foundation to create and build more creatively that will suit any environment, application, or object being managed. This chapter will cover the following topics:

- Types of widgets
- Widget settings
- Creating custom dashboards

Why use custom dashboards?

One of the greatest features of vCOps 5.x is still available in vROps 6.0, and this is, of course, the ability to create custom dashboards. The power of custom dashboards is being able to display relevant information to the different areas of your organization.

Let's look at some of the reasons why we would want to create custom dashboards, and how it will help you manage your environment more efficiently.

Generally, IT support is split up into different sections. While this does vary from environment to environment with size and complexity, typically, one would see the following infrastructure teams in an enterprise environment:

- The Wintel server team
- The Linux server Team
- The storage team
- The database team

- The messaging team
- The application's middleware team
- The network team
- The monitoring team

Many of these teams will generally call on the VMware/Virtualization team or person when things go wrong, requesting metrics on disk, network, memory, and CPU to assist with troubleshooting issues. Alternatively, they will blame the sole cause of a problem due to it being a virtual machine; this is simply part of the philosophy that in IT operations, generally the team lower down the stack is used as a scapegoat.

What if a dashboard or two could be supplied with only the relevant information that each of those teams need? It will free up time and hopefully make all the other teams more self-sufficient and less reliant on the VMware admins. As such, creating dashboards for different teams or functions is a great way to provide self-service for performance management of a virtualized environment.

Widgets

Although dashboards are a powerful concept, a dashboard on its own is just a blank canvas. It is the ability of a dashboard to host widgets and their associated configuration that makes the difference. Widgets display the information we want to show in a variety of different ways. In vROps 6.0, we have 42 widgets available to us out of the box, which is up from the 26 widgets that were available in vCOps 5.x.

Most widgets display metric information in the form of scores, graphs, or lists. Widgets can also be linked by interactions, which means that when an object like a virtual machine is selected in one widget, the linked widgets will change their data based on the selected object. Some widgets though do require the use of an additional XML file to show the specific information that may be required.

Types of widgets

We will now have a look at all the available widgets and see a quick explanation on each type:

- **Object List**: As the name suggests, this widget lists objects, and by default it will show every object available in vROps, but can be limited to show specific objects by tags. This widget is designed to be used as an interactive widget, allowing the user to see what is displayed within the other widgets on the dashboard.

- **Metric Chart**: This widget has the ability to show multiple charts of any metric based on a selected time period. This widget is a common choice for an interactive troubleshooting type dashboard.
- **Environment Status**: This widget shows general numerical statistics, such as the number of active objects, active alerts, configured metrics, and so on.
- **Metric Picker**: This widget displays all metrics for the selected object. It is commonly used in conjunction with the **Metric Chart** widget.
- **View**: This widget displays views based on selected objects. The use of views and how they apply to widgets will be covered in *Chapter 8, Reporting and Views*.
- **Alert List**: This widget displays alerts associated with the selected object(s).
- **Heatmap**: This widget displays metrics represented as a color range grouped and sized by different object types, for example, colored by CPU Usage, sized by the VM, grouped by the host, and so on.
- **Tag Picker**: This widget is similar to the **Object List** widget, but lists all of the tags instead of object types. This widget cannot be modified.
- **Sparkline Chart**: This widget displays a small chart over time, which has just visual details, with the metric name to the right of the small chart. It can display multiple metrics from multiple objects.
- **Health Chart**: This widget displays the historical health, risk, or efficiency badge data for a selected time period.
- **Anomaly Breakdown**: This widget shows the volume and anomaly score of selected object.
- **Forensics**: This widget shows the 75th, 90th, and 95th percentile values overlaid with the objects metrics value to see how it compares.
- **Weather map**: This widget is similar to the **Heatmap** widget, but shows specific metric values over time like an animated GIF.
- **Container Overview**: This widget shows selected objects with the Health, Risk, and Efficiency badges with sparklines.
- **Rolling View Chart**: This widget is same as the **Metric Chart** widget, but only shows one chart at full size and allows manual selection of other charts, which can be cycled through automatically on a timer.
- **Mashup Chart**: This widget displays events that are overlaid on a health chart over time, alongside anomalies over time for the object.
- **Top-N**: This widget allows us to display the top x amount of objects by a specified metric or health score.

- **Object Relationship**: As the name suggests, this widget shows the parent and child relationships of the selected object, along with the health, risk, and efficiency of all related objects.
- **Scoreboard**: This widget is a table of boxes in which we can display any metric value with a custom label and a sparkline, if needed. The box color values are also chosen, or left to the state of symptom to determine.
- **Scoreboard Health**: This widget is similar to the **Scoreboard** widget, but displayed in circles. While we can choose custom metrics, it's created primarily to badge health with a number.
- **Container Details**: This widget shows all of the child objects of the selected container object with a summary of metrics, objects, and alarms for that container.
- **Object Relationship (Advanced)**: This widget is identical to the **Object Relationship** widget but displays the information differently.
- **Environment Overview**: This widget was part of the earlier versions on Operations Manager in what was called the vSphere UI. It shows all the objects in a hierarchy, highlighting an object and all its relationships.
- **Test Display**: This widget can display other web pages by supplying a URL or supply file contents using the file's location.
- **Health**: This widget can be seen on the default home screen of vROps and shows the Health badge for the object.
- **Workload**: This widget displays the minor workload badge details for the selected object.
- **Capacity Remaining**: This widget displays the capacity remaining details for the selected object.
- **Stress**: This widget displays the minor badge with a heatmap over 24/7.
- **Anomalies**: This widget displays the anomaly minor badge with anomalies over time for the selected object.
- **Faults**: This widget displays the faults minor badge with a list of all the faults for the selected object.
- **Efficiency**: This widget displays the efficiency minor badge with a breakdown of what makes up the efficiency score via a pie chart.
- **Reclaimable Capacity**: This widget displays the minor badge with a breakdown of what type of waste was reclaimable in a pie chart.
- **Risk**: This widget displays the minor badge with the risk trend over time graph.

- **Time Remaining**: This widget displays the time remaining minor badge with days remaining for resource types.
- **Density**: This widget displays the minor badge with details on current density configurations.
- **Symptom Volumes**: This widget displays the volume of symptoms over time for the selected object.
- **Current Policy**: This widget displays the current effective policy on the selected object.
- **Environment**: This widget lists the number of all the object types related to the selected object.
- **Top Alerts**: This widget shows the top alerts for the selected object or the dependents of the selected object.
- **Data Collection Results**: This widget lets you run an action and view the results of the actions that are initiated. The results of the past actions are stored in the database.
- **Topology Graph**: This widget shows a relationship mesh of all parent and child objects of the selected object.
- **Property List**: This widget displays configuration metrics on the selected object.

The widget settings

Each widget has a group of settings that will impact on both how the widget displays information and what information a widget will display. In this section, we will go through the common setting types and the layout of a widget.

Most widgets will have the following settings:

- **Title**: This is what is displayed as the title of the widget on the dashboard.
- **Refresh Content**: When enabled, this widget will refresh with the latest data automatically. This is recommended unless the widget is used in an interactive manner.
- **Refresh Interval**: This determines the regular time interval after which the widget will refresh data.
- **Self Provider**: When set to **On**, this widget becomes its own provider and will only show data on the objects and metrics selected within the widget itself, and will not participate if linked to another widget.

These settings, for one such widget, are shown in the following screenshot:

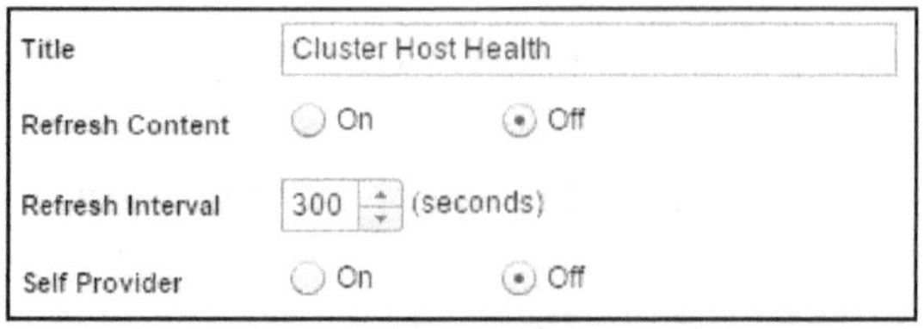

> It is recommended to set the refresh interval to the same value as your collection interval. This is the reason why 300 seconds is the default. If the widget is not displaying data that changes every data collection, such as capacity, it would be recommended not to enable refresh content.

Next, the two more common settings we will come across are as follows:

- **Mode**: This has the following three subsettings:
    - **Self**: This displays information/metrics of the object, for example, Host A.
    - **Children**: This displays the children of the selected object, for example, if Host A is the object, it's children would be virtual machines and datastores on Host A.
    - **Parent**: This displays the parent of the object, if Host A is the object, it's parent would be Cluster A.
- **Res. Interaction Mode**: This setting is a drop-down menu of XML files that contains metrics we want to display for an object, and is only used when **Self Provider** is set to **Off** and linked to another widget through interactions.

These settings are shown in the following screenshot:

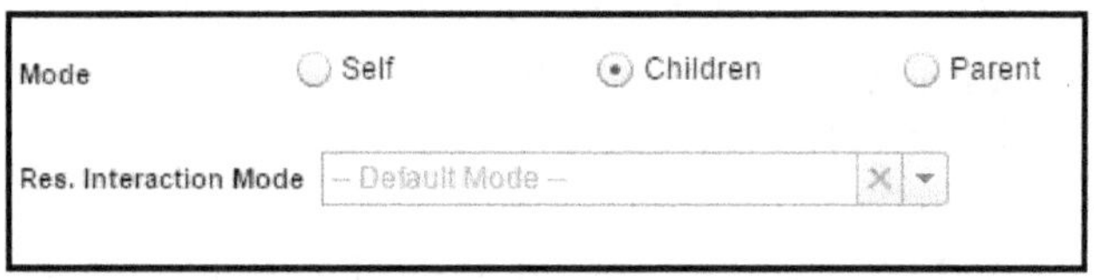

Particular widgets will have specific settings related only to that widget, for example, a generic scoreboard widget contains settings for box size, text size, decimal places, and period length.

Widgets will generally have two or three sections. Settings at the top, followed by object(s) or tags. If there is a third section, it generally has additional settings such as box labels, measurement units, or to change the display order of metrics.

An example widget with three sections is shown in the following screenshot:

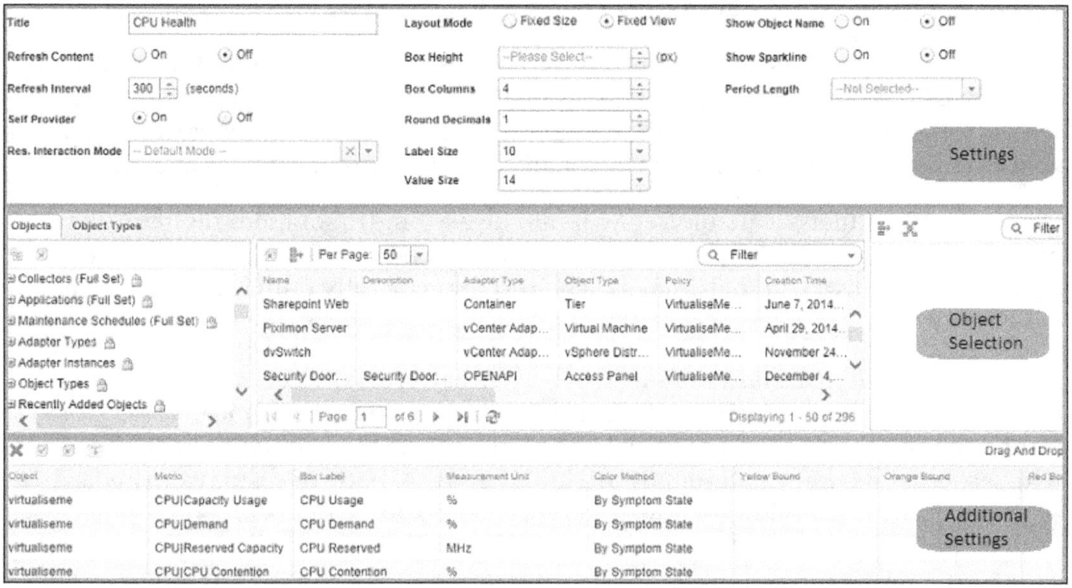

The following screenshot shows an example of a widget with only two sections to it, which is settings and tag selection:

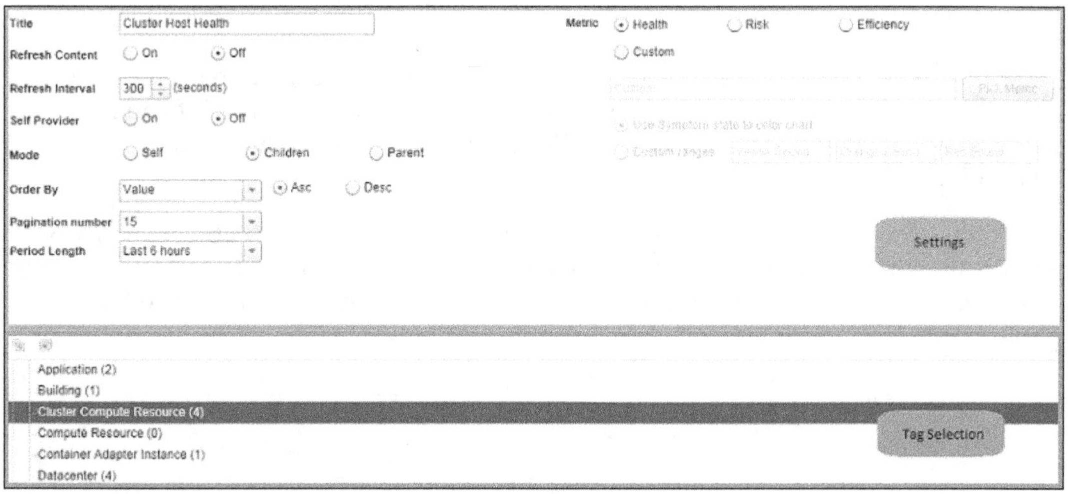

> Widget settings will vary based on the widget, but most will share the previously mentioned configuration settings.

Creating a custom dashboard

Creating a dashboard is a relatively simple exercise, and will require tuning and some tweaking. The tricky part is displaying the information needed on a single screen, which is one of the biggest challenges when creating a dashboard. The first goal when creating a dashboard is to get all of the information across in a glance.

Out of the 42 widgets available, we will only use a handful of them regularly. The most commonly used widgets from experience are the scoreboard, metric selector, heatmap, object list, and metric chart. The rest are generally only used for specific use cases.

There are basically two types of dashboards we can create: an interactive dashboard and a static dashboard. An interactive dashboard is typically used for troubleshooting or similar activities, where you expect the user to interact with widgets to get the information they are looking for. A static or display dashboard typically uses self-providing widgets such as scoreboards and heatmaps, which are designed for display monitors, or other situations where an administrator is keeping an eye on environment changes.

Each of the widgets has the ability to be a self-provider, which means we set the information we want to display directly in the widget. The other option is to set up interactions and have other widgets provide information based on object or metric selection.

Until the end of this chapter, we will focus on the interactive dashboard and we will be looking at creating a dashboard that looks at vSphere cluster information, which at a glance will show us the overall health and general cluster information an administrator would need.

Working through this will give us all the knowledge needed to be able to go away and create either type of dashboard. The dashboard we are about to create will show how to configure the more common widgets in a way that can be replicated on a greater scale.

Interactive dashboard

To get started with creating an interactive dashboard, perform the following steps:

1. Navigate to the dashboard page and click on the green plus icon, as shown in the following screenshot:

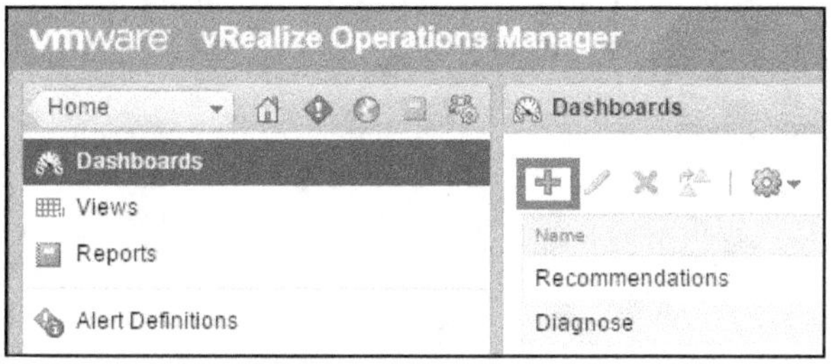

2. Under **Dashboard Configuration**, we need to give a meaningful name and choose the column count. For this dashboard we will be selecting **3**, as shown in the following screenshot:

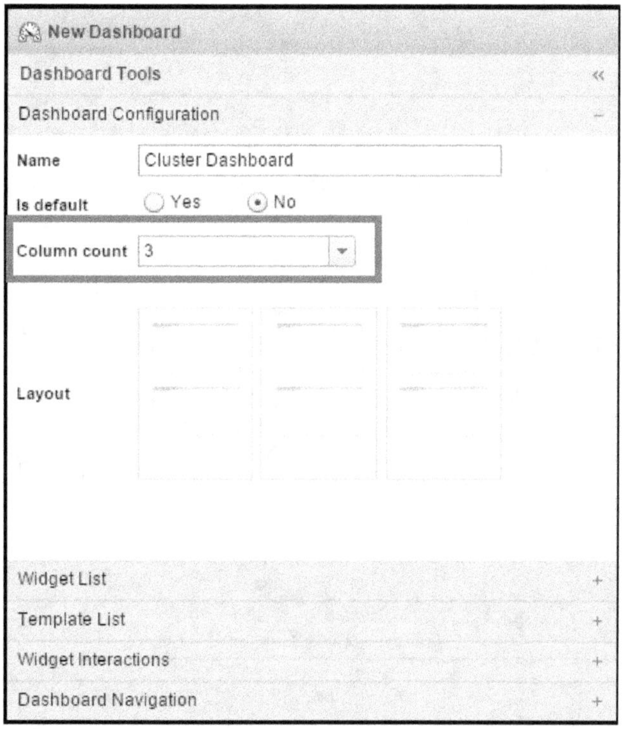

> Next to **Layout** you will see the three columns that you can actually click and drag, in order to adjust the width of these columns if required.

3. Next we click on **Widget List** to bring up all the available widgets. Here we will click and drag the widgets we need from the left pane to the right. Used in the following screenshot are:
    - **Object List**
    - **Metric Picker**
    - **Metric Chart**
    - **Generic Scoreboard**
    - **Heatmap**

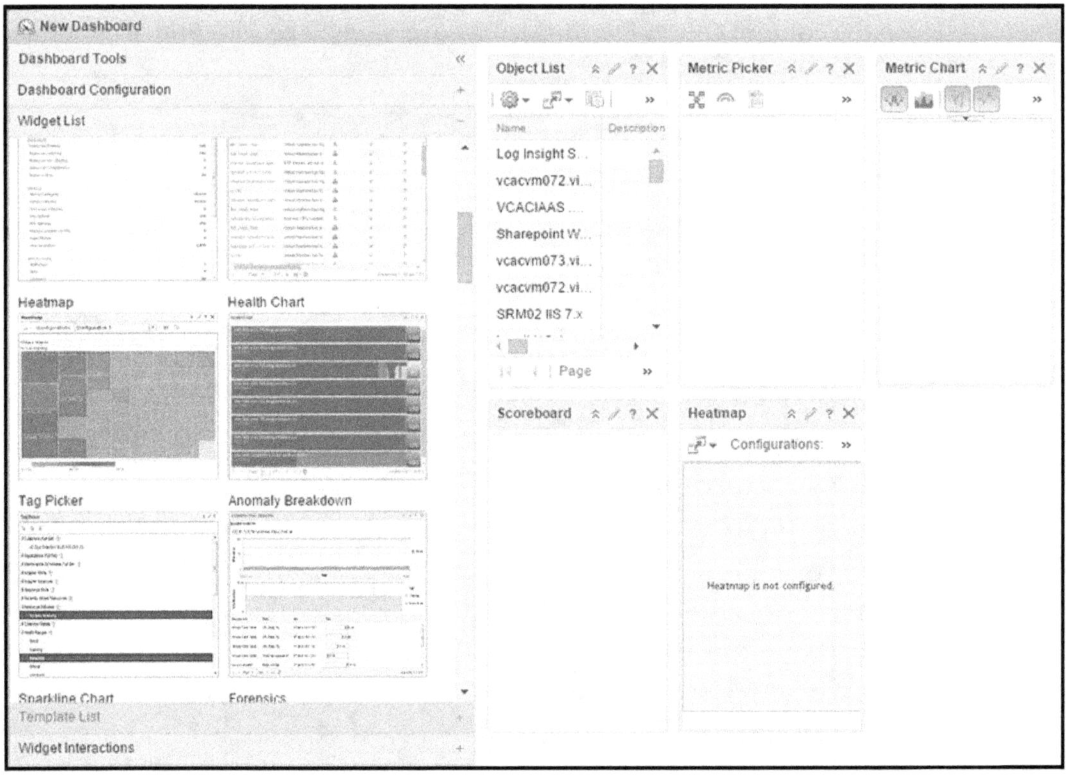

One big improvement in dashboard creation over previous versions is being able to configure the widgets during the creation stage. In vCOps 5.x, we had to lay out the widgets first and configure them later.

To edit the widgets, we click on the little pen icon sitting at the top of widget.

Editing Object List

1. Click on **Object List** and the **Edit Object List** window will appear. Here, edit the **Title**; select **Auto Select First Row** and select **Cluster Compute Resource** under the **Object Types** tag. We should have something similar to the one shown in the following screenshot. Click on **Save** to continue.

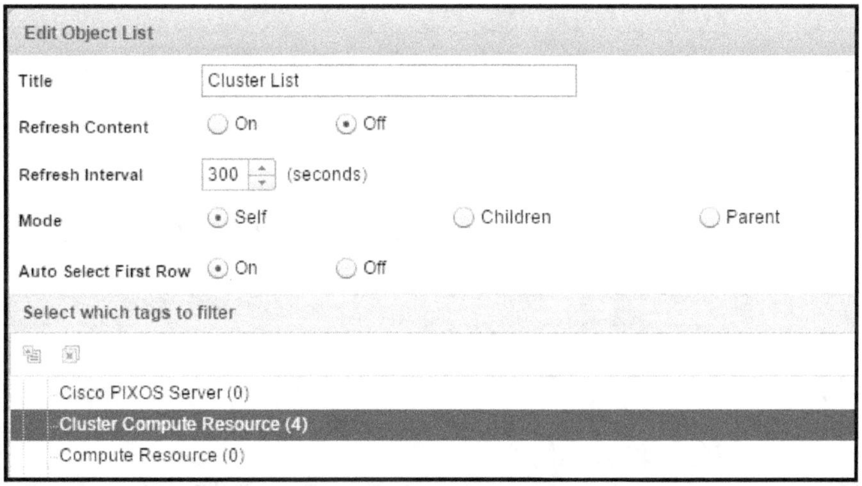

> With tag selection, multiple tags can be selected, and if this is done, only objects that fall under both tag types will be shown in the widget.

2. The next thing we want to do is click on **Widget Interactions** on the left pane. This is where we go to link the widgets: for example, if we select a virtual machine from an object list widget, it would change any linked widgets to display the information of that object.

   We will see **Selected Object(s)** with a drop-down list followed by a green arrow pointing to our widgets. This means that what we select in the drop-down list will be linked to the associated widget.

3. Here our new **Cluster List** will feed **Metric Picker**, **Scoreboard**, and **Heatmap**, while **Metric Picker** will feed **Metric Chart**. We will also notice that a widget like **Metric Chart** can be fed by more than one widget. Click on apply and we should end up with something similar to the following screenshot:

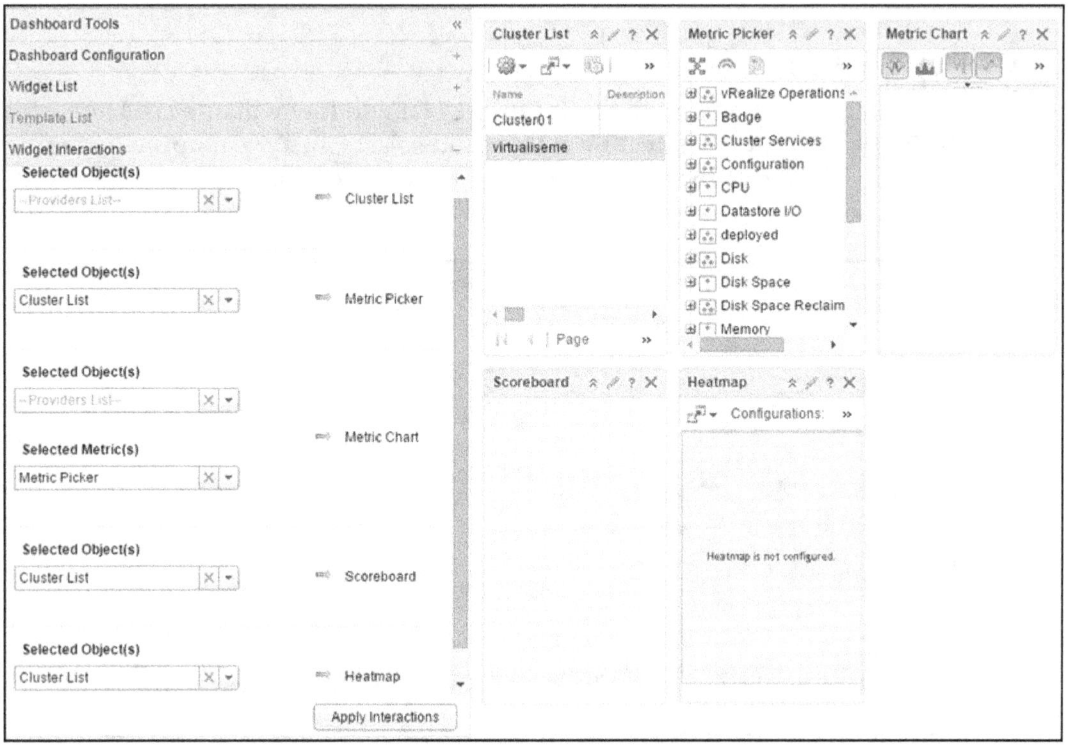

Editing Metric Picker

Now if we select a metric under the **Metric Picker** widget, it should show the metric in the **Metric Chart** widget, like the one displayed in the following screenshot:

> The Metric Picker widget will contain all the available metrics for the select object like an ESXi host or a virtual machine.

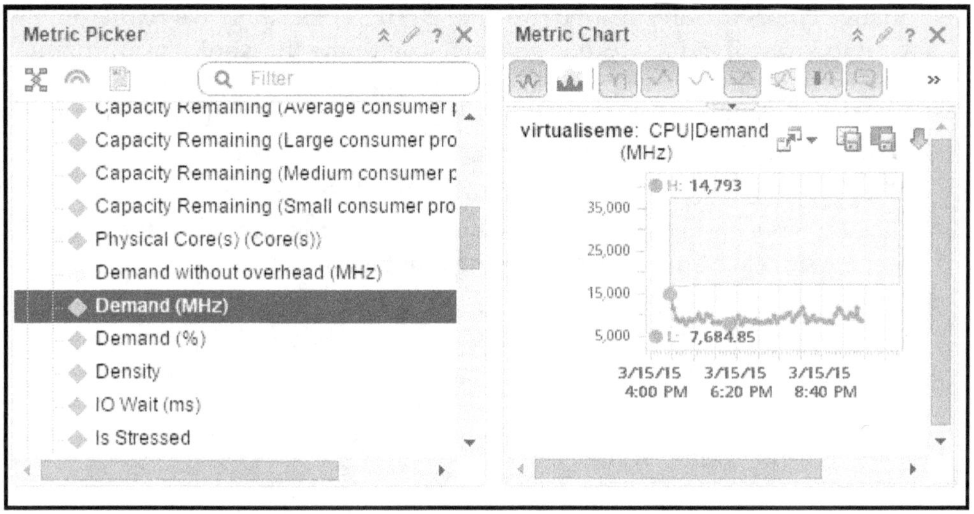

Editing Heatmap

Next up, we will edit the Heatmap widget. In this example, we will use the Heatmap widget to display the capacity remaining for the datastores attached to the vSphere cluster. This is the best way to see at a glance that none of the datastores are over 90 percent used or getting close. We need to make the following changes:

1. Give the widget a new name describing what we are trying to achieve.
2. Change **Group By** to **Cluster Compute Resource**: This is what we want the parent container to be.
3. Change mode to Instance: This mode type is best used when interacting with other widgets to get its objects.
4. Change object type to Datastore: This is the object we want displayed.
5. Change attribute kind to Capacity remaining: This is the metric of the object we want to use.

6. Change colors around from 0 (min) to 20 (max): Because we really only want to know if a datastore is getting close to the threshold, minimizing the range will give us more granular colors. Change the colors around making it red on the left and green on the right. This is done by clicking on the little color square at each end and picking a new color. The reason this is done is because we have capacity remaining, so we need 0 percent remaining as red.
7. Click on **Save** and we should now have something similar to the following image, with each square representing a datastore:

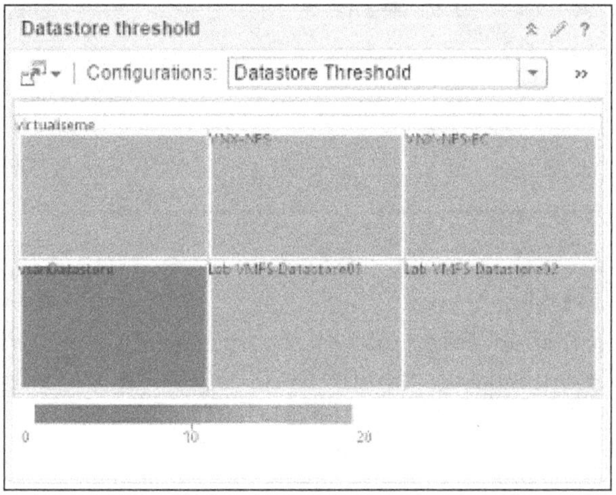

> Move the mouse over each box to reveal more detail on the object.

XML editing

A lot of the widgets are edited through the GUI with the objects and metrics we want to display. But some require an XML file to define what metrics the widget should display.

It is time to modify the last widget. This one will be a little more complicated due to the way we display what we want, while making sure it remains interactive. When we configured the widget interactions, we noticed that the **Scoreboard** widget was populated automatically with a bunch of metrics, as shown in the following screenshot:

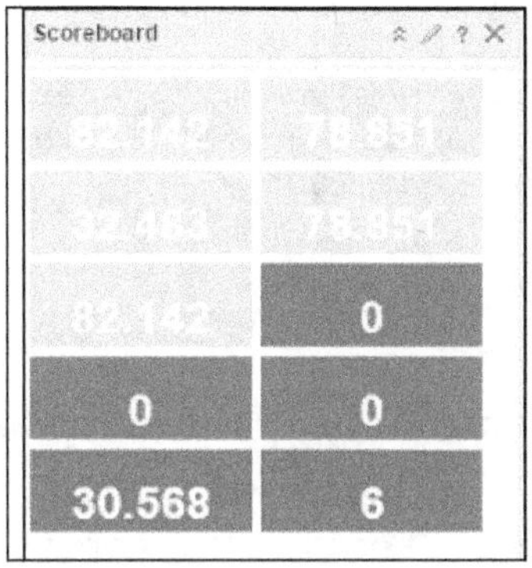

To get the widget to display the information we want while continuing to be interactive to our selections in the cluster list, we have to create a specific XML file and upload it to the vROps 6.0 nodes.

To keep this simple, we will configure four metrics to be displayed, which are as follows:

- CPU usage for the cluster in percentage
- CPU demand for the cluster
- Memory ballooning
- CPU usage for the cluster in MHz

Let's begin by performing the following steps:

1. Open a text editor and add the following code and save it as an XML file; in this case, we will call it `clusterexample.xml`:

```
<?xml version="1.0" encoding="UTF-8" standalone="yes"?>
<AdapterKinds>
  <AdapterKind adapterKindKey="VMWARE">
    <ResourceKind resourceKindKey=
      "ClusterComputeResource">
```

```
        <Metric attrkey="cpu|capacity_usagepct_average"
          label="CPU" unit="%" yellow="50" orange="75"
          red="90" />
        <Metric attrkey="cpu|demandPct" label="CPU Demand"
          unit="%" yellow="50" orange="75" red="90" />
        <Metric attrkey="cpu|usagemhz_average"
          label="CPU Usage" unit="GHz" yellow="8"
          orange="16" red="20" />
        <Metric attrkey="mem|vmmemctl_average"
          label="Balloon Mem" unit="GB" yellow="100"
          orange="150" red="200" />
      </ResourceKind>
    </AdapterKind>
  </AdapterKinds>
```

2. Using WinSCP or another similar product, upload this file to the following location on the vROps 6.0 virtual appliance:

   `/usr/lib/vmware-vcops/tomcat-web-app/webapps/vcops-web-ent/WEB-INF/classes/resources/reskndmetrics`

   In this location we will notice some built-in sample XML files, as shown in the following screenshot:

   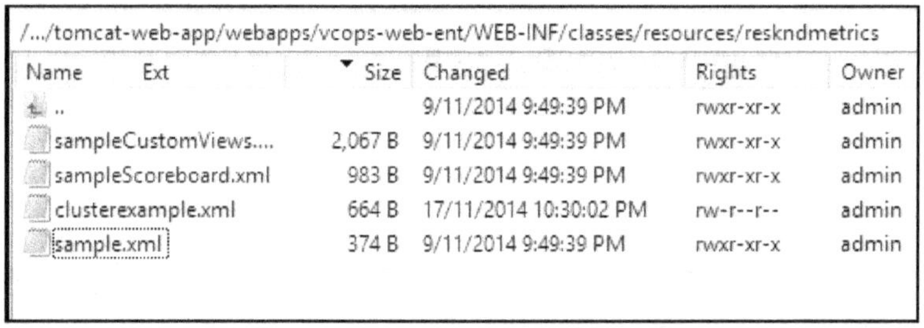

3. Now let's go back to our dashboard creation and edit the **Scoreboard** widget. We will notice quite a lot of configuration options compared to others, most of which are how the boxes are laid out, such as the number of columns, box size, and rounding out decimals. What we want to do for this widget is as follows:

   ◦ Name the scoreboard something meaningful

- Round the decimals to 1; this cuts down the amount of decimal places returned on the displayed value
- Under **Res. Interaction Mode**, choose the XML file we just uploaded from the drop-down list

We should now see something similar to the following screenshot:

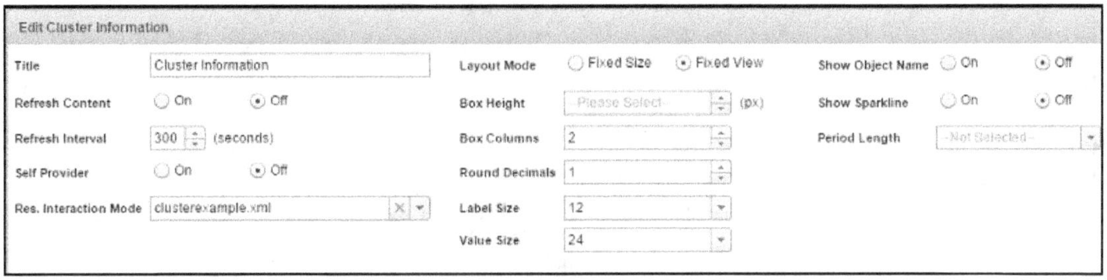

But what about the object selection you may have noticed in the lower half of the **Scoreboards** widget? These are only used if we make the widget a self-provider, which we can see as an option to the top left of the edit window. We can choose objects and metrics, but they are ignored when **Self Provider** is set to **No**.

1. If we now click on **Save**, we should see the new configuration of the scoreboard widget, as shown in the following:

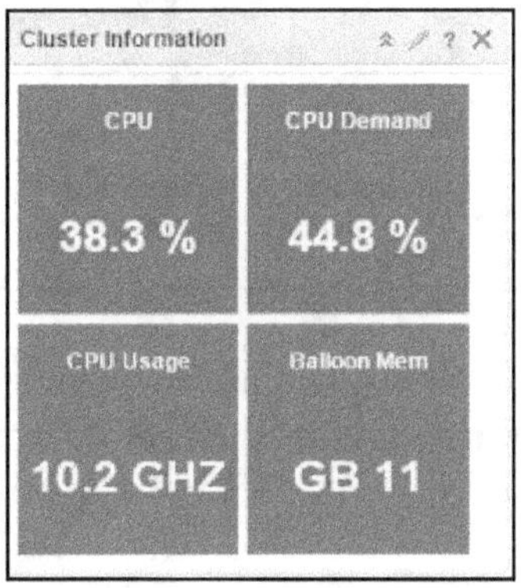

2. We have now completed the new dashboard. Click on **Save** on the bottom right to save the dashboard. We can go back and edit this dashboard whenever we need to. This new dashboard will now be available on the home page, as shown in the following screenshot:

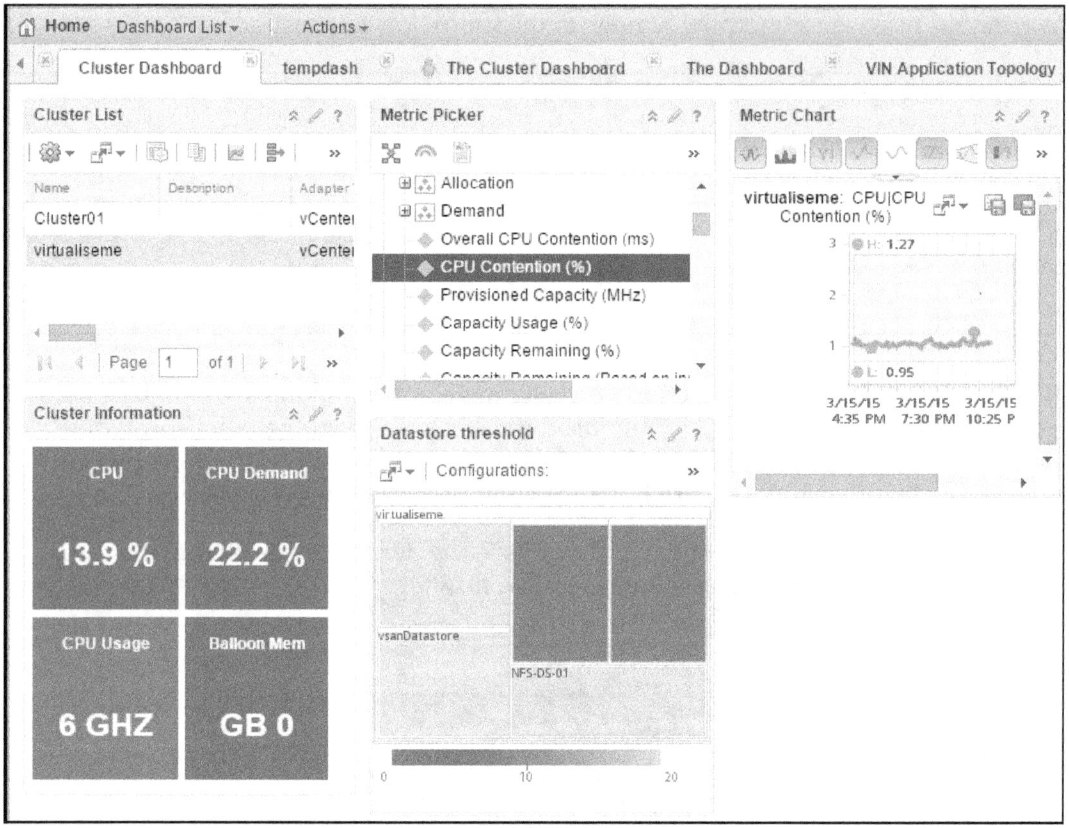

For the **Scoreboard** widget, we have used an XML file, so the widget will display the metrics we would like to see when an object is selected in another widget. How can we get the correct metric and adapter names to be used in this file?

Glad you asked. The simplest way to get the correct information we need for the XML file is to create a non-interactive dashboard with the widget containing all the information we want to display. For example, let's quickly create a temporary dashboard with only one scoreboard widget and populate it with what we want by manually selecting the objects and metrics with **Self Provider** option set to **On**.

1. Create another dashboard and drag and drop a single scoreboard widget into it. Edit the scoreboard widget and configure it with all the information we would like. Search for an object in the middle pane and select the widgets we want in the right pane.
2. Configure the box label and measurement unit. A thing to note here is that we have selected memory balloon metric, as shown in the following screenshot, but we have given it a label of GB. This is because of a new feature in 6.0, which will automatically upscale the metrics when shown on a scoreboard, which also goes for datastore GB to TB, CPU MHz to GHz, and network throughput from KBps to MBps. Typically, in 5.x, we would create supermetrics to make this happen.

   The downside to this is that the badge color still has to be set in the metrics base format.

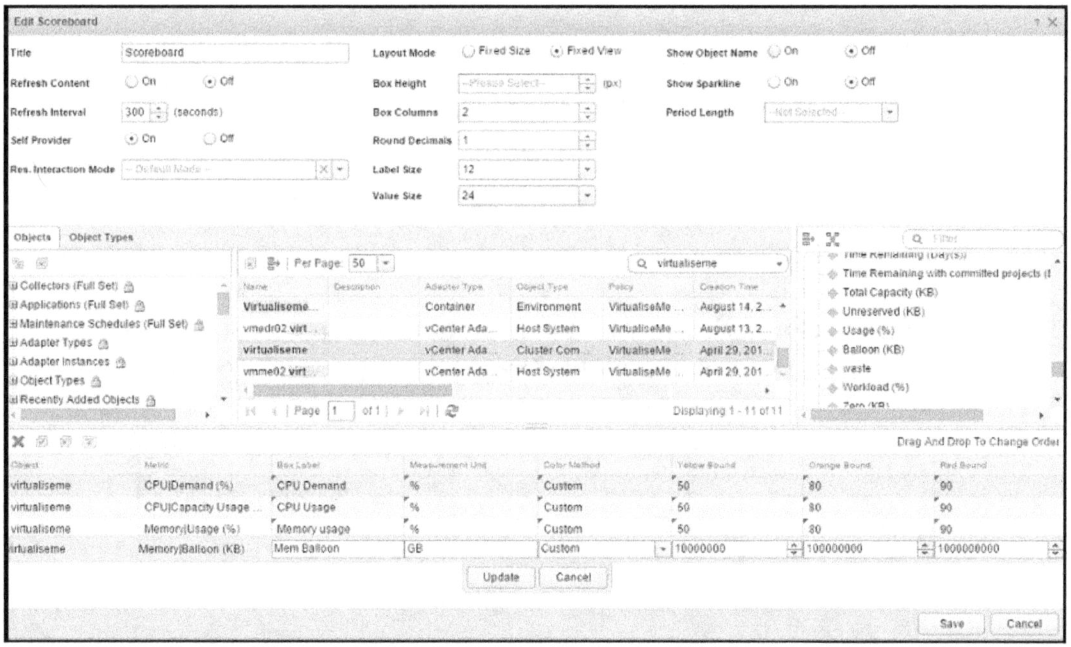

3. Save this dashboard once we have the metrics we want. Locate it under our dashboard list and select it, click on the little cogwheel, and select **Export Dashboards**, as shown in the following screenshot:

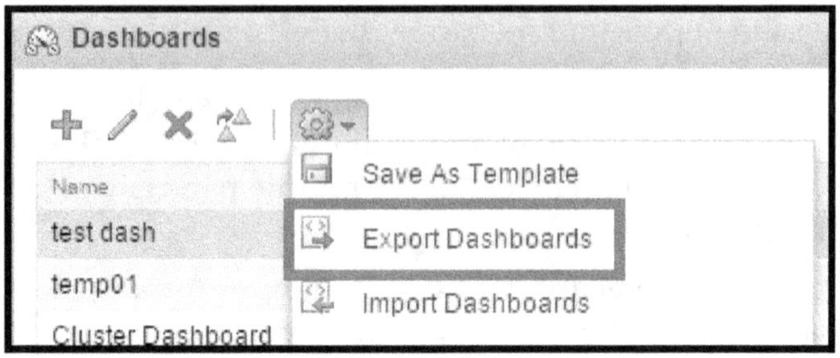

This will automatically download a file called Dashboard<Date>.json.

Open this file in a text editor and have a look through it. We will see all the information we require to write our XML interaction file. First is our resourceKindKey and adapterKindKey, as shown in the following screenshot. These are pretty self-explanatory; resourceKind being a cluster resource, while adapter is the one that's collecting the metrics, in this case, the inbuilt vCenter called VMWARE.

```
"entries": {"resource": [{
    "resourceKindKey": "ClusterComputeResource",
    "internalId": "resource:id:0_::_",
    "adapterKindKey": "VMWARE",
    "identifiers": [
        {
            "value": "domain-c26",
            "key": "VMEntityObjectID"
        },
```

Next are our resources, as we can see from the following screenshot, we have metricKey, which is the most important one, as well as the color settings, unit and label:

```
"resourceMetrics": [
    {
        "yellowBound": 50,
        "resourceId": "resource:id:0_::_",
        "unit": "%",
        "metricName": "CPU|Demand (%)",
        "metricKey": "cpu|demandPct",
        "resourceKindName": "",
        "resourceName": "virtualiseme",
        "resourceKindId": "",
        "label": "CPU Demand",
        "redBound": 90,
        "orangeBound": 80,
        "colorMethod": false
    },
```


The following is how we can get the information we require for the XML file:

```
<?xml version="1.0" encoding="UTF-8" standalone="yes"?>
<AdapterKinds>
  <AdapterKind adapterKindKey="VMWARE">
    <ResourceKind resourceKindKey="ClusterComputeResource">
      <Metric attrkey="cpu|capacity_usagepct_average" label="CPU"
        unit="%" yellow="50" orange="75" red="90" />
      <Metric attrkey="cpu|demandPct" label="CPU Demand"
        unit="%" yellow="50" orange="75" red="90" />
      <Metric attrkey="cpu|usagemhz_average" label="CPU Usage"
        unit="GHz" yellow="8" orange="16" red="20" />
      <Metric attrkey="mem|vmmemctl_average" label="Balloon Mem"
        unit="GB" yellow="100" orange="150" red="200" />
    </ResourceKind>
  </AdapterKind>
</AdapterKinds>
```

Any widget with the setting **Res.Interactive Mode** available can use the XML files you create. The XML format is as per the preceding code. The XML file can also have multiple adapter kinds as there could be different adapter metrics that you require.

The following screenshot shows a more complex dashboard, which is operationally more useful than the quick one we went through. Using the same things we learnt previously, we can make a dashboard like the one shown in the following screenshot:

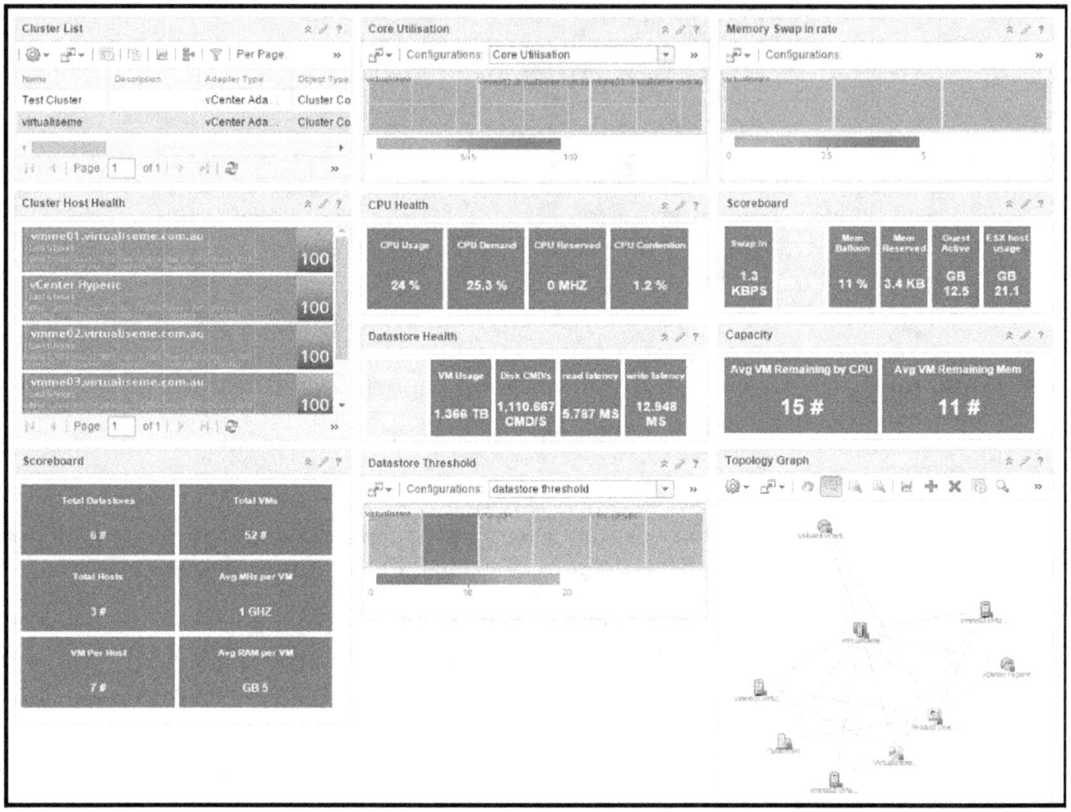

Summary

In this chapter, you learned why one would want to create dashboards (mainly to get all the other support teams off our backs!). You learned how each of the widgets function, and then how to link them together to make a dashboard that is interactive, based on selections made within widgets.

We also unraveled the mystery of the interaction XML file and how to get the information we require into it.

We satisfied the techies in this chapter. In the next chapter, we will take a trip through creating reports and views, which will keep even the fussiest executive happy with the new custom reporting.

8

Reporting and Views

This chapter will cover the new vROps 6.0 features of views and reports, and discuss how they assist in easily proving any piece of information about your environment at any time. You will discover the major improvements that these features bring, thereby effectively managing your environment along with examples on how to create your own report and views.

Changes to views and reports in Operations Manager 6.0

I just stated that views and reports are among the new features of vROps 6.0, however that is not entirely the case. Although views and reports, to a degree, existed in vCOps 5.x, their new 6.0 equivalents are so much better that we should probably just pretend that the old versions did not exist. However, let's quickly cover the major differences and new features of views and reports in vROps 6.0.

Views in Operations Manager 5.x versus 6.0

Views did exist in Operations Manager 5.x, however they were mostly a component of the original CapacityIQ product, and as such were generally based on capacity information. These views had display types similar to the new views system such as lists, summaries, trends, and distributions (which will we discuss soon), however they had many limitations. These views were not configurable around the data that was displayed, and as they were part of the vSphere UI, they only showed prebuilt information around vSphere components. An example of views in Operations Manager 5.x is shown in the following screenshot:

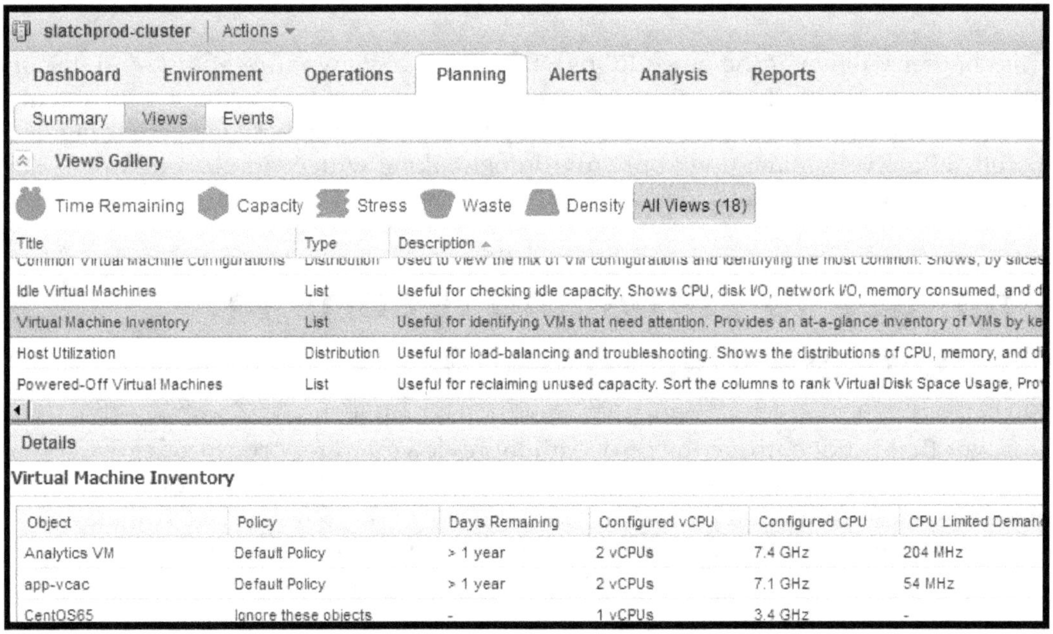

In Operations Manager 6.0, views are now fully configurable against any subject (which is the new term for object type or resource kind). A helpful UI is provided for administrators to construct these new views and apply them as a standalone object, part of an existing tab or included in a report. Out-of-the-box, there are well over 150 views that come prepackaged with Operations Manager 6.0 as part of the vSphere Solution pack. These views provide an amazing amount of information for the most common operation scenarios as well as provide great examples to create your own views. An example of the new view builder UI is shown in the following screenshot:

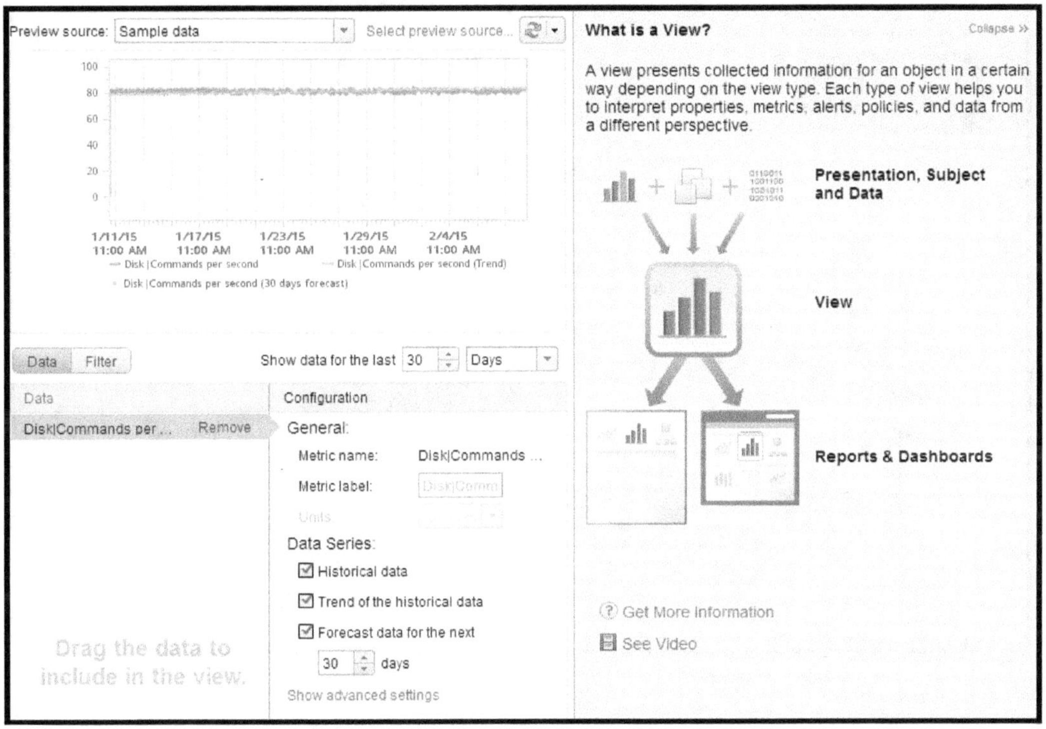

Reports in Operations Manager 5.x versus 6.0

In Operations Manager 5.x, reports were heavily limited to mostly capacity type reports based on the original CapacityIQ product. In Version 5.6, experimental support was provided to allow users to create custom reports using XML queries (no UI support). These custom reports were very complicated to create and often provided little value as they were not associated with an object type.

In Operations Manager 6.0, a fully functional UI is available to build and deliver reports of any type. The report builder UI leverages views for the content of the reports as well as to add format and layout options. An example of the new report builder UI is shown in the following screenshot:

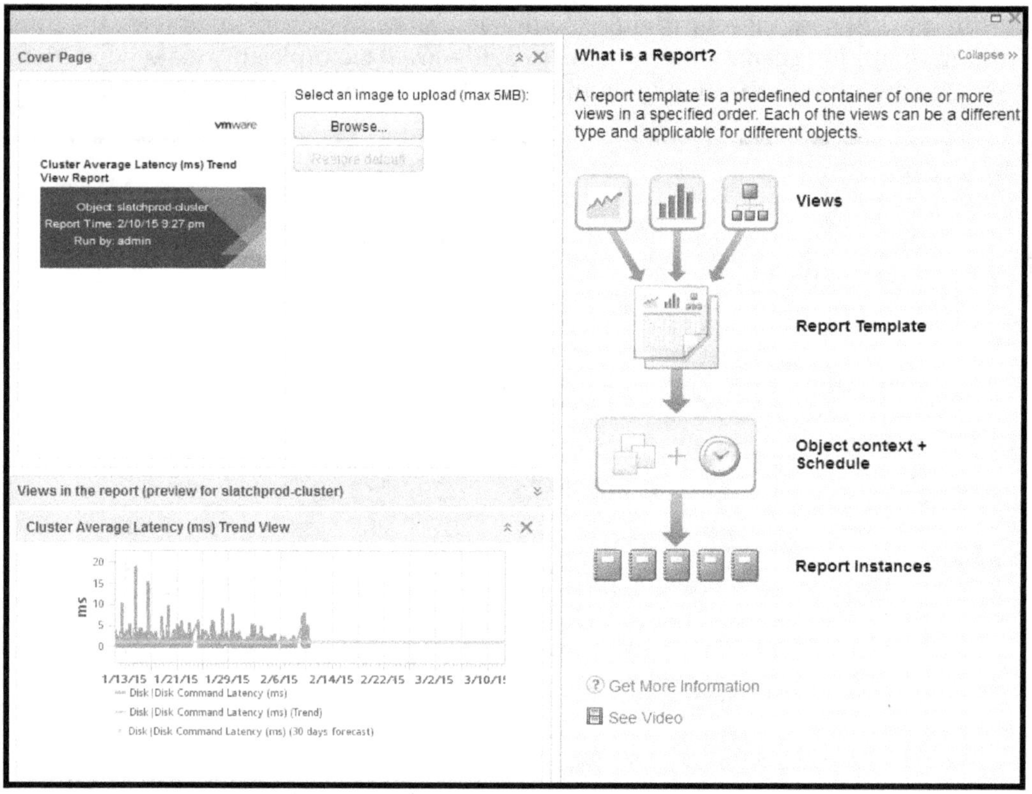

Views in Operations Manager 6.0

Although it may seem repetitive to see the getting started window in the product, a view can best be described as follows:

> *A view presents collected information for an object in a certain way depending on the view type. Each type of view helps you interpret properties, metrics, alerts, policies, and data from a different perspective.*

Another way to interpret this is considering a view as a window or container that takes data from an object or group of objects and presents it in a way that provides useful information to the administrator. The first thing to take away from this statement is that a view is a container or an object in its own right. It is the smallest component of a dashboard or report but it can be linked to directly from other sections of vROps showing just that individual view or used on its own.

It is also important to point out that, like all facets of Operations Manager 6.0, views can be applied to any object type from any adapter. Different object types can even be combined or compared in the same view if the objects have the same data types. These views can then be added to different parts of Operations Manager to ensure that they are available to administrators at the right time. We will discuss how to link views to other parts of the UI shortly.

Defining and building views

Before you start creating views, it pays to have an understanding of the components that they are comprised of. So, first let's walk through the parts required to define and build a view and then apply them to real work situations.

Name and description

Although it might seem obvious, the first thing you need to define when creating a report is the name and description. Before you dismiss this requirement and simply enter `My View` or `Scott's Test`, you should be aware that the name and description fields are very useful in defining the scope and target of the view. This is because many views are not really designed to be run/applied on the subject, but rather on one of its parents. This is especially true for the lists and distributions that we will cover in just a moment.

Subjects

Although the subjects are generally selected after the presentation, it makes sense to describe them first. A subject is "the base object whose information is shown by the view". In other words, a subject is a vROps object type with the data field based on vROps attribute kinds. Any object type from any adapter can be selected. It is important to keep in mind that you may be designing a view for a parent object, however the subject is actually the data of a child object. For example, if you wish to list all the datastore free space in a vSphere cluster itemized by the datastore, the subject will be the datastore not the cluster compute resource. This is because although the list will always be viewed
in the context of a cluster, the data listed is from datastore's objects. An example of selecting subjects is shown in the following screenshot:

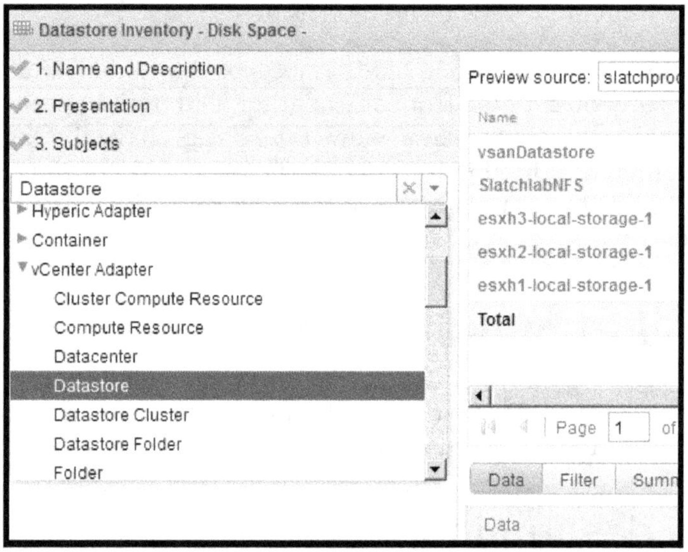

When selecting a subject, an option is provided to select multiple object types. If this is done, only data that is common to both object types will be available.

Presentation

The presentation is the format in which the view is created and how the information is displayed. In Operations Manager 6.0, there are six different presentation types that are as follows:

- List
- Summary (or list summary)
- Trend
- Distribution
- Text
- Images

List

A list is one of the simplest presentation types to use and understand, and is also one of the most useful types. A list provides a tabular layout of values for each data type, with the ability to provide an aggregation row, such as sum or average, at the end. Lists are the most useful presentation type for a large number of objects and are able to provide information in the form of metrics and/or properties. Lists are also most commonly used for presentations when showing a collection of objects relative to their parent. An example of a list can be seen in the following screenshot:

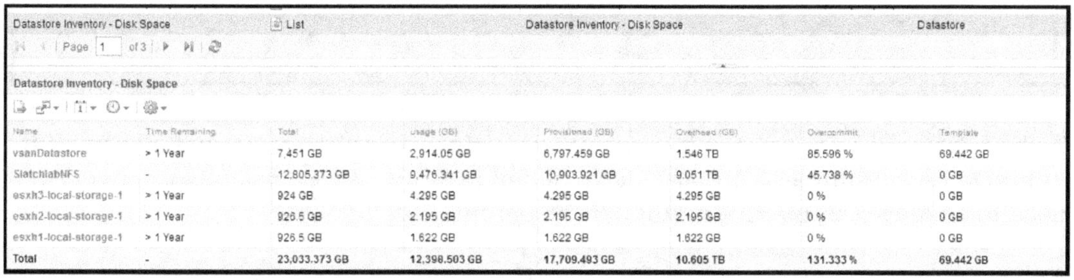
Datastore Inventory - Disk Space | List | Datastore Inventory - Disk Space | Datastore

Page 1 of 3

Datastore Inventory - Disk Space

Name	Time Remaining	Total	Usage (GB)	Provisioned (GB)	Overhead (GB)	Overcommit	Template
vsanDatastore	> 1 Year	7,451 GB	2,914.05 GB	6,797.459 GB	1.546 TB	85.596 %	69.442 GB
SlatchlabNFS	-	12,805.373 GB	9,476.341 GB	10,903.921 GB	9.051 TB	45.738 %	0 GB
esxh3-local-storage-1	> 1 Year	924 GB	4.295 GB	4.295 GB	4.295 GB	0 %	0 GB
esxh2-local-storage-1	> 1 Year	926.5 GB	2.195 GB	2.195 GB	2.195 GB	0 %	0 GB
esxh1-local-storage-1	> 1 Year	926.5 GB	1.622 GB	1.622 GB	1.622 GB	0 %	0 GB
Total	-	**23,033.373 GB**	**12,398.503 GB**	**17,709.493 GB**	**10.605 TB**	**131.333 %**	**69.442 GB**

List summary

A summary is similar to a list, however the rows here are the data types (rather than the objects) and the columns are the aggregated values of all children of that subject type. Unlike a list, a summary field is compulsory as the individual objects are not presented in the view. The summary view type is probably used least commonly; however, it is useful when you simply care about the end result and not the detail of how it was calculated. The example from the following screenshot shows datastore space usage from the cluster level; information such as the average gigabytes used across each datastore can be displayed without the need to show each datastore present in a list. Take a look at the example shown in the following screenshot:

Datastore Space Usage Breakdown

	Average Value	Peak Value	Standard Deviation
Disk Space|Capacity (GB)	4,606.675 GB	12,805.373 GB	4,815.772 GB
Disk Space|Provisioned Space	3.459 TB	10.648 TB	4.419 TB
Disk Space|Total used (GB)	2,479.701 GB	9,476.341 GB	3,675.545 GB
Disk Space|Virtual Machine used	309.94 GB	1.31 TB	521.948 GB
Disk Space|Virtual Disk Used (GB)	307.856 GB	1,330.86 GB	517.832 GB
Disk Space|Snapshot Space (GB)	1.286 GB	6.429 GB	2.572 GB
Disk Space|Swap File Space (GB)	0 GB	0 GB	0 GB
Disk Space|Overhead	2.121 TB	9.051 TB	3.516 TB

Although it will be discussed in more detail in the next chapter, the availability of the option to create simple summary views of child resources has partially removed the need to create super metrics to roll data to parent objects.

Trend

A trend view is a line graph representation of metrics showing historical data that can be used to generate trends and forecasts for those metrics. Unlike some of the other presentation types, a trend can only show data from that subject, as such trend views do not filter to parent objects.

A trend view in many ways is similar to a standard metric chart widget with a set of combined preconfigured data types, with one major exception: the trend view has the ability to forecast data into the future for a specified period of time as well as to show the trend line for historical data for any object type.

This allows the trend view to provide detailed and useful capacity planning data for any object in the vROps inventory. When selecting the data types to use in the view, it is recommended that if multiple data types are used, then they must support the same unit of measurement. Although this is not a requirement of the tool, views that have different unit types on the same scale are relatively hard to compare. An example of a trend view is shown in the following screenshot:

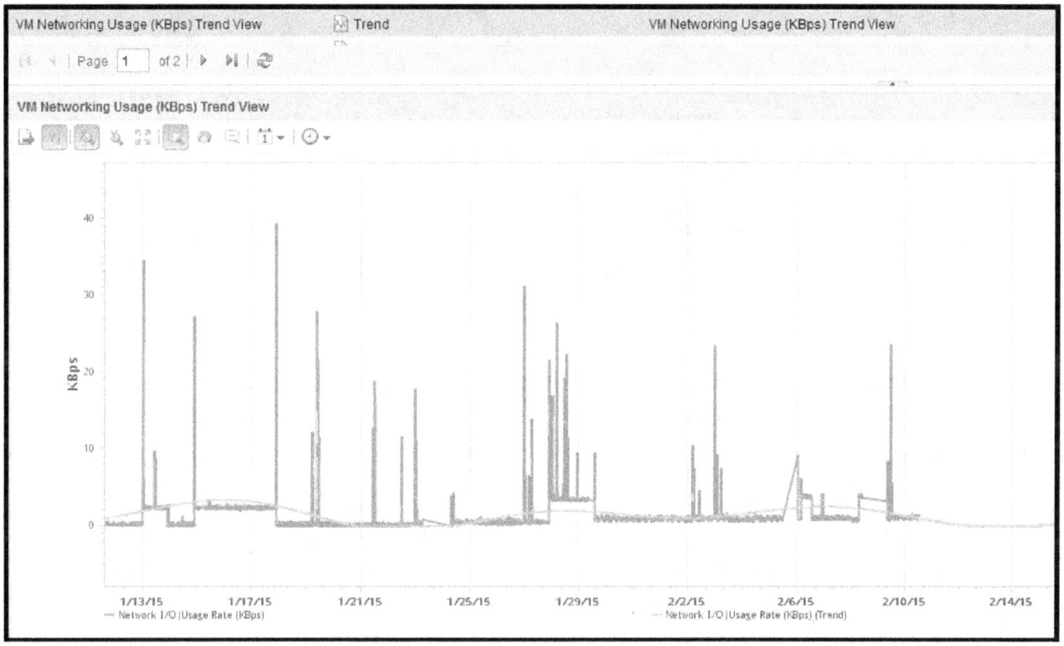

Distribution

A distribution view is a graphical representation of aggregated data and how resources fall within those aggregation groups. This essentially means that vROps finds a way to graphically represent a particular metric or property for a group of objects. The example from the following screenshot shows the distribution of virtual machine OS types in a given vSphere cluster. A distribution view like a summary is very useful in displaying a small amount of information about a large number of objects.

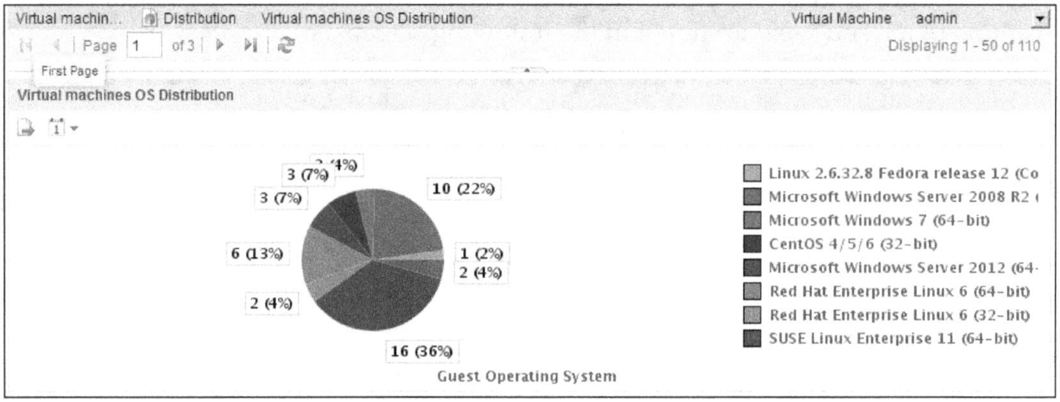

An important point when creating distribution views is that the subject must be a child of the preview or target object. This means that you can only see a view for a distribution on one of the subject's parent objects.

When selecting a distribution, two methods for visualization of the data are available, the bar chart and pie graph. Both methods essentially group the subjects into buckets with the number of buckets and their values based on the distribution type. The three distribution types include:

- **Dynamic distribution**: vROps automatically determines how many buckets to create based on either an interval, a min/max value, or a logarithmic equation. When dealing with varying data values, this is generally the recommended display.
- **Manual distribution**: This type allows the administrator to manually set the range of each bucket in the display.
- **Discrete distribution**: This type is used for displaying exact values of objects rather than ranges. A discrete distribution is recommended if most objects have only a few possible values such as properties or other binary values.

Text and images

The text and image views are used to insert static text or image content for the purpose of reports and dashboards. They allow an administrator to add context to a report in combination with the dynamic views that are inserted when the reports are generated.

Data

Data is the content that makes up the view based on the selected subject. The type of data that can be added and the additional options available depend on the selected presentation type. An important feature with views is that they are able to display and filter presentations based on properties, and not just on standard metrics. This is particularly useful when wanting to filter a list or distribution group. For example, the following screenshot shows badge information in a given vSphere cluster as long as they contain a vSphere custom tag of `vrmManagedMachine=True`. This allows a view to be filtered to only virtual machines that are deployed and managed by vRealize Automation.

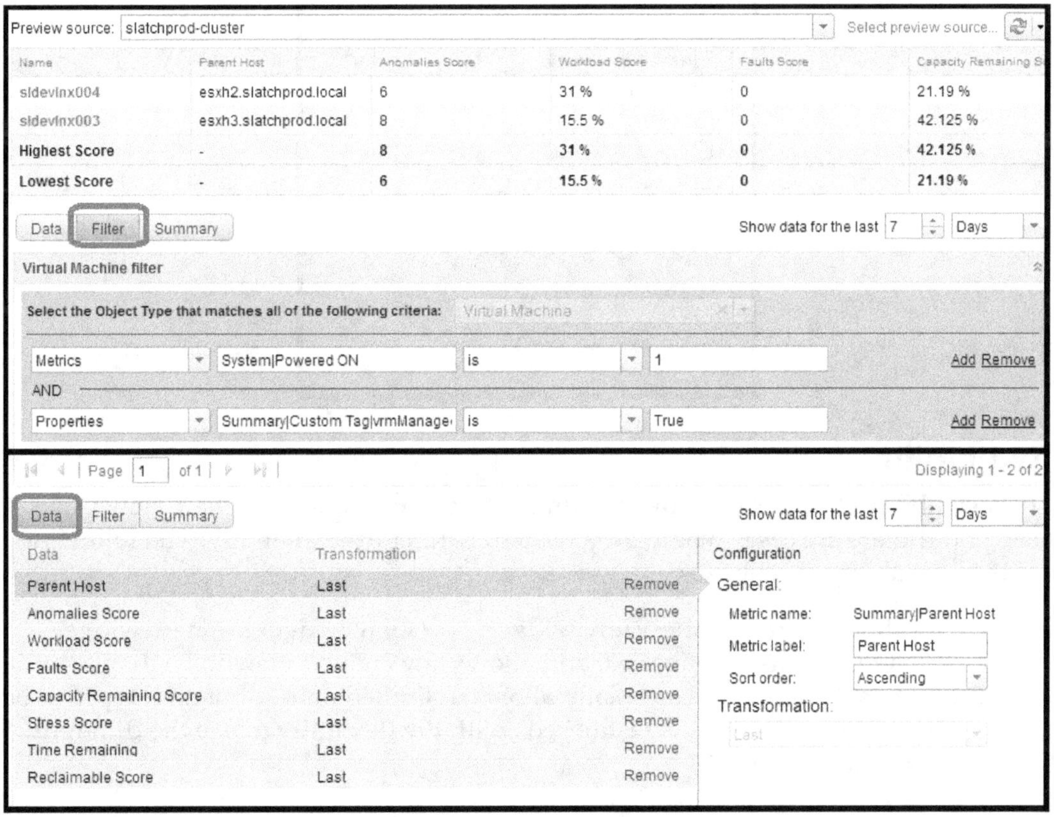

Visibility

One of the most useful features of views is that you have the ability to decide where they show up and where they can be linked from. The visibility layer defines where you can see a hyperlink to a view in vROps based on a series of checkboxes.

The visibility step is broken into three categories as **Availability**, **Further Analysis**, and **Blacklist** as shown in the following screenshot:

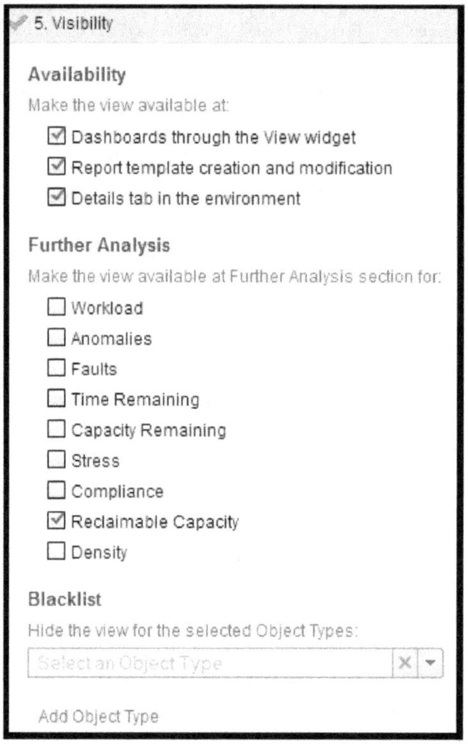

Availability

The availability checkboxes allow an administrator to devise how their view can be used and if there are cases where they wish to restrict its availability. The following are the availability checkboxes:

- **Dashboard through the View widget**: The View widget is a new widget with Operations Manager 6.0 and allows any created view to be displayed on a dashboard. This essentially allows unlimited amount of data types to be displayed on the classic dashboards with the flexibility to use the different presentation types.

- **Report template and modification**: This setting allows views to be used in reports. If you are creating views to be used explicitly in reports, ensure this box is checked.
- **Details tab in the environment**: This is the default location that administrators will use for views. It is also the location where the **Further Analysis** links will take an administrator if this checkbox is selected. In most cases, it is recommended that this option be enabled unless a view is not yet ready to be released to other users.

Further Analysis

The checkboxes under **Further Analysis** are a feature that allow an administrator to link views that they have created to the minor badges in the Object Analysis tab. Although this feature may seem comparatively small, it allows users to create relevant views for certain troubleshooting scenarios and link them directly to the location where administrators will be working. This then allows administrators to leverage views more quickly to troubleshoot rather than simply jump to the All Metrics tab and look for dynamic threshold breaches. The following screenshot shows the options available under **Further Analysis**:

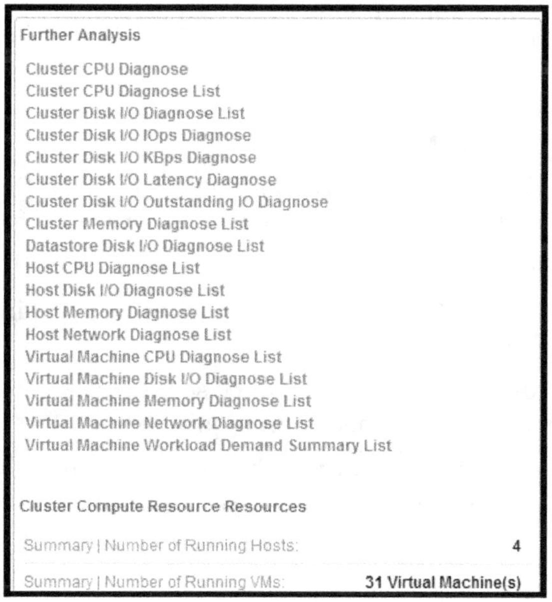

Blacklist

The blacklist allows administrators to ensure that views cannot be used against certain object types. This is useful if you want to ensure that a view is, for example, only partially promoted up to a parent and not a grandparent.

Reports in Operations Manager 6.0

With the introduction of Operations Manager 6.0, the ability to create custom reports for any object type with a simple UI is now available. Out-of-the-box, with Version 6.0, there are over 50 report templates to leverage straight away or use as examples for your own reports.

The creation of reports is very simple, as views are used as the delivery container for content in the reports. This includes the text and image presentation types, which can be used to add context and detail to manual or scheduled reports.

Like views, report templates can be imported and exported from other vROps systems allowing administrators to share system configuration across environments.

As the majority of the configuration for setting up reports is creating relevant views, the reporting functionality can simply be seen as a delivery engine for multiple views as well as custom content.

Scheduling reports

One common reason for creating reports for views is to allow them to be generated automatically on a schedule. Scheduling reports can bring the following benefits to administrators:

- Allows views and data to be easily captured at a point in time and sent to interested stakeholders
- Allows CSV copies of information to be sent to external systems that might also consume the data for their own requirements
- Allows different tailored reports to be sent to different teams, such as capacity management, on a regular basis without the need to log in to vROps

When setting up a schedule report, the easiest way is to find the object in the environment and select the **Reports** tab. From there, an administrator can select the relevant report template and select **Schedule Report** under **Actions**. An example of this workflow is shown in the following screenshot:

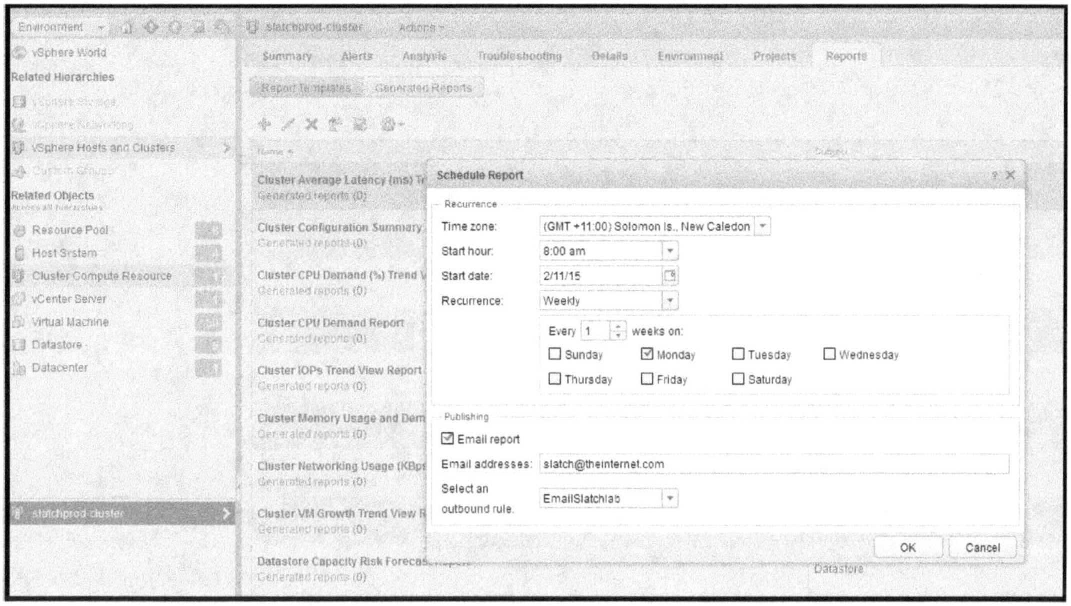

Summary

In this chapter, we covered the new powerful features of views, and looked at how they can be used in reports. We covered the different view presentation types and their strengths and weaknesses for varying data types. In the next chapter, we will cover the super world of super metrics.

9
Super Metrics

As the name would suggest, super metrics are no ordinary metric, and with great power come great opportunities. Super metrics have been around since vCOps 1.0 and VMware have maintained this functionality due to their usefulness. In this chapter, we will discuss the following topics:

- Metric terminology and definitions
- Types of super metrics
- Comparing super metrics to views
- Building your own super metrics
- Applying super metrics in vROps 6.0

What are super metrics and when do I use them?

A super metric is an administrator-created custom metric based on a mathematical formula, using existing metrics that can then be applied via a policy. A super metric can be derived from either a single object or multiple objects across multiple environments.

A super metric is usually defined when an administrator notices a gap in the available metrics on a given object. For example, an administrator notices high CPU ready value on a virtual machine, and is curious to know if it may be common across all VMs on the host or even the vSphere cluster. The administrator might check what the average CPU ready value is for all VMs across the cluster to see if this has changed recently or has progressively been getting worse.

Unfortunately, a suitable metric to perform this analysis is not available on a vSphere host or cluster (although other useful metrics may be available) and, therefore, the administrator is forced to look through several VMs individually to get this data. In this case, the administrator could create a super metric that rolls up the average CPU ready value of all VMs to the cluster level, saving a lot of time by not having to view each object individually.

Although this represents valid example of when creating a super metric may be required, generally the quality of the solution (aka adapter) will determine how many super metrics are required.

Although there are different types of super metrics, a high quality adapter will define most attribute types an administrator should need for that object type. For example, this may include taking two opposite raw values, such as used capacity and free capacity, and dividing them to produce used capacity percentage. However, if this is not the case or an administrator is importing custom data via the API or HTTP Post adapter, super metrics can be very useful in providing a complete set of metrics to benefit from.

Metric terminology and definitions

Now, granted this section heading may not sound like the most interesting subject, but before we get into building super metrics, we need to understand the various definitions around metrics. Too many administrators find super metrics difficult, not because they fail to have use cases or struggle with the math, but because they fail to understand the different terminologies surrounding metrics and how they should be built.

On top of this, during this book, and especially this chapter and the previous chapter, terms such as objects and attribute types are often used, and if you are still aren't 100 percent sure about their meaning, it is time to put that to bed. We will also cover some of the terms that have changed their name between Operations Manager 5.x and 6.0.

Objects

First up is understanding what an object is and what an object type is. An object is a single entity in vROps such as a virtual machine, a datastore, a switch, and so on. The individual object has a name and set of identifiers that make it unique inside vROps, and even if there are multiple objects with the same name (for example, vCenter folders), they will all still be a unique objects in the vROps inventory.

As mentioned in *Chapter 1, vROps – Introduction, Architecture, and Availability*, an object shares its GemFire shard key with its FSDB metric data and alarm data, and this ensures that all elements that make up an object are persisted together on the same vROps node. In previous versions of Operations Manager, an object was referred to as a resource, and as such you may see the two terms are used inter-changeably.

Metrics

An object has metrics that are added to the FSDB and can be retrieved on request. Object metrics are the main concept that drives vROps and includes examples such as VM CPU co-stop (ms), VM Host Disk Usage rate (Kbps), and VDI desktop pool average PCoIP latency (ms).

Metrics are used in all areas of vROps including dashboards, views, widgets, and alarms. An individual metric always has a 1:1 mapping with its parent object, as shown in the following figure:

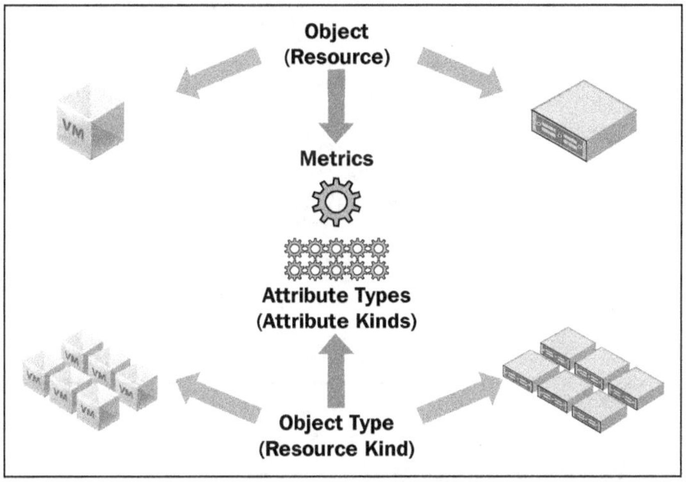

An object type is a group of objects that share the same set of properties and metrics. This can also be seen as a category and includes examples such as virtual machine, datastore, and vSphere Distributed Switch. When creating and applying super metrics, object types are the most common selection, as they allow super metrics to be applied to all objects of the same object type with a single formula, rather than creating individual formulas for individual objects. Following the same name change said earlier, object types were previously referred to as resource kinds. An object has a one to many relationship with an object type.

Attribute types

Attribute types (previously known as attribute kinds) are the definition of the array of metrics an object type generally supports. Attribute types can be seen as the list of metrics you would expect an object to have; however, there is no guarantee that all objects in the given object type have data for every single attribute. For example, if an administrator selects a virtual machine and wishes to view the snapshot space used (GB) metric, and that VM has never had a snapshot, the **No Data** message will be displayed in the metrics graph window. Following the same use cases as object types, attribute types are commonly used in super metrics as they allow the formula to be applied to more than one object. One careful consideration when using attribute types in super metrics is that an object may have more than one instance of an attribute, for example, when a VM has more than one CPU or network adapter, as shown in the following figure:

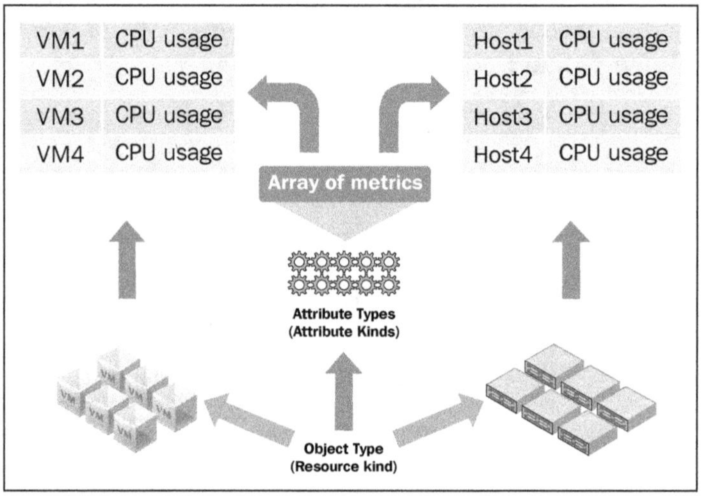

Super metric types

Now that we are ready to get into the detail of super metrics, let's quickly discuss the following three main types of super metrics:

- Rollup
- Generic resource
- Specific resource/Pass-through

Rollup

A rollup super metric is the most common example of a super metric. It uses transformation type functions such as sum, avg, min, count, and so on, and then applies them through a looping function of all child objects matching the object and attribute type. The result of this calculation is then available as a super metric on the object where the super metric is applied.

Let's go through an example using Datastore Free Disk Space (cluster level). Now, before you e-mail me and point out that this metric already exists by default in the vCenter adapter, and that there is no need to create a super metric, I will point out that you are correct; however, the following figure well illustrates the point of rollups. We will go through a more unique example of this later. Take a look at the following figure:

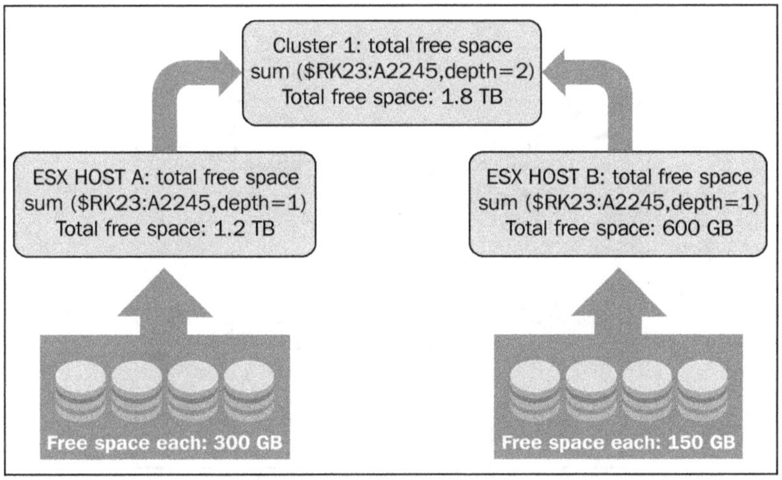

This figure shows an example of two different super metrics of the rollup type applied at different levels. There are two different ESX hosts (A and B), both with only local storage. Each datastore on host A has 300 GB free space and each datastore on host B has 150 GB free space. The administrator wishes to know at a cluster level how much free space is remaining. The administrator creates a super metric that uses the sum function to loop through all instances of free space for the datastore object type. A depth value is also provided to indicate how many generations the super metric has to travel to loop through all of the objects. This super metric is then applied to the vSphere cluster via a policy, and the result of 1.8 TB is given by the super metric.

Generic resource

A generic resource super metric is used when you combine existing metrics using mathematical operators and apply them back to the same object or another object with the same attributes. This essentially allows an administrator to create a completely new metric for an object type where a gap has been identified. What makes a generic resource super metric different from others is the use of the `This` option, which is substituted for the object type. The use of the `This` option allows the super metric to be placed on any object; however, it depends on all objects sharing an attribute with exactly the same name. On top of this, an administrator needs to ensure that the attribute has the same meaning or result if applied to different objects, as sometimes the context of an attribute can be important. As with views, it is recommended that administrators provide a meaningful name that indicates which object types can be associated with the super metric. An example of a generic super metric is shown in the following figure:

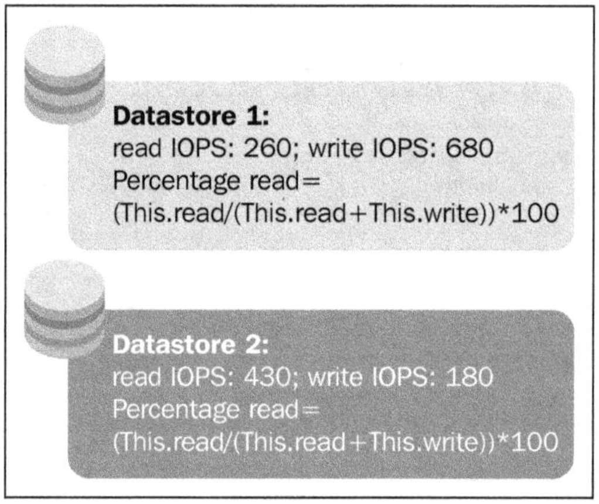

> It is common when defining generic super metrics that an error is received: **Cannot convert aggregated result to number,** This is due to the fact that an object may have multiple instances of an attribute, so use of an additional sum, avg, max, or count operation is required to instruct the formula for how to handle these occurrences, for example, `sum(avg($This.CPUUsage)/(avg($This.CPULimit)).`

Specific resource/pass-through

A specific resource or pass-through is a super metric that is targeting a particular object rather than an object type. It is also referred to as pass-through, as a particular object is being targeted and this super metric can be applied anywhere without the need to specify depth as with the rollup super metric. Unlike the other super metrics, this type generally also targets specific metrics, rather than an attribute, as the super metric is already unique to an object.

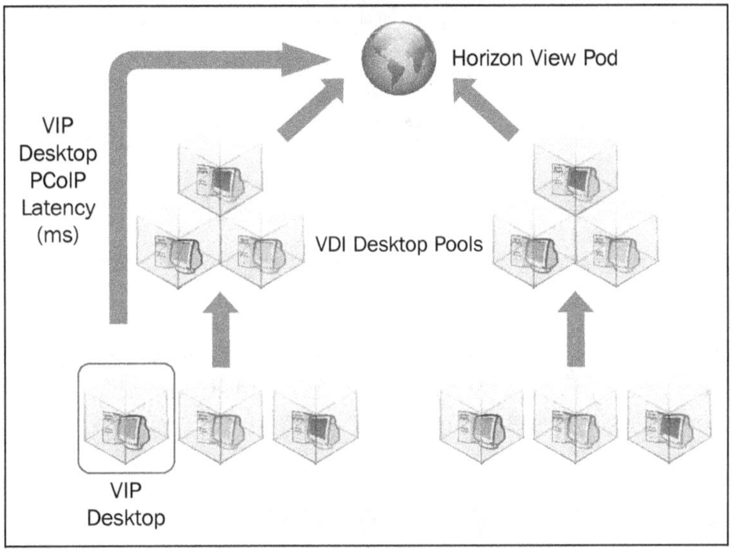

Building your own super metrics

Now it is time to start building your own super metrics, and we can walk through the process of doing so. The first step in designing and building a super metric is to have a clear use case or problem that you are trying to solve. In our example, an administrator is keen to know if the CPU percent ready (or CPU contention) is increasing on all VMs in a cluster as the amount of provisioned VMs increases. Because the administrator wants to know the maximum value of a metric that is present on all virtual machines, a rollup super metric is the most appropriate.

When creating rollup super metrics, understanding parent/child relationships is critical as it helps determine the depth of the looping algorithm that is being defined. The parent/child relationships can be seen in the All Metrics view, the relationship widget, and the object relationships section under administration. An example of these relationships is shown in the following image:

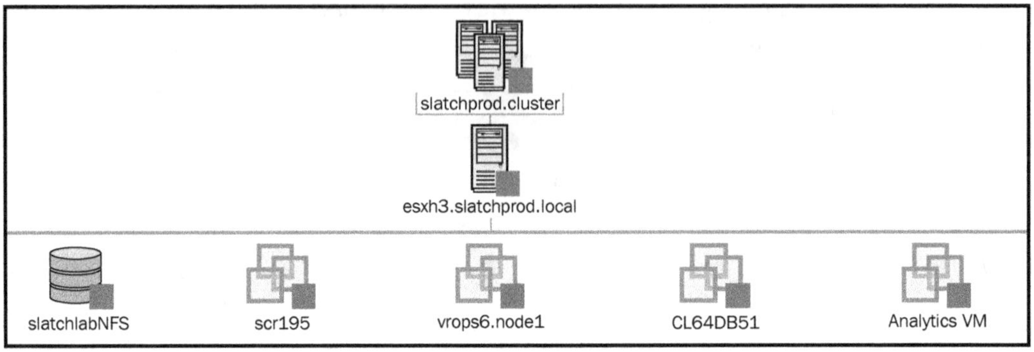

In our example, the administrator has DRS set to fully automatic, so the administrator is most interested in seeing if the maximum CPU ready across the VMs in increasing at the cluster level rather than at the host level. For the super metric to apply correctly, the administrator needs to, set the depth to a value of 2.

Defining a new super metric

To define a new super metric select **Content** | **Super Metrics** in the navigation bar and then select the plus symbol to open the wizard. Now let's step through the seven steps in creating the metric formula. These steps refer to the following example screenshot:

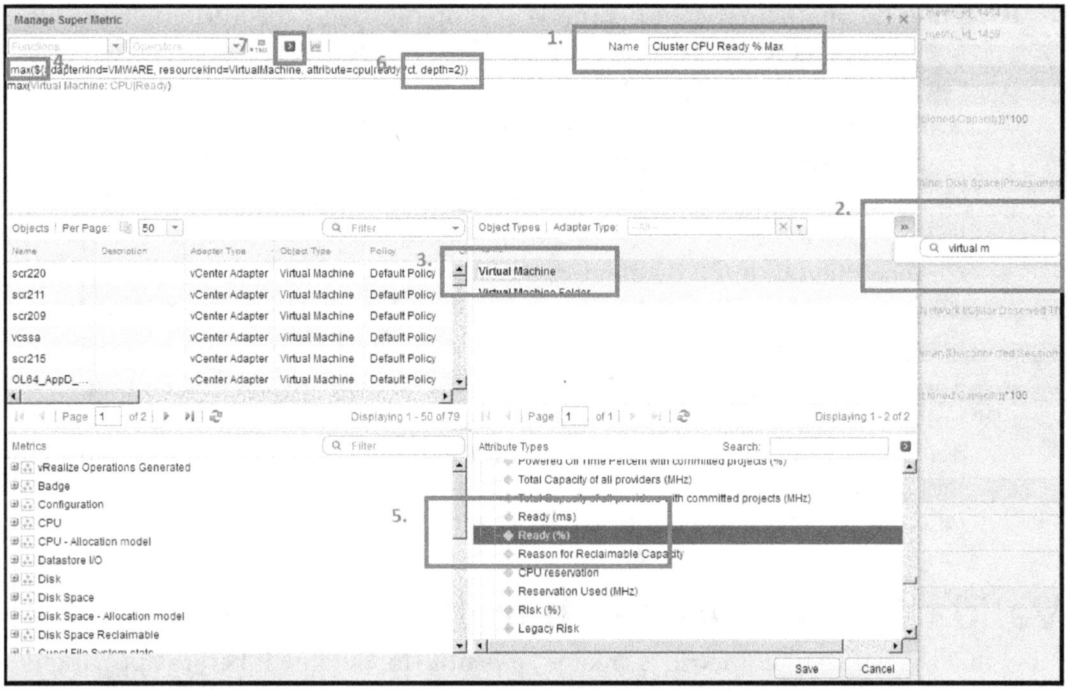

Let's look at some important sections of this screenshot:

- **Name the super metric** (1): Remember from earlier discussion that naming is critical in describing where a super metric should be applied and what its function is. Unlike views, super metrics do not have a description field, so make good use of the name field.
- **Filter on object types** (2): As there are a lot of object types out there, you can leverage the filter field to cut down the options.
- **Select the virtual machine object type** (3): We know that we are after the maximum value of CPU ready across a cluster from each virtual machine. As our metrics are coming from virtual machines, it's apparent that we select the virtual machine object type.

- **Enter the mathematical operand** (**4**): Before we select the attribute type, we need to open the mathematical operand by typing out the `max` function or selecting it from the functions menu.
- **Add the object type to the super metric** (**5**): With the `max()` operand in place, we can now scroll through the list and find the attribute type we are interested in, for example, **Ready (%)**. Double-clicking it will add it to the workspace.
- **Change the depth** (**6**): By default, the depth is **1**, and, therefore, this super metric can only be applied to the vSphere host level. Update the value to `2` to ensure we can add it at the cluster level.
- **Show formula description** (**7**): Selecting the show formula description button will allow a more human readable version of the super metric to be displayed and also perform some basic validation. If a generic resource super metric was being created and multiple instances of an attribute were not taken into account, this step would give an error.

Validating the new super metric

Now that the basic super metric is created, it is time to validate it before applying it to real-world objects. Validation is important as it allows you to see the result of your formula and can help you easily pickup major formulaic errors.

As mentioned earlier, super metrics do not start having a value until they are applied to an object through a policy; therefore, it is impossible the see the value of a super metric before it is created. There is one exception to this rule, however: the super metric validation allows you to model the value of a super metric from any time period. This is useful in ensuring that the result is what you expect before you apply the super metric and find out the formula is incorrect, after waiting four weeks for dynamic thresholds to be calculated. These steps will refer to the following example screenshot:

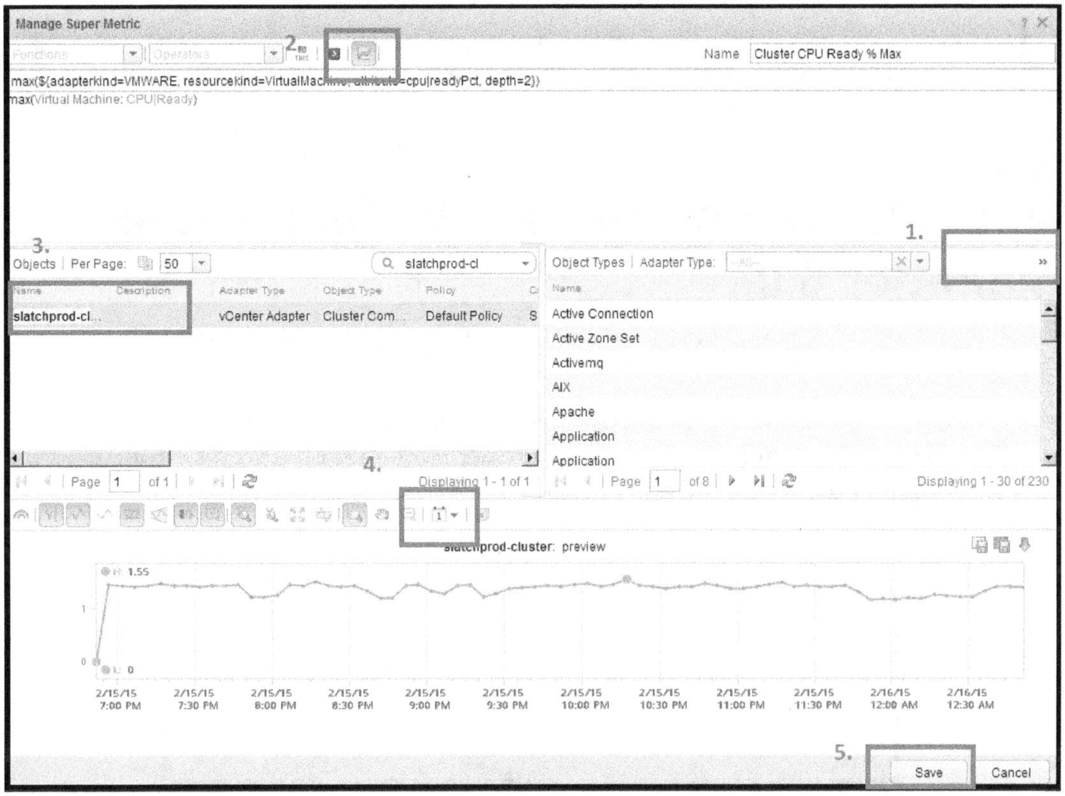

Let's look at some important sections of this screenshot:

- **Clear the object type filter** (**1**): Now that we are ready to visualize the super metric (validate it), we need to first clear the object type filter to allow us to select a cluster object.
- **Open the super metric visualizer** (**2**): Sounds a bit sci-fi, but even so select the button at the top of the wizard to replace the metrics and attribute type windows with the metric visualizer.
- **Select a target object** (**3**): Find and select a target object which matches the object type of where the super metric will be applied. A preview of the super metric will now be shown.
- **Set the time range** (optional) (**4**): Set the time range if you wish to preview data from a longer or different time period.
- **Save the super metric** (**5**): If you're happy with the super metric, it is now time to save and close the wizard.

> It is important to preview your super metric and check that it shows the data you expect. Super metrics can be misleading if proper care is not taken when defining the formula.

Applying super metrics in Operations Manager 6.0

Finally, we are at the last stage of applying our recently created super metric into a policy and applying it to active objects.

1. After you have saved and closed your super metric, select the **Object Types** tab at the bottom of the screen and select the green plus sign button, as shown in the following screenshot:

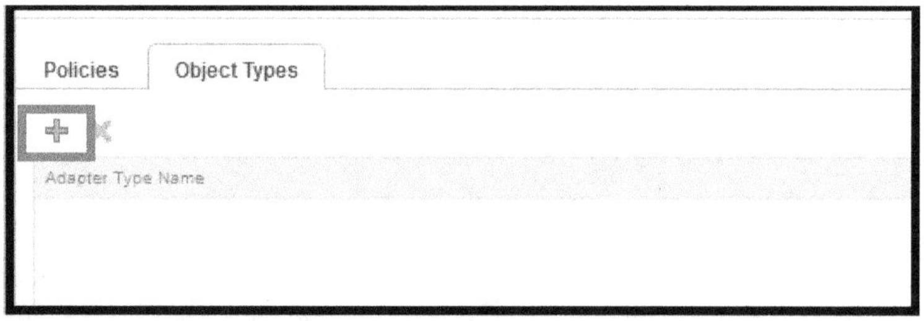

2. Browse or search for the object type you wish to add to the super metric, as shown in the following screenshot. This will allow us to specify that the super metric will only apply to certain object types and, therefore, will not be calculated on object that will not support it, such as datastores:

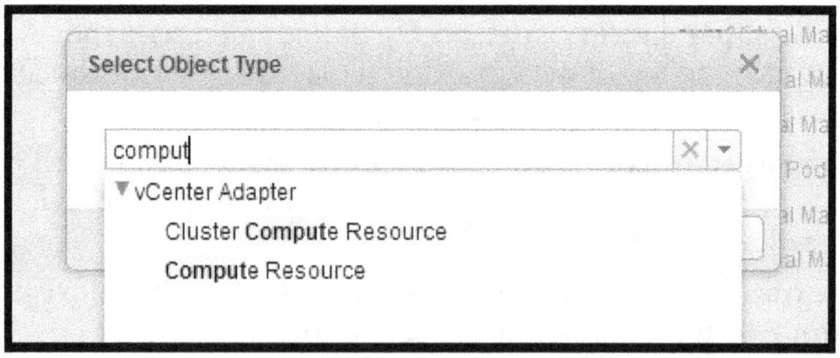

3. From the policy library, find the appropriate policy to add the super metric to and select the pencil icon, as shown in the following screenshot. For more on policies see *Chapter 5, Policies in vRealize Operations Manager 6.0*.

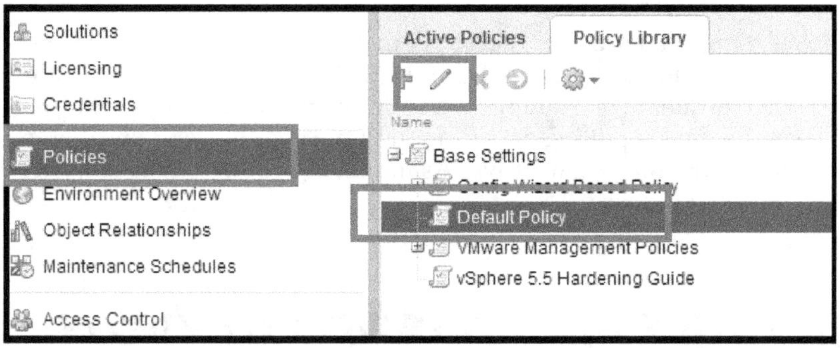

4. Under the **Override Attributes** section, select the **Attribute Type** dropdown and deselect **Metric** and **Property** to heavily reduce the number of attributes to select from. Finally, find your created super metric that matches your resource type and set the state to **Local** (enabled), and save and close the policy, as shown in the following screenshot:

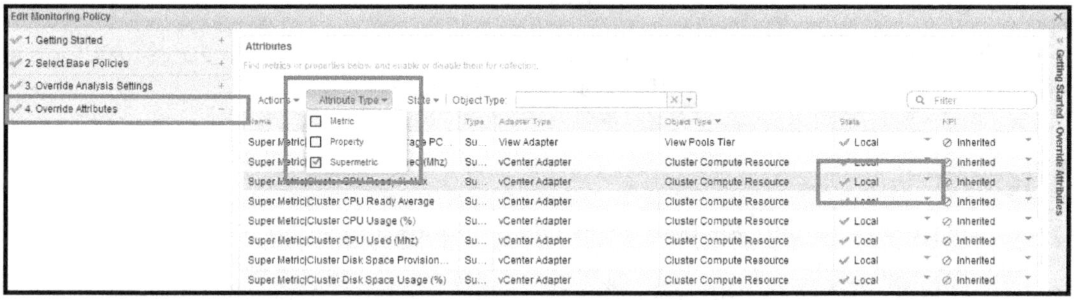

5. After a few collection cycles (5–10), your super metric should begin showing on the selected object types within the inventory, as shown in the following screenshot:

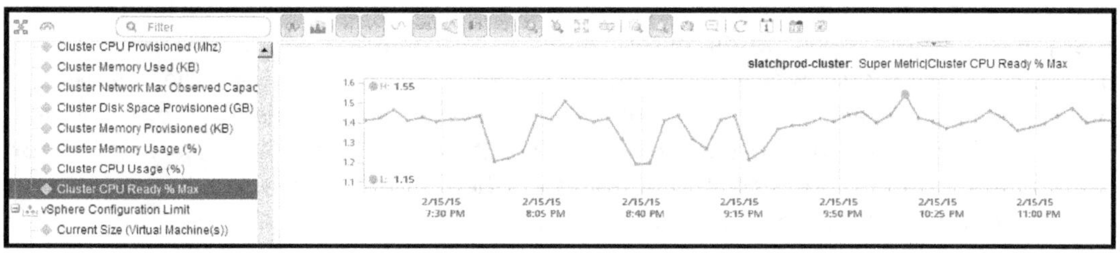

> It is important to note that super metrics depend on accurate and consistent data collection from the metrics that are being transformed in a formula. For example, if an administrator is using a rollup super metric that is pulling data from multiple adapters and one goes offline, the metric may skew heavy. As the saying goes, "garbage in, garbage out," so take care.

Comparing super metrics to views

Before ending our journey on super metrics, I think now would be a great time to explain how they are different from views. As views were only properly introduced in Operations Manager 6.0, and super metrics have been around for a while, you might assume that views are the new natural replacement for super metrics. A good example of this was in the last chapter, where we mentioned that the summary type view allows data from multiple objects to be transformed with operators such as sum, avg, max, and so on in the same way that a rollup super metric does.

So, using a rollup super metric as an example, let's compare super metrics and views, comparing the advantages and disadvantages of each.

Views

Views are quick and easy to create especially compared to super metrics, and when created, they also have the ability to show past, present, and future data (trends). This is a big distinction from super metrics, who only have data when they are created and attached to an object, and as such you can't see the value of a super metric before it was applied.

Super metrics

A super metric is a metric in its own right, and unlike views, which are only dynamically generated when requested by a dashboard or report, a super metric once applied is always being calculated and stored in the FSDB as if it were a normal metric. Although the drawback of this is, as mentioned earlier, that an administrator has no data for a super metric before it was applied, it does however allow for a variety of benefits that views cannot provide.

First and foremost, a super metric is a real metric and both dynamic thresholds (once enough time has passed) and alerts can be applied to super metrics. This allows vROps to detect anomalies and alert accordingly on a user-created super metric if the need arises. A super metric also has the granularity and regularity of any standard metric, which makes it very easy to combine with other metric charts on the All Metrics window.

Because of these pros and cons for both super metrics and views, it depends on the use case and situation that will decide the best fit for you. If you are in a situation where you need some basic data transformation on a group of objects, it might be a good idea to start with a view, and if the information is required on a regular basis, convert it into a super metric. However, if you need functionality such as advanced mathematical operands, or dynamic thresholds and alerts, skip straight to super metrics. Ensure that you put on a lab coat when defining them and do it on a whiteboard first, this will ensure you gain the respect of your colleges who see how smart you really are.

Summary

From this chapter, I hope you have vRealized (couldn't help it) why they are called super metrics and how they can be defined. I recommend before moving onto the next chapter to try, if possible, defining a few of your own super metrics based on what we have gone through.

10
Administering vROps 6.0

Until now, we have just been learning about what puts the word super in super metrics. We also discussed various topics, such as dashboards, policies, capacity management, and reporting. However, we have generally been discussing these topics from an administrator's point of view (someone with access to all components). In this chapter, we will focus on other users who should only be able to view and edit certain components based on their role in an organization. To enable this, we are going to discuss authentication and authorization of vROps 6 and walk through the process of setting up **role-based access controls** (**RBAC**).

Overview of role-based access

Role-based access is the principle of allowing least-privilege access based on a user's role within an organization. vROps 6.0 comes with a twofold advantage: out of the box roles as well as the ability to define your own roles based on a very granular set of permissions.

There are three main ways to authenticate users against vROps. These include:

- Authentication via vCenter (vCenter Single Sign On)
- Direct Active Directory (LDAP)
- Local vROps users

The only users we can't really manage directly through vROps are vCenter users. Just like in vCOps 5.x, when vROps 6.0 registers with vCenter, new roles get added to the vCenter server and users can be given these roles that allow them to log in to vROps with the associated permissions.

There are two levels of access in vROps 6: access to objects such as hosts or virtual machines and access to permissions within vROps, such as the ability to edit dashboards or create alarms.

Roles are not that different from the access rights that you could grant in vCOps 5.x under the Custom UI. Roles are used to define which permissions a user or group has access to. For example, a role can grant the ability to create dashboards, delete dashboards, create alarms, or restrict a user to only the ability to read or view alarms.

Objects, however, are new in vROps 6.0 and unlike the previous versions of Operations Manager, we can now grant users and/or groups access to an individual object. This access gives purely the ability to access and see the object in vROps. This goes for every object of every solution and as such, is not limited to vSphere objects.

The role-based access system is broken down as users and groups being assigned to objects and roles first, and then roles are assigned their respective permissions. It is recommended, like any role-based access, that you use groups wherever possible, as assigning permissions directly to the users can become difficult to manage over time. This role-based access system is summarized in the following figure:

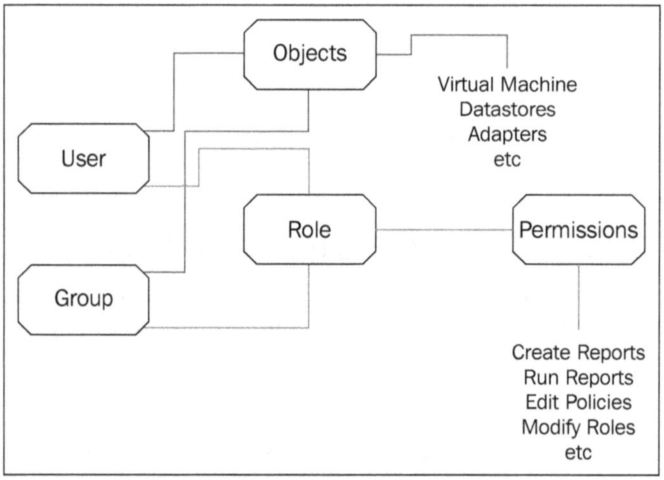

Configuring an LDAP source

Before we look at how to configure users, groups, and roles, we will configure an LDAP source that will give us a third user source we can work with since we already have local and vCenter users:

1. Log in to the vROps 6.0 instance as admin, navigate to the administration section, and select **LDAP Import Sources**.

2. Click on the little green plus symbol, which will open up the **Add Sources for User and Group Import** box. There are two options we can choose: **Basic** or **Advanced**. Selecting the **Basic** option will determine the base **Distinguished Name** (**DN**) and will auto discover the host based on only the domain name that we enter, while selecting the **Advanced** option lets us manually enter all the connection details typically seen with LDAP sources.
3. As seen in the following screenshot, basic was used and all the information was discovered. Once all the correct information has been entered, click on **Test** and we should get back a successful test message. Make sure that the checkbox is checked to synchronize group membership, so that vROps automatically keeps the AD groups and the members synced.

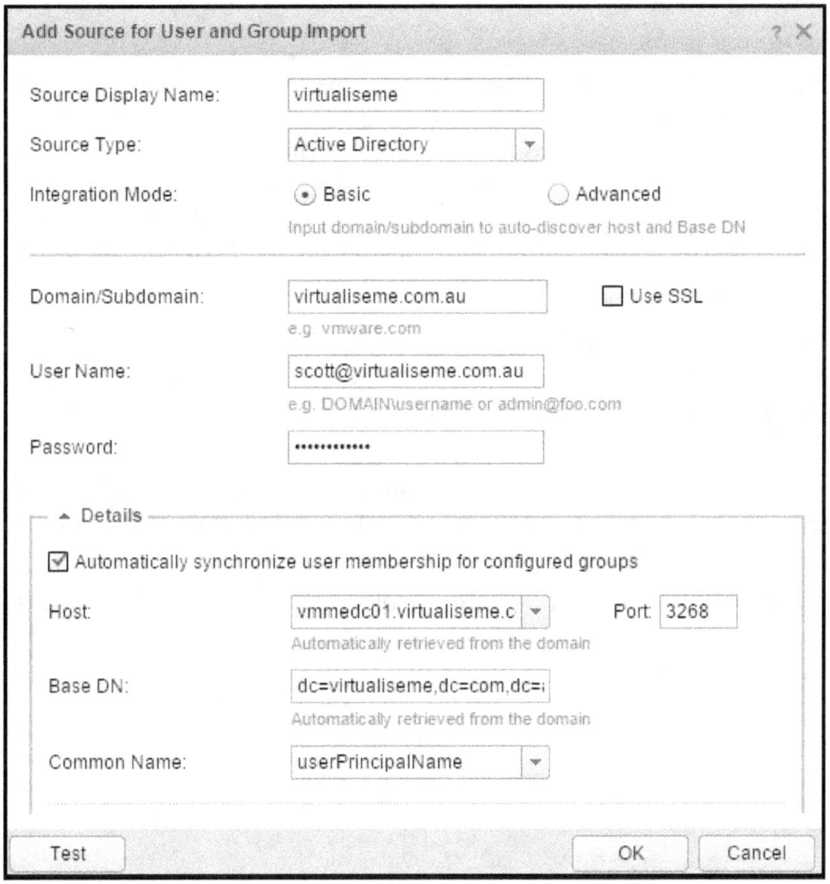

Configuring users and groups

Now that we have our third provider, let's look at how to grant permissions. We will work backwards from roles to users. This makes more sense when you see what the selections are while adding groups and users.

1. Log in to the vROps 6 instance and navigate to the administration section to select **Access Control**. We have the **User Accounts** tab, the **User Groups** tab, the **Roles** tab, and the **Password Policy** tab.
2. Let's now look at the **Password Policy** tab. Within this tab, we can configure the password policy that only applies to the local vROps user accounts. We will not be touching this topic today. If you do want to make changes in the password policy, make them in line with the existing AD password policy of your environment.
3. Next, we will select the **Roles** tab. You can see that there is a bunch of out-of-the-box roles that have been created such as **ReadOnly**, **PowerUserMinusRemediation**, and **GeneralUser-1**. If we select any one of these, it will show all the users assigned to this role on the bottom-left side of the window. All the user groups that are assigned to this role are shown at the bottom center, and the list of permissions the role currently has at the bottom right of the window.

   Permissions are listed in three parts, **Administration**, **Content**, and **Environment**, which are aligned to different areas of vROps that have been used throughout this book. *Chapter 4, The Merged UI*, specifically looks at the UI sections.

   To change these permissions, we will just check or uncheck the boxes next to specific actions, such as the ability to cancel alerts or to create dashboards. Then click on **Update**.

   Your **Role** tab should now look something like the one shown in the following screenshot:

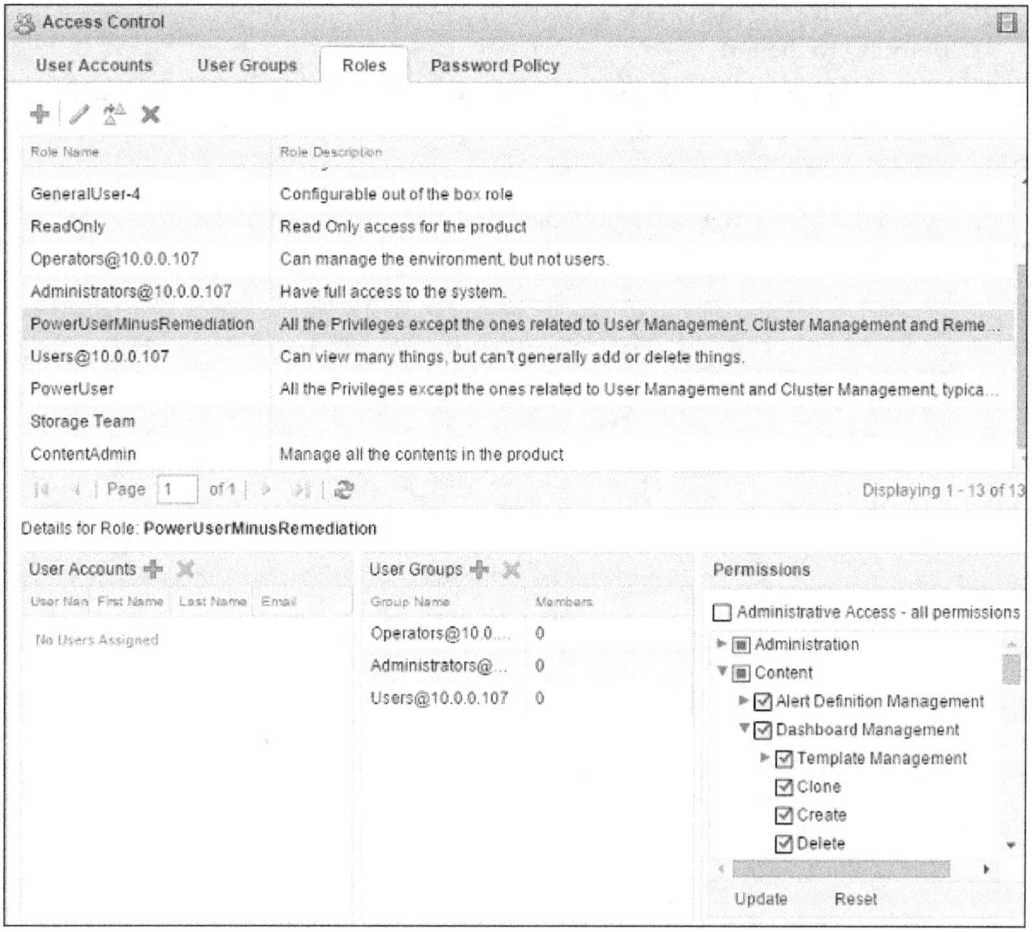

These were the roles; when defining custom roles, sorting through all the relevant permissions can take some time. However, on the other side of the equation, a granular permission model allows only the required permissions to be applied to a role.

1. Now, we select the **User Groups** tab, and then we click on the green plus sign, which would create a local group, but for this example, we will import an Active Directory group, which would be a more efficient way to grant access to vROps.

2. So, we will click the icon that looks like two people with a green arrow pointing to the left.

   This will bring up the **Import User Groups** dialog box. In here, we will select the LDAP source we configured previously and search for the group we want.

3. Select the relevant groups and click on **Next**, as shown in the following screenshot:

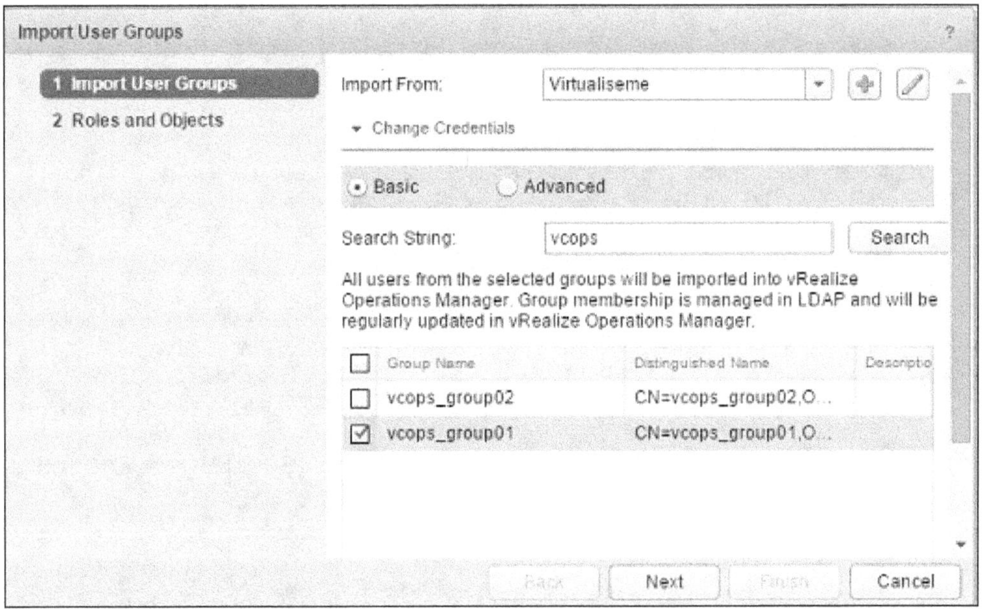

4. We next have to select roles and permissions for the group we want to import. Under **Roles**, check the roles we want in the group, as shown in the next screenshot.

   Note that a group or user can have multiple roles. The permissions will be combined and in areas of contention, the most restrictive right or permission will be the most effective.

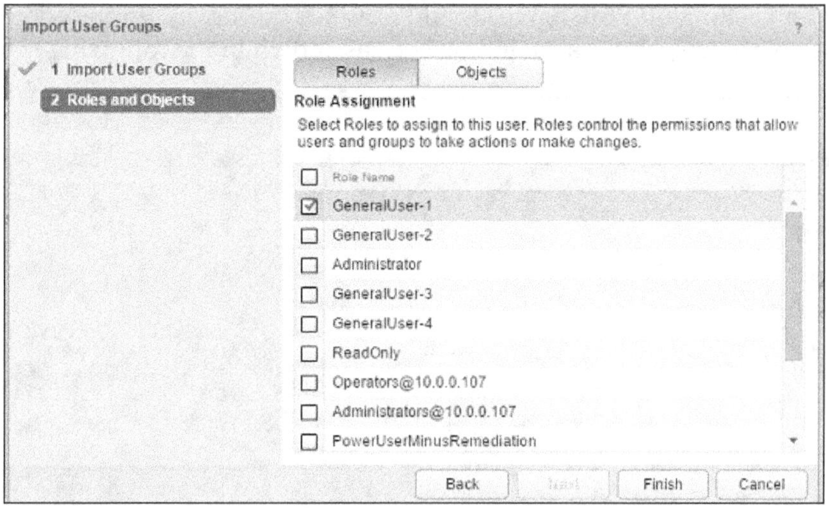

5. Now, we need to click on the **Objects** tab. This is where we will allow the group and users access to specific objects or to all objects. On the left-hand side, we have the object hierarchies, which will be different depending on which solutions we have installed. On the right-hand side, we have all the objects associated with the solution.

   Check the checkboxes next to the objects of your choice to grant the group or users the ability to view and interact with them when users are logged in to vROps. This is shown in the following screenshot:

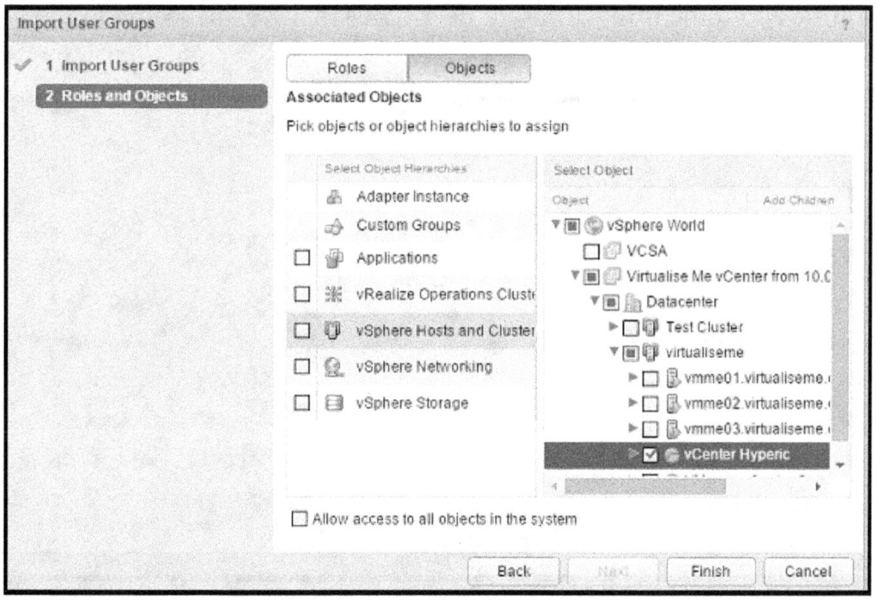

6. After clicking on **Finish**, we should now see our newly imported group with the role, users, and associated objects, as shown in the following screenshot:

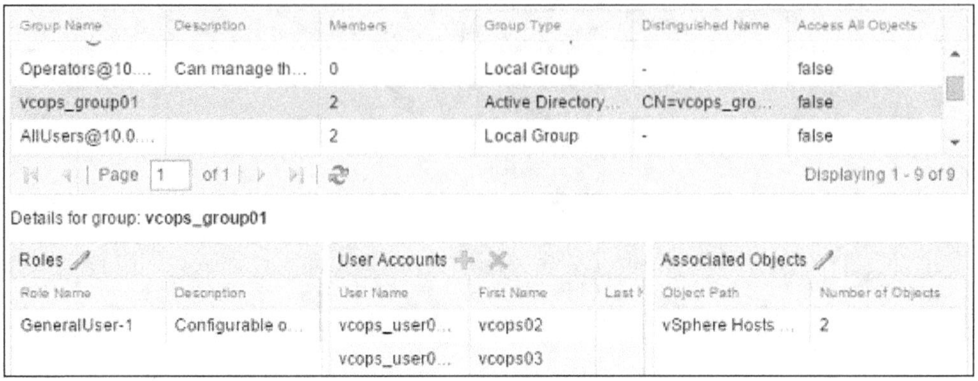

> In the previous screenshot, you may have noticed that there are groups such as `ALLUsers@10.0.0.107`. These are the groups that were created in vCOps 5.8.x and have migrated over.
>
> Due to the significant change in the way permissions now work, it is recommended that you create new groups.

On the **User Accounts** tab, as you can see in the following screenshot, the users from the AD group we just imported have also been brought in. We won't go through the process of adding a user as it is exactly the same as adding groups. However, we will explain a little about the three different user types that we are seeing in the following screenshot.

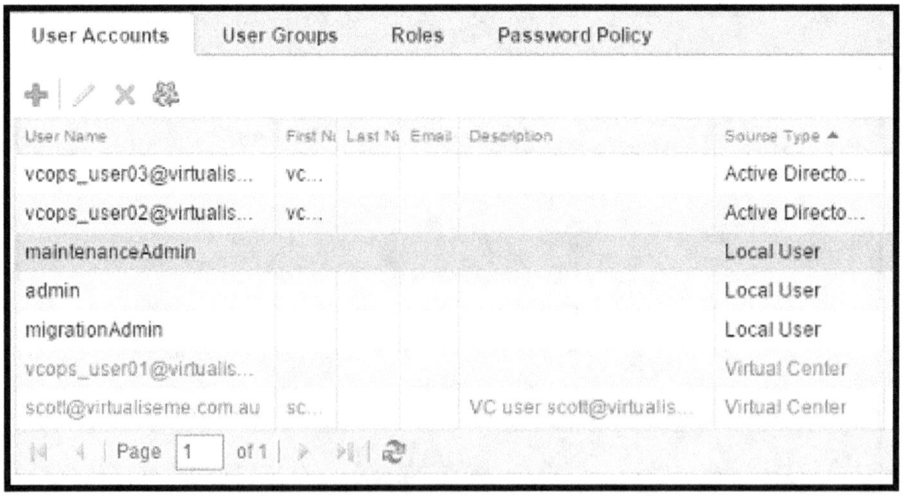

The grayed out users are the ones from vCenter. These cannot be added to roles, groups, or objects. vCenter users can *only* see vSphere objects associated to the vCenter server they have permission to and their access comes from the roles imported into vCenter at the time of the vROps 6.0 registration.

The AD users are just like local users; they can be added to local groups and are not limited to only the AD groups they may have been imported from.

As we use AD for vCenter authentication (via Single Sign On) and the same AD for vROps authentication, what happens to a user who is both a vCenter user and an LDAP user? Good question! In this particular case, even though technically it's the same network domain account, it is treated as two completely separate vROps users, as it all depends on what authentication source we choose at login.

That's general user administration, but what if you want to share dashboards to particular groups? In such case, perform the following steps:

1. Navigate to the content section of the UI and select dashboards. On the right-hand side pane, select the cogwheel icon and choose **Share Dashboards**. This will open up a new window. Here, we can see the groups on the left and the dashboards on the right.

   To share, click and drag the dashboard from the right and drop it into the group to the left with which we want to share the dashboard, just like we would when dragging and dropping files into a folder. This is shown in the following screenshot:

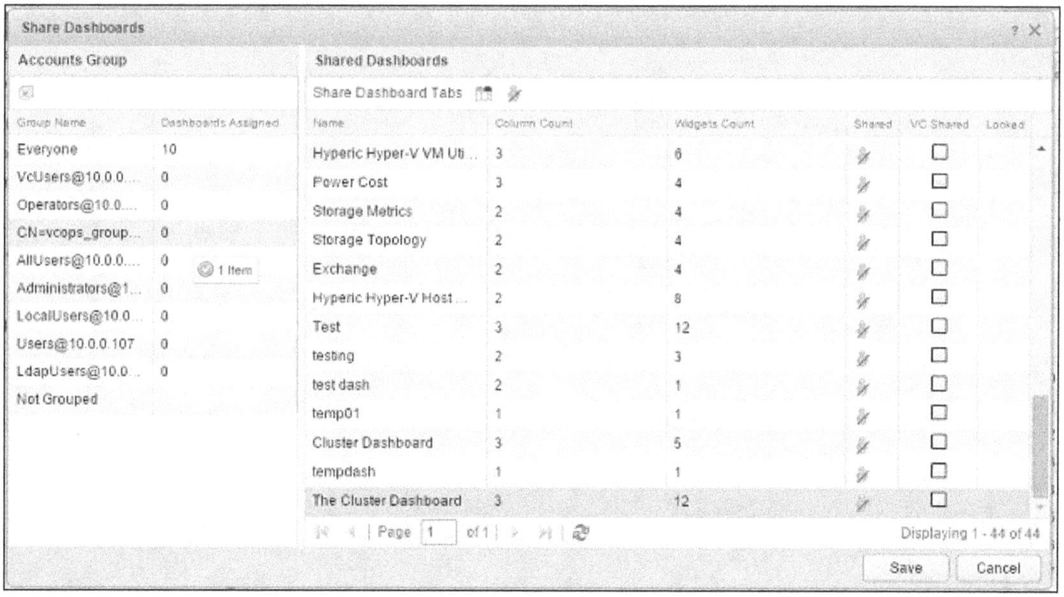

2. To unshare the dashboard, we simply have to select the group on the left-hand side of the window, then select the dashboard we no longer want to be shared, and click on the little icon at the top that looks like a little man with a line through it, as shown in the following screenshot:

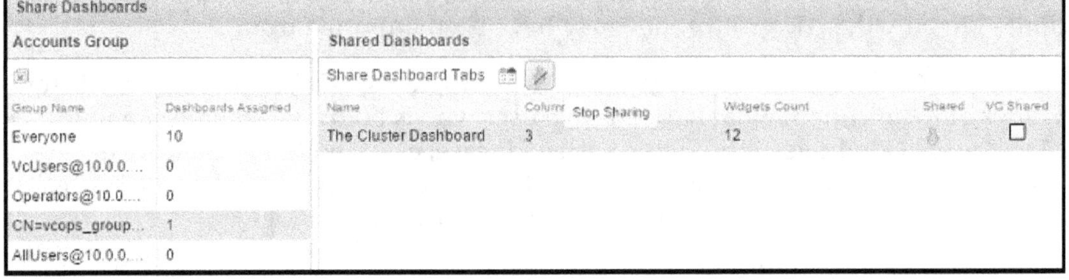

Summary

In this chapter, we took a quick look at how we can use role-based access. We also learned how to grant users and groups access to objects and apply roles to give them privileges to vROps' features and views. Next up, we will be diving into solutions, which is the vROps 6.0 version of management packs or adapters.

11
Expanding vROps with Solutions

Operations Manager has always supported adapters for other sources than just those of vSphere. Not only does this give us the ability to pull in metrics from other data and metric collectors, such as HP BAC and Microsoft SCOM, but it also allows direct connection to other systems, such as storage arrays and network switches.

While this expandability was great, there was always an issue. All adapters were treated as second-class citizens because they could only be displayed in the Custom UI. As such, these metrics from other adapters didn't have access to the same intuitive tabs or features, such as capacity management and reporting. Now, with vROps 6.0, this is no longer the case; all the adapters are now referred to as solutions, including the vCenter adapter, and are considered equal.

VMware supplies a number of these solutions for other products, such as vRealize Hyperic, VMware Horizon View, and Log Insight. While all adapters have access to all the features of vROps, it's completely up to the developers of the solution as to what they want to take advantage of, for example integrating adapters with the capacity management engine.

The important enablers that allow different solutions to share the same vROps instance are the improvements made to the vROps licensing engine. Previously, vROps was only licensed via vCenter, and as such, administrators sometimes experienced issues when the licensing vCenter was unavailable. vROps 6.0 now supports fully independent licensing that allows both the decoupling of vCenter as a dependency as well as the ability to license individual solutions and objects. With individual objects or object groups now available for licensing, administrators no longer have the restriction to deploy multiple instances of Operations Manager due to the licensing constraints.

Why collect additional data?

Why would an administrator want to import data from other monitoring systems or data sources into vROps? Especially, when the data for those systems is already being managed by an existing monitoring solution.

This is a fair question given the absence of some nice to have features like all the data being in one place and on a single pane of glass, but the real power of vROps is the way it handles relationships and the benefits that it provides to the administrators out there.

Say, we have installed vROps and it's doing what it does well, importing vSphere data and providing various types of useful information and reports. When an incident ticket comes in saying that there is a problem with the performance of a VM or a number of VMs, we can look at these VMs in vROps and see which cluster it belongs to, what host it is currently sitting on, and on which datastore the VMs' disks are located. We can see the health and metrics of all the areas of the hypervisor and rule out any anomalies or bottlenecks that might be occurring.

Then, the ticket starts its journey to the SAN team, the network team, and the application team, generally, with everyone saying that everything is fine at their end.

However, what if we could go deeper than the logical datastore, further than the physical NIC or up into the application in the guest OS of the VM? Well, we can, and this is done through solutions.

Picture for a moment, what can currently be seen when you look at the health relationship objects of a VM. We get stopped at the datastore level. However, if we use the EMC Storage Analytics solution, we could then break through the datastore and keep moving down to see the array that the datastore belongs to, then to the disk pool the datastore/VM belongs to. Then, finally, we would hit the physical disks themselves. All the while having access to all the metrics, logs, and alerts for all of these objects.

Then, on the networks, what if we could see the upstream switch, the port that the NIC is plugged into, and all the metrics and data that goes along with it. Then, using a solution, such as VMware Hyperic, we could reach inside the guest and see the services that make up the application and all the relevant application-level metrics. For example, for Microsoft Exchange, you will be able to see a number of incoming and outgoing messages, a number of people logged in, the response times, and so on.

Having all this data on a single pane of glass is great, but having a full end-to-end view of the infrastructure that supports a virtual machine and the applications within it allows the service desk or the server administrator to more accurately pinpoint where in the stack the problem most likely is.

Solutions can also take advantage of the different vROps analytics, such as dynamic thresholds and capacity management. While these are really good added bonuses, relationship linking is the key to make a big difference in the day-to-day operational running of the environments. The following screenshot shows a view with a storage solution added, and the extra data and health we can see beyond the datastore is great:

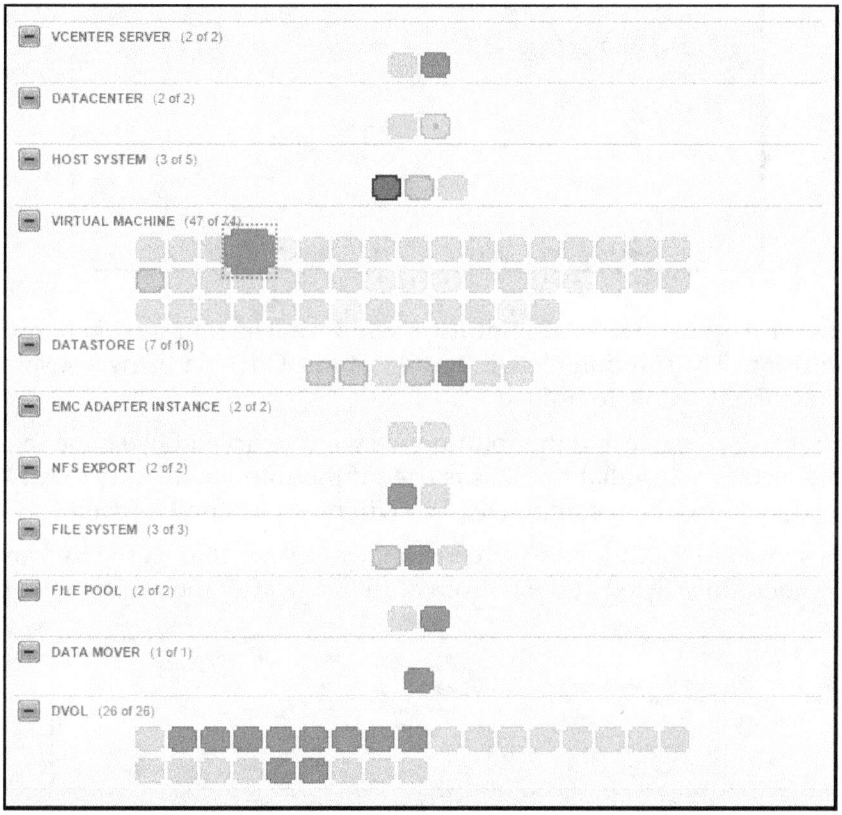

Installing solutions

Let's now have a look at how to install a solution. The solution we are installing here is the Hyperic solution. Just like in vCOps 5.x, solutions are simple to install. Follow the given steps to install a solution:

1. By now, the vROps 6.0 interface will be familiar to you. The first step to install a solution is to navigate to the admin section and select **Solutions**. There, we will see the installed solutions, as shown in the following screenshot. At the top of the page, we will find a green plus icon. Click on it.

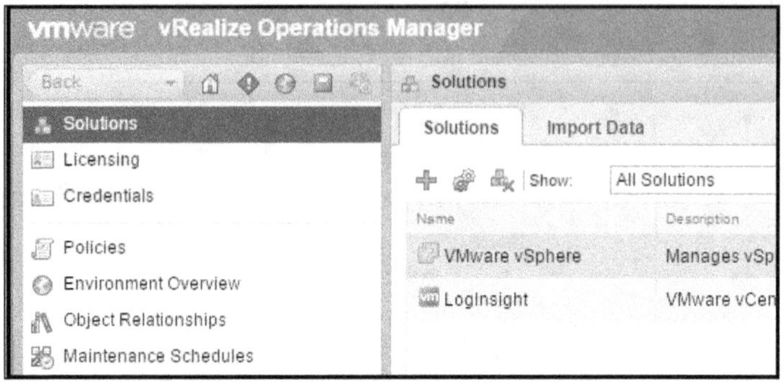

2. This will open up the **Add Solution** window. The first section here is **Select Solution**. The solution file will be a PAK file. Click on **Browse a solution** and locate the PAK file to upload.
3. After we have selected the solution we want to upload, we have the option to select force installation. This is used if the solution already exists and we need to overwrite it completely. We will now click on **Upload**.

   As shown in the following screenshot, we can see that all the information of the solution is listed at the bottom of the page after the solution is uploaded:

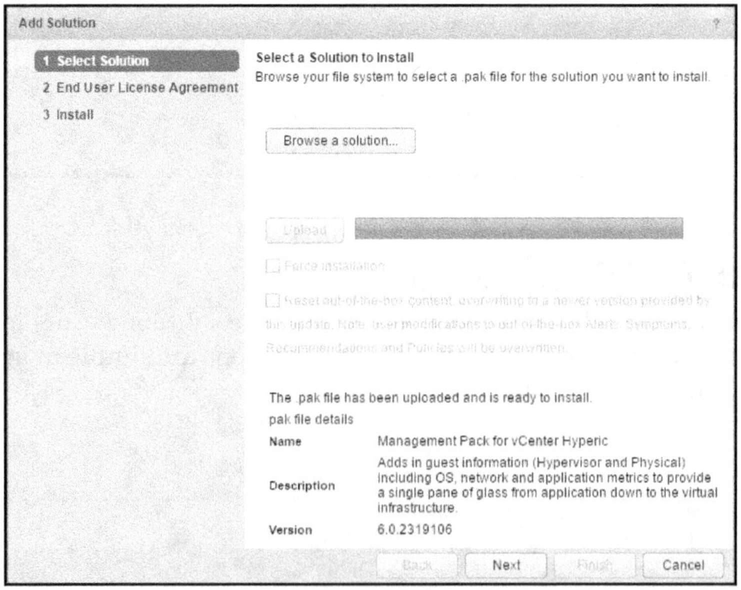

4. Click on **Next** and we are then presented with the EULA. Accept the agreement and click on **Next** again.

   Once you click on the **Next** button, the installation will instantly start, as we can see in the following screenshot, and we can see the progress of the installation. It's important to remember that this procedure installs the solution on every node in the cluster and the logs will reflect that.

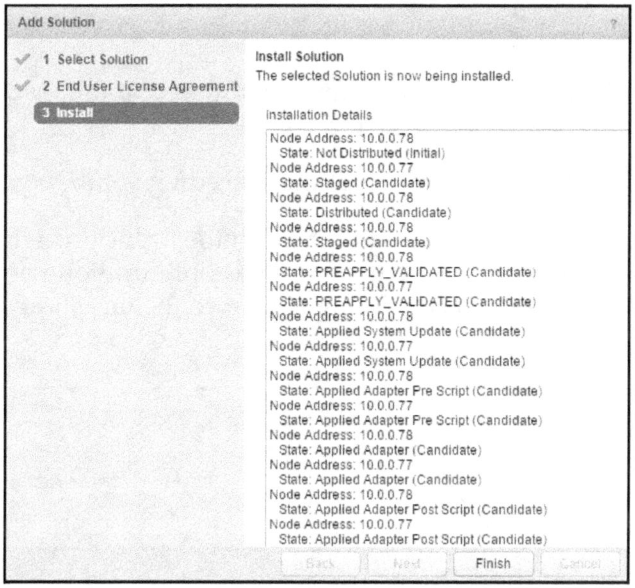

5. When the installation is done, click on **Finish** and we are then directed to the **Solutions** page where we will be able to see our newly installed solution. This is shown in the following screenshot:

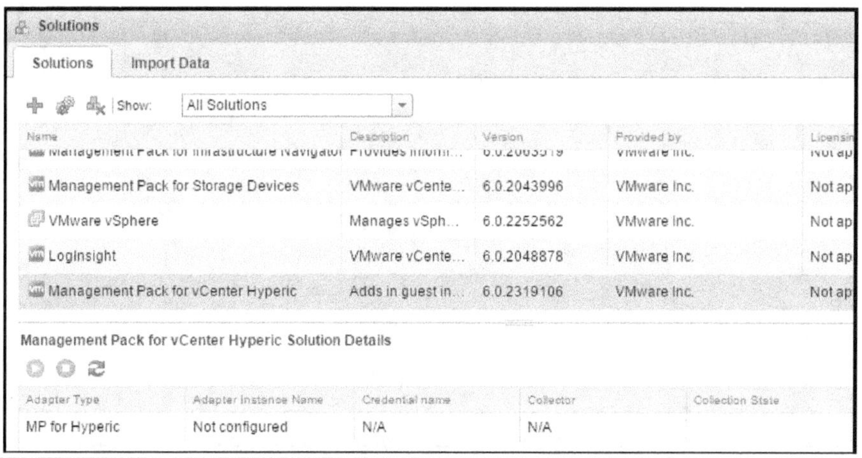

The solution is now installed; this installation process will be identical for other solutions. However, before a solution starts collecting data, it needs to be configured.

Solution configurations will vary greatly between each solution and the next; some will require license keys and others will require a connection to multiple servers or devices. For example, the Universal Storage solution requires authentication and connections to vCenter(s) and fabric switch(es), while for the vRealize Hyperic solution, we need to configure the connection to the Hyperic Server, certificate, and additional advanced settings.

All the solutions will vary and it is recommended that you follow the solution documentation from the supplying vendor.

Let's now go through the configuration of the preceding solution we just installed:

1. While having the solutions highlighted in the **Solutions** window, click on the little cogwheel icon to open up the configuration window for that solution. We should get something similar to the one shown in the following screenshot:

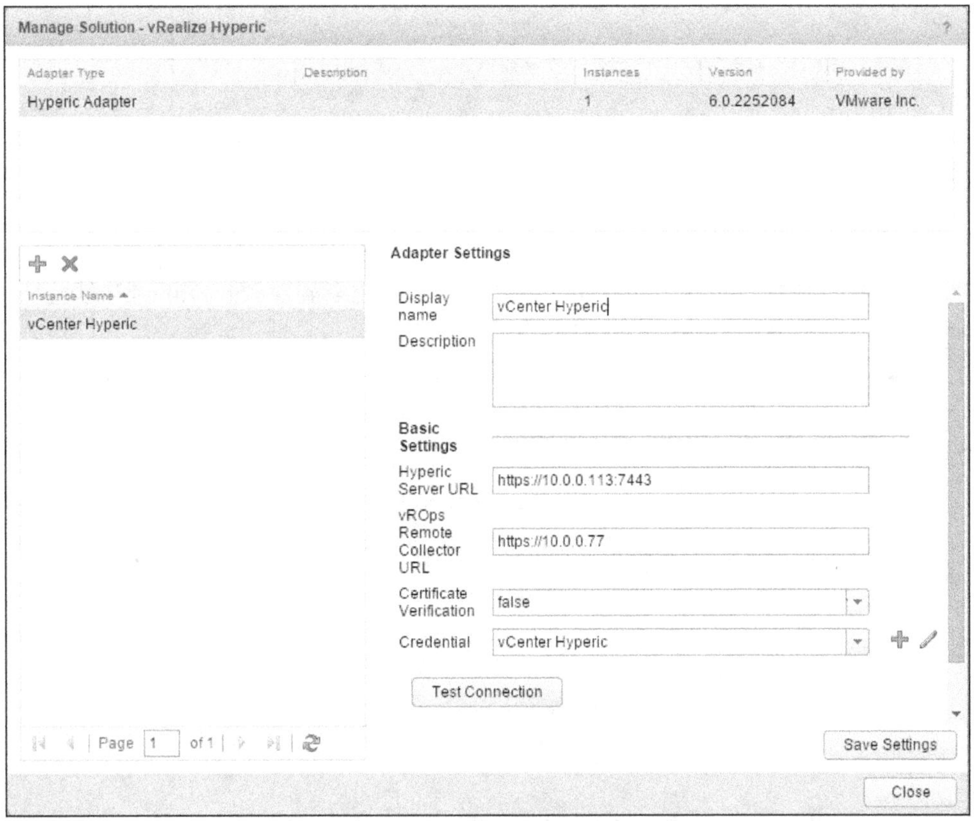

2. After filling in all the details the solution requires, we can hit the **Test Connection** button, which will tell us whether everything is configured correctly. Once we are happy with the changes in the settings, click on **Save Settings**.
3. Click on **Close** after the settings are saved.

Now, looking at the **Solutions** page again, we find a small difference from what we saw earlier. With the newly installed solution selected in the lower solution detail pane, we will now be able to see its status. Assign the solution a single cycle (which is 5 minutes by default) and we should see that data is being collected and received.

As shown in the following screenshot, the rainbow looking (semicircle) icon under the **Collection State** column is in the data collection state, and the ball icon under the **Collection Status** column is showing whether data is being received correctly. Both should appear green if everything in the solution is configured correctly.

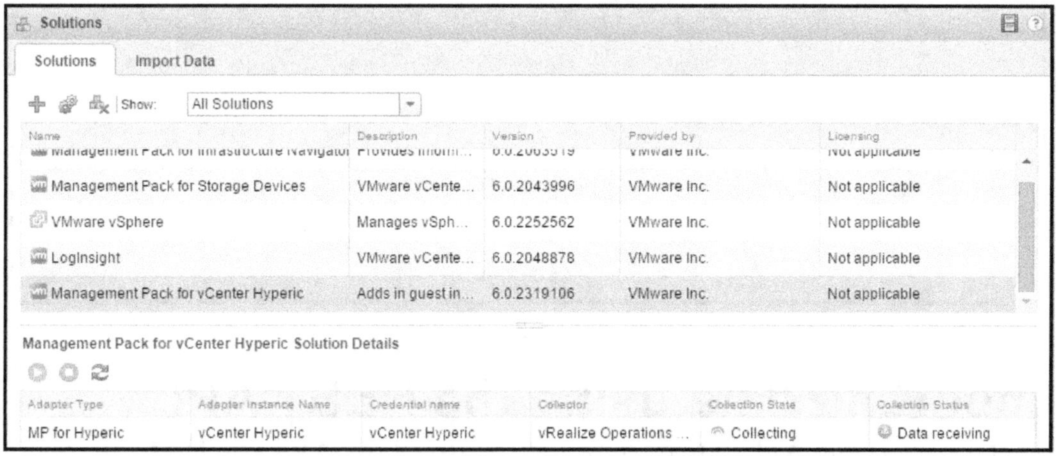

The solution is now installed and has started collecting data. The solution we covered here is the vRealize Hyperic solution. As explained at the start of this chapter, what a solution provides will vary, but at the very least, it will generally provide new object types and new attribute types (these are defined in *Chapter 9, Super Metrics,* in case you have forgotten the differences). A more feature complete solution also provides a good selection of out-of-the-box dashboards, and the most mature solutions, for example, will take advantage of other features, such as the open capacity management framework.

Let's now take a look at which dashboards this Hyperic solution has given us. To do this, click on the home icon and cycle through the available dashboards. By default, the new dashboards will be placed on your home screen. Alternatively, we can navigate to the content section and select dashboards.

In the following screenshot, we can see the default Exchange dashboard that the Hyperic solution creates, which shows the exchange server and all the associated metrics.

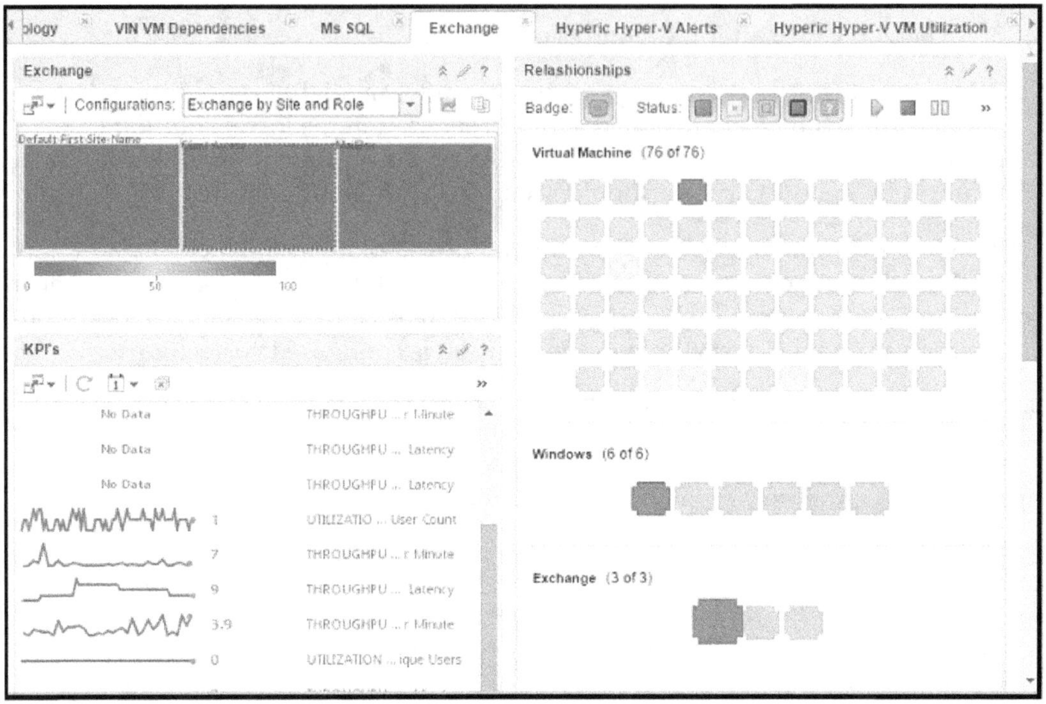

Importing data using the REST API

What if there is information that we would like to import in vROps, but there is no solution available? This is fine as vROps 6.0 supports multiple ways to import any data that we like. However, doing this will require some scripting if it's a regular import.

Prior to vROps 6.0, in vCOps 5.x, we had the HTTP POST adapter and the Text adapter and both could import data into vCOps 5.x.

In vROps 6.0, we still have access to the HTTP POST adapter. This adapter has remained unchanged since vCOps 5.x for legacy support, and the import of any current scripts data that is configured, should still work using this adapter.

The new and preferred way to import our own data is through the new vROps REST API. This is a highly functional API using which most GUI tasks can also be done if required.

All the vROps nodes that can be deployed have a detailed REST guide built in and, which can be found by navigating to `https://<vROPS-FQDN/IP>/suite-api/docs/rest/index.html`, as shown in the following screenshot. We can find sample code and information on all the rest functions at this location.

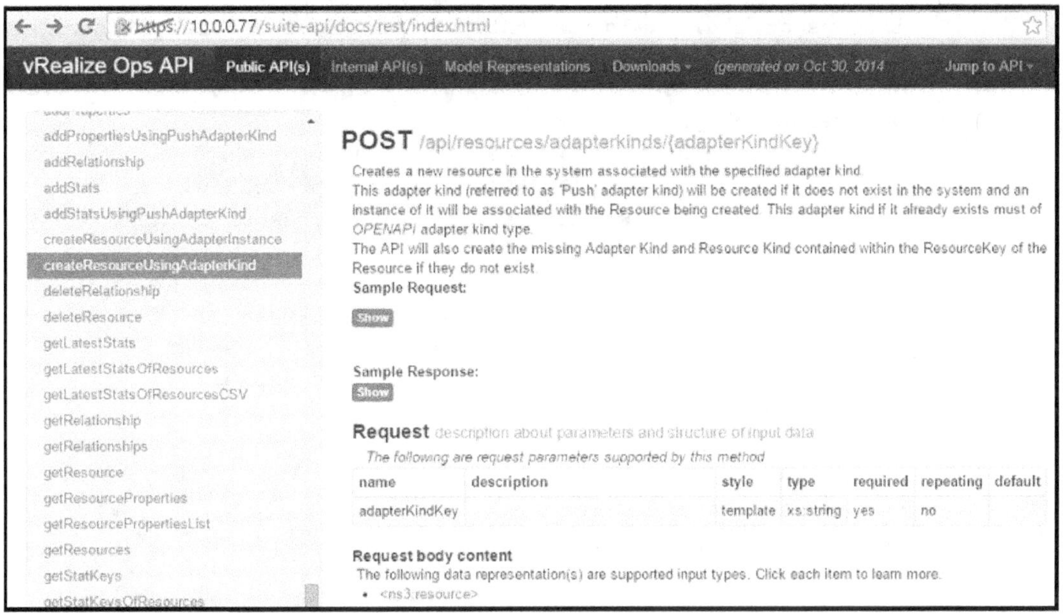

If we currently are not importing anything via the HTTP POST adapter, it is highly recommended that anything new be done through the new REST API or as it's commonly referred to, the OPEN API solution.

We are now going to go through the process of using a script to import custom data using this OPEN API solution. Believe me when I say that this data can be anything! For this example, we will pick something that we wouldn't normally see in an infrastructure monitoring and reporting tool. We will import an example security system data, such as swipe locks on doors.

It is worth noting that we will make up this data and have it manually entered. Obviously, if this was something that requires continuous metric uploads, the device/system/object would require some way to pull the information out and into vROps in a scripted fashion. We will now step through the process of importing our own custom data with the following steps:

1. The first step we want to take is to create an object using the REST function. We will use PowerShell 3.0 or a higher version here to upload the data. Anything that can make standard REST calls will work, such as cURL in Linux or a browser with the right plugins.

The first object we will create is a security door. vROps accepts both XML and JSON formats; here, we will use XML. The body of our request will be as follows:

```
<?xml version="1.0" encoding="UTF-8"?>
<ops:resource xmlns:ops="http://webservice.vmware.com/
vRealizeOpsMgr/1.0/" xmlns:xs="http://www.w3.org/2001/XMLSchema"
xmlns:xsi="http://www.w3.org/2001/XMLSchema-instance">
   <ops:description>Security Door swipe console</ops:description>
   <ops:resourceKey>
      <ops:name>Security Door D09</ops:name>
      <ops:adapterKindKey>OPENAPI</ops:adapterKindKey>
      <ops:resourceKindKey>Access Panel</ops:resourceKindKey>
      <ops:resourceIdentifiers>
         <ops:resourceIdentifier>
            <ops:identifierType name="EntityName"
dataType="STRING" isPartOfUniqueness="true" />
            <ops:value>Security Door D09</ops:value>
         </ops:resourceIdentifier>
      </ops:resourceIdentifiers>
   </ops:resourceKey>
   <ops:resourceStatusStates />
   <ops:dtEnabled>true</ops:dtEnabled>
</ops:resource>
```

The key takeaways from this XML code are:

- `description`: This is the description that the object will have in vROps.
- `name`: This is the name of the object.
- `adapterKindKey`: This is the adapter we want the resource to be referenced under (this could be `VMWARE` or any other adapter type).
- `resourceKindKey`: This is the type of resource. Anything can be entered here, but it is best to make it descriptive, for example, `Virtual Machine` is a resource kind key. If it doesn't already exist, it will be created automatically.
- `identifierType`: In this, multiple identifier types can be added and these will be unique values.

For reference, the JSON equivalent for the preceding XML code would be as follows:

```
{
    "description": "Security Door swipe console",
    "resourceKey": {
      "name": "Security Door D09",
      "adapterKindKey": "OPENAPI",
      "resourceKindKey": "Access Panel",
      "resourceIdentifiers": {
        "resourceIdentifier": {
          "identifierType": {
            "name": "EntityName",
            "dataType": "STRING",
            "isPartOfUniqueness": "true"
          },
          "value": "Security Door D09"
        }
      }
    },
    "dtEnabled": "true"
  }
```

2. We will now post this up to vROps with the following code:

   ```
   Invoke-restmethod -uri https://<vROPS FQDN or IP>/suite-api/api/
   resources/adapterkinds/OPENAPI -Headers $headers -body $body
   -contenttype "application/xml" -Method post
   ```

   Here, `$headers` is just the authentication username and password and `$body` is a string that contains the XML code that was shown previously.

3. The returned information we should get will contain data similar to the following when you use PowerShell:

   ```
   xsi                  : http://www.w3.org/2001/XMLSchema-instance
   xs                   : http://www.w3.org/2001/XMLSchema
   ops                  : http://webservice.vmware.com/
   vRealizeOpsMgr/1.0/
   identifier           : 42a2f291-d4be-48c4-b60e-2a8aa3b9d3fa
   description          : Security Door swipe console
   resourceKey          : resourceKey
   resourceStatusStates :
   dtEnabled            : true
   links                : links
   ```

The most important part of the returned information is the identifier. This is what will be used to upload metrics to this object and to create relationships.

If we now look in vROps, we will be able to see our new object, as shown in the following screenshot:

4. Cool right? Especially the icon! So, we have a new object, but what about some metrics, as there aren't any in here. Now, let's add some metrics to our object.

   To do this, we will use the following XML code for the body:

```
<?xml version="1.0" encoding="UTF-8" standalone="yes"?>
<ops:stat-contents xmlns:xs="http://www.w3.org/2001/XMLSchema"
xmlns:xsi="http://www.w3.org/2001/XMLSchema-instance"
xmlns:ops="http://webservice.vmware.com/vRealizeOpsMgr/1.0/">
    <ops:stat-content statKey="swipeIN|numhr">
      <ops:timestamps>1417586855784</ops:timestamps>
      <ops:data>5</ops:data>
    </ops:stat-content>
    <ops:stat-content statKey="swipeOUT|numhr">
      <ops:timestamps>1417586855784</ops:timestamps>
        <ops:data>7</ops:data>
```

```
    </ops:stat-content>
    <ops:stat-content statKey="swipeIN|Totalfailures">
      <ops:timestamps>1417586855784</ops:timestamps>
        <ops:data>20</ops:data>
    </ops:stat-content>
</ops:stat-contents>
```

As you can see, we are importing multiple metrics in one hit, which is a lot more efficient than the HTTP POST adapter, as that can only import one metric per post. It is also worth noting that we can enter multiple timestamps and data values for each metric, for example, consider the following structure:

```
    <ops:stat-content statKey="swipeIN|numhr">
      <ops:timestamps>1417586855784</ops:timestamps>
<ops:timestamps>1417586856784</ops:timestamps>
<ops:timestamps>1417586857784</ops:timestamps>
      <ops:data>5</ops:data>
<ops:data>8</ops:data>
<ops:data>12</ops:data>
    </ops:stat-content>
```

The key takeaways from the preceding XML code are:

- `statKey`: This is the metric. Here, the first part is the base metric type and the second is the metric itself, for example, `cpu|usage%` would be the usage of CPU.
- `timestamps`: This is the timestamp of the data so we could enter old data if we wanted. The important part of the timestamp is that it's epoch time in milliseconds.
- `data`: This is the value of the metric.

The reference JSON format for the preceding XML code would be as follows:

```
{
  "stat-content": [
      {
        "statKey": "swipeIN|numhr",
        "timestamps": [1417586855784],
        "data": [5]
      },
      {
        "statKey": "swipeOUT|numhr",
        "timestamps": [1417586855784],
        "data":[7]
      },
      {
```

```
            "statKey": "swipeIN|Totalfailures",
            "timestamps": [1417586855784],
            "data": [20]
          }
        ]
      }
```

To add multiple metric inputs, the following example code is used with JSON:

```
          {
            "statKey": "swipeOUT|numhr",
            "timestamps": [1417586855784, 1417586856784,
1417586857784],
            "data":[7,6,3]
          },
```

> If a metric and type does not exist, they will be created. If they currently exist, the metric data will be added.

5. Now, we need to post the preceding XML body to vROps. To do this, we require the identifier that was returned when we created the object. This will create the URL shown as follows:

   Invoke-restmethod -uri https://<vROPS FQDN or IP>/suite-api/api/resources/42a2f291-d4be-48c4-b60e-2a8aa3b9d3fa/stats -Headers $headers -body $body -contenttype "application/xml" -Method post

Let's now head over to the vROps UI and see if our object now has some metrics. As we can see in the following screenshot, the metrics are now available and we have our first data point:

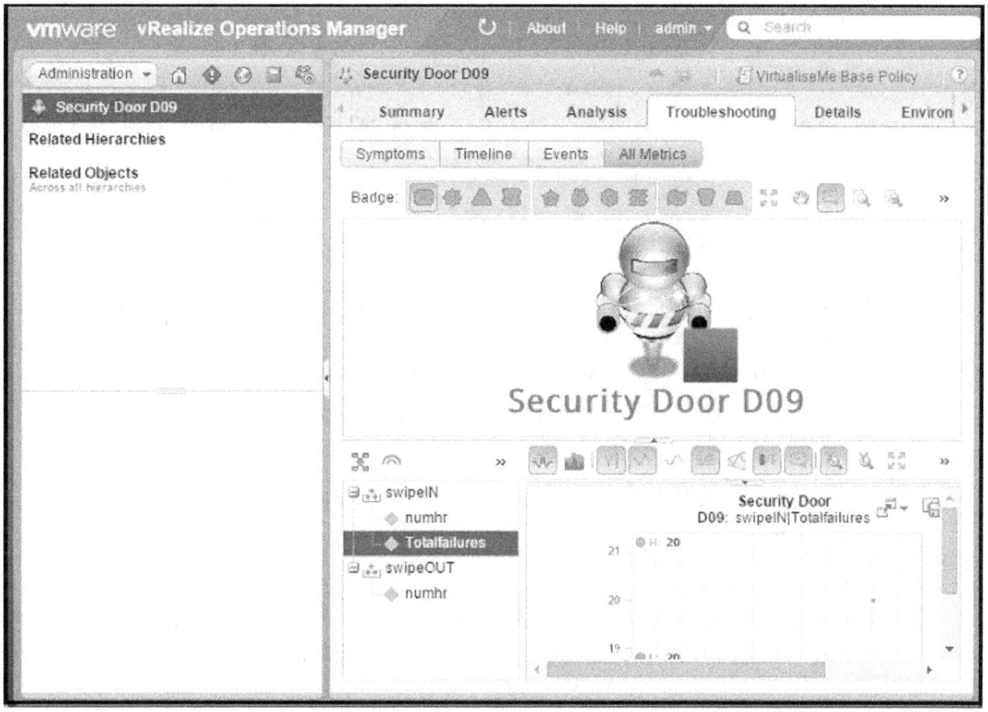

Great stuff, let the data importing begin! As we can see from this very simple example, we can enter just about any data into vROps.

1. Let's now do a little more with the REST API. We now want our object to be related to a building or office or something else, such as a data center, if this is where our swipe door was. Similar to how an ESXi server is related to a cluster and data center.

To do this, we need the ID of this object and the ID of the object we want to relate it to. Use the following XML body to post to vROps:

```
<?xml version="1.0" encoding="UTF-8" standalone="yes"?>
<ops:uuid-values xmlns:xs="http://www.w3.org/2001/XMLSchema"
xmlns:xsi="http://www.w3.org/2001/XMLSchema-instance"
xmlns:ops="http://webservice.vmware.com/vRealizeOpsMgr/1.0/">
    <ops:uuids>42a2f291-d4be-48c4-b60e-2a8aa3b9d3fa</ops:uuids>
</ops:uuid-values>
```

The only takeaway from the preceding XML code is the UUID, which is the unique object identifier. We can specify multiple UUIDs with only a space between them if we had multiple children to add to a parent to.

The JSON format would be as shown in the following code:

```
{
    "uuids": ["42a2f291-d4be-48c4-b60e-2a8aa3b9d3fa"]

}
```

2. Once we have the body, we need to post it as a child to the parent resource. A similar URL as shown in the following command would be used where the UUID or ID is the parent object's ID:

   ```
   Invoke-restmethod -uri https://<vROPS FQDN or IP>/suite-api/api/
   resources/86095817-509a-43a4-8b44-d96028ee79b4/relationships/
   children -Headers $headers -body $body -contenttype "application/
   xml" -Method post
   ```

   Post this to vROps and only a 204 return code is received, which is no content as we have nothing to receive from this.

3. Let's now navigate back to our object and see if we now have a relationship mapped. We should see something similar to the following screenshot:

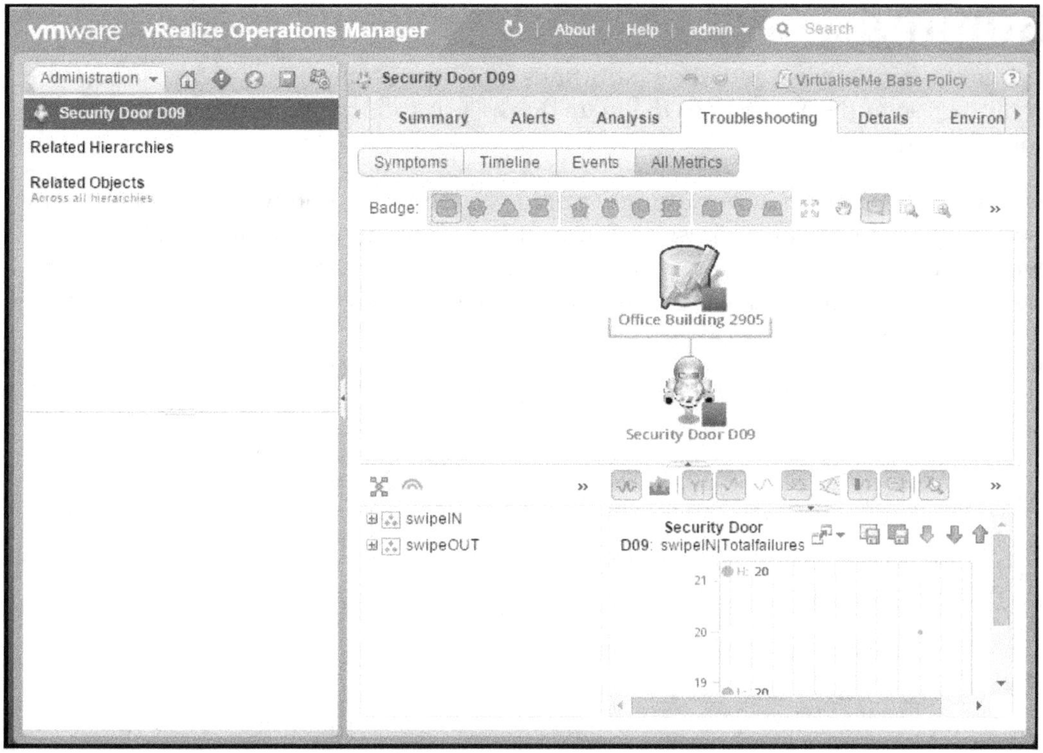

This is a very basic overview of what can be achieved if there is no official solution for the data we would like to import. Most of what people want to import will be IT-related in some way, but vROps is definitely not limited to computer data; we can import weather, power usage, parcel deliveries, and anything to which we can apply relationships and metrics.

Summary

In this chapter, we learned about solutions and how helpful they can be to an organization and especially to the team on the ground that monitors and supports your infrastructure.

We then moved on to import our own data when no solution was available or when we want to get back at the boss and import how long his/her lunch breaks are every day and display them on the big screen. With dynamic thresholds enabled, we can get warnings whenever the lunch breaks get longer or shorter than what is considered "normal."

Next up, we will go through how to configure and work with applications in vROps.

12

Application Management in vROps 6.0

In the previous chapter, we looked at solutions, and how data can be fed into vROps from various sources other than just vSphere's performance data. Now, we will look at how to leverage these different data sources, and how to group them together in a single application that allows simple navigation and troubleshooting.

To achieve this, we will leverage additional solutions to be installed and configured in vROps. The most useful solutions in application monitoring is **vRealize Hyperic (vRH)**. vRH is an agent-based monitoring solution that focuses on an operating system's application-level performance and availability. Although the use of Hyperic or other solutions is not compulsory while creating applications in vROps, their benefit to create an end-to-end picture of a business application's performance and availability is very powerful.

By default, when the vRealize Hyperic agent is installed, it will auto discover the installed applications and begin collecting relevant metrics along with typical OS-level metrics in order to send them to the Hyperic Server. These platforms and components are also created in vROps via the vRealize Hyperic adapter essentially using the Hyperic Server, a single collection point, and proxy for the data.

The vRealize Hyperic agent supports both 32-bit and 64-bit versions of Windows and Linux, as well as a large array of enterprise applications. When an application is discovered in Hyperic, it is added as a server (Hyperic's term for an application or a component) that then it translates into a vROps object type, such as IIS, .NET, WebLogic, vPostgres, and so on.

In this chapter, we will not go through the installation or configuration of vRealize Hyperic, but we will show the end result of using Hyperic application monitoring combined with vROps.

> Like vROps, Hyperic also supports management packs that provide additional application support. These packs are installed on the Hyperic Server and then pushed out to the agents.

Creating applications

Before we move on to look at what vRH brings to the table, we are going to look at how to create an application in vROps. This feature is available in the previous versions as well, and allows us to create containers or objects that can contain a group of virtual machines or other objects in different tiers. This new application object can then be managed as a single object, and have all its health badges and alarms aggregated from the child objects of the group.

For example, we could create a standard 3-tier application with a web app and database tier or we could just have a single-tier application. There is really no limit to how we can configure applications, and it is down to what will best fit the application that you want to monitor.

By creating applications, vROps allows the application teams to monitor the health of the application as a whole and gives an overall view of the health of the application or entire platform, as well as the individual objects if needed, thus removing the hassle of the team having to wade through vROps to find individual objects in order to check how they are running.

Let's now create an application in vROps:

1. To view or create new applications, navigate to the **Environment** section and select the **Applications** tab. This is shown in the following screenshot. Here, we can see all the created applications and we can create a new application. To create an application, click on the small green plus icon.

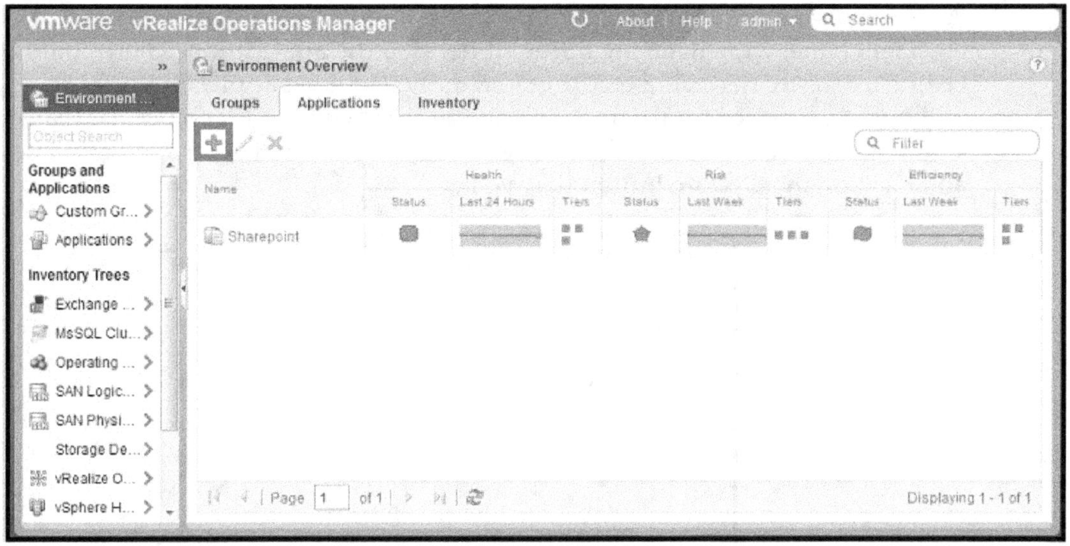

2. This will bring up the dialog box where we can select the application type, as shown in the following screenshot. The choices shown provide an application with precreated tiers, in which we can drop objects. For this example, we will select **Custom** and click on **OK**, which will allow us to create our own tiers.

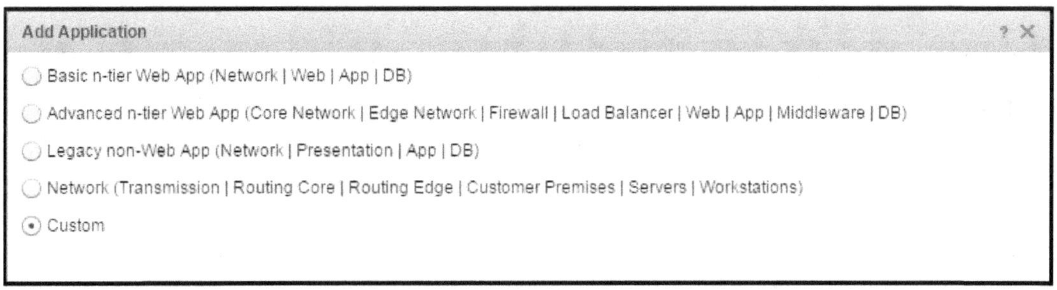

3. We should now see the **Application Management** window. In the first pane, the **Tiers** pane, we will create different tiers for the application. There could be one tier or there could be 20, but generally, for most applications, there will only be three or four tiers. Click on the icon with the green dot to create a new tier. As shown in the following screenshot, we will enter the tier name and click on the **Update** button to save it.

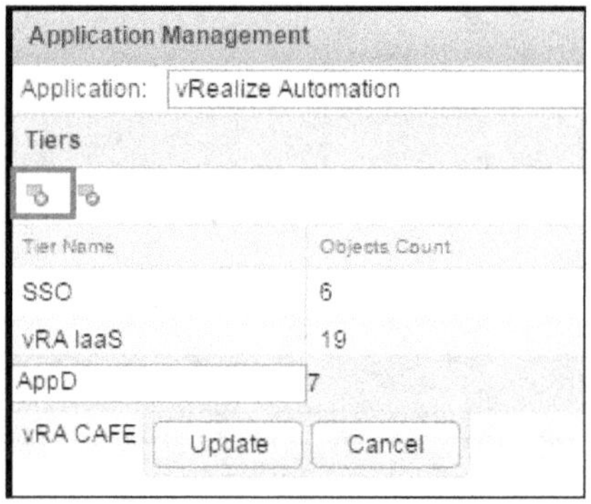

4. Now, it's time to drag and drop the object we would like to see from the bottom pane of the window into the different tiers, as shown in the following screenshot. Once all the objects are placed, click on **Save**. This will create the application.

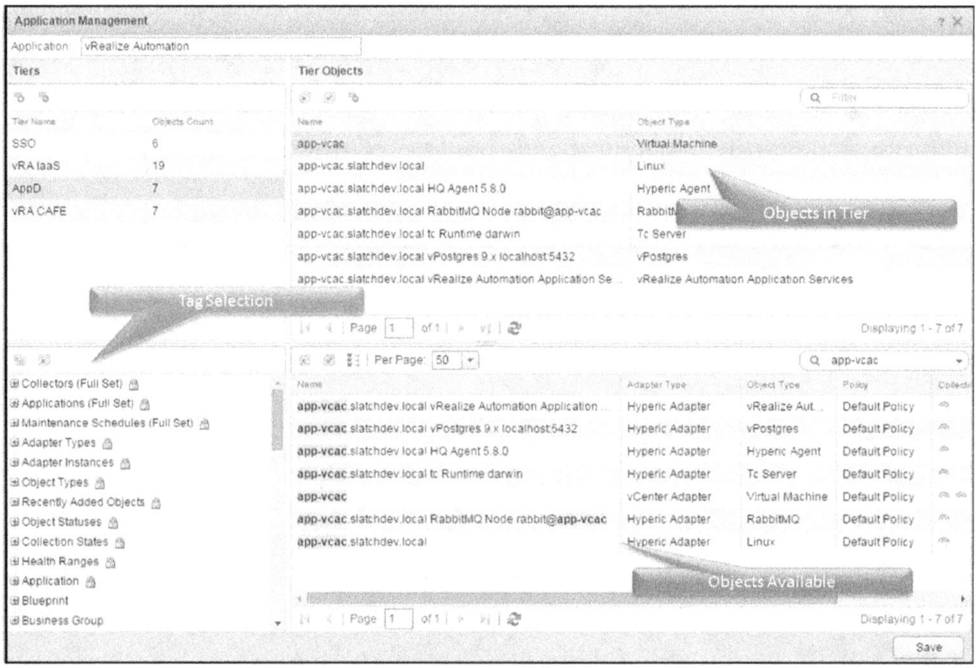

5. Once the application is created, we will be directed back to the **Applications** tab, where we notice that the Health, Risk, and Efficiency information is represented in gray. This will only be the case for a couple of collection cycles and then all the health data will be available. This is shown in the following screenshot:

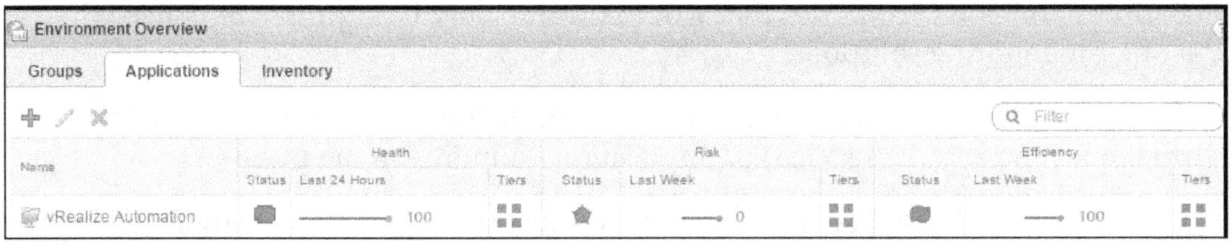

The application is now created. This will now allow us to report, alert, and monitor all the objects that make up the application as a single logical object. We can see the environment overview with relationships that show us on which host, datastore, or vCenter the objects reside. An example is shown in the following screenshot:

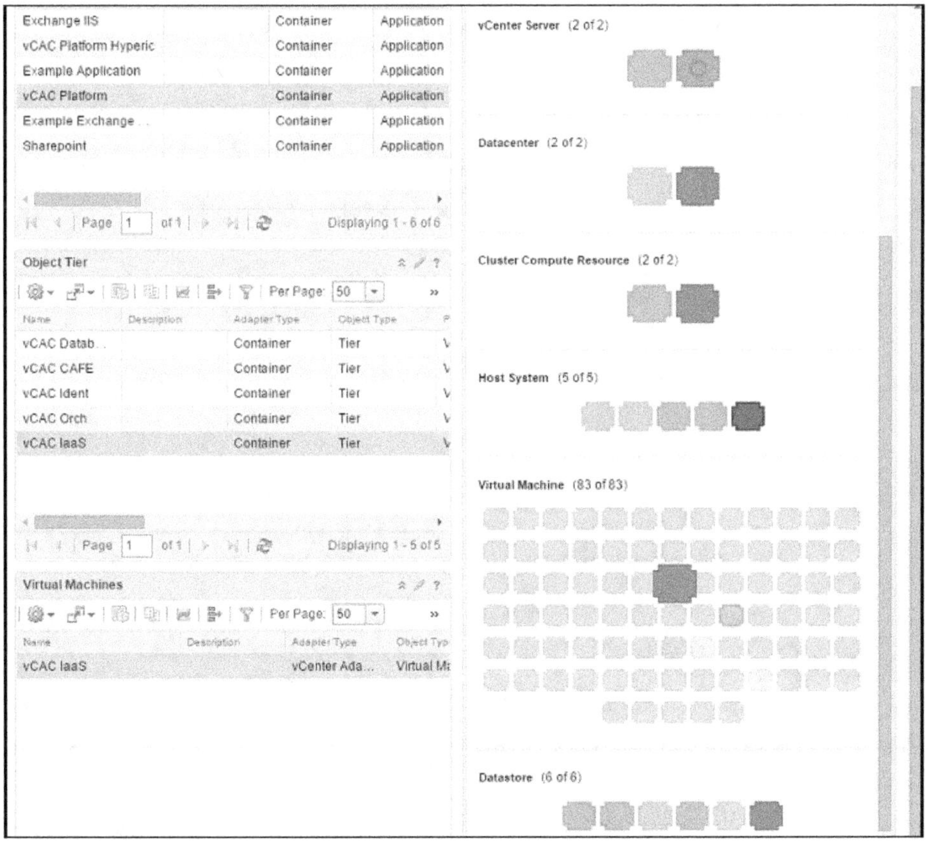

The preceding screenshot is what we would typically see with a normal virtual machine object. This way we can monitor the infrastructure that hosts the applications we want to monitor, and this is what the vCOps is traditionally used for.

If we now use the same application that we created, but have the vRH solution installed in it, we not only get all the guest OS metric counters, but we also get application-specific metrics that would traditionally be supplied or collected via other monitoring solutions.

The icing on the cake is that there is now a relationship established between the virtual machine and the services or applications running on the guest OS.

Compared to what is seen in the previous screenshot, we can now analyze the health of all the related objects in the following screenshot, which shows a Windows box that runs IIS and .NET applications:

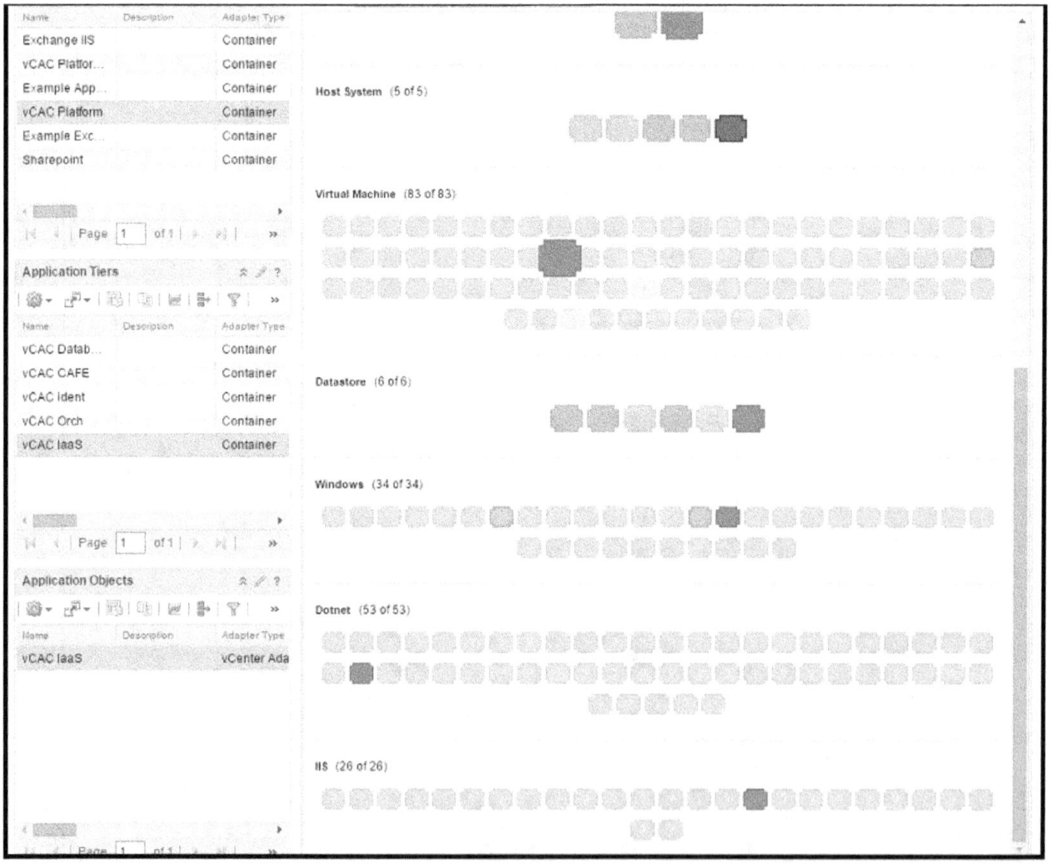

Just like any object, we can attach policies to an application to limit or increase alarms, collect specific metrics, or change the way capacity management is applied to them. We can also have security for applications and allow only specific application teams access in order to see the applications they need to monitor.

Importing applications

Instead of creating applications manually in vROps, you can import them from **VMware Infrastructure Navigator** (**VIN**), which is also a part of vRealize Management Suite. VIN is a small appliance that uses VMware Tools in virtual machines to see which services and ports are listening and which active connections are present within the guest OS.

VIN then uses this information to draw maps of virtual machine dependencies that can be grouped together to form an application. VIN also uses a database of known executables and ports to determine which applications are running on various virtual machines, which can then provide critical information to the dependency map.

The VIN application dependency data can be brought into vROps using the VIN solution that allows automatic creation of application-like topologies without the need of manually defining applications.

In this section, we will not set up VIN, but will show how we can leverage this information in vROps:

1. After the installation of the application and after it has run for a couple of days, select any VM that you know to be a part of an application you want to configure, and it should now have a detailed map of the incoming and outgoing dependences, as shown in the following screenshot. I will be using VMware vCAC, which is now called vRealize Automation or vRA as my "application" but it can be anything. This liberty to choose our VM is *only* available through vSphere Web Client.

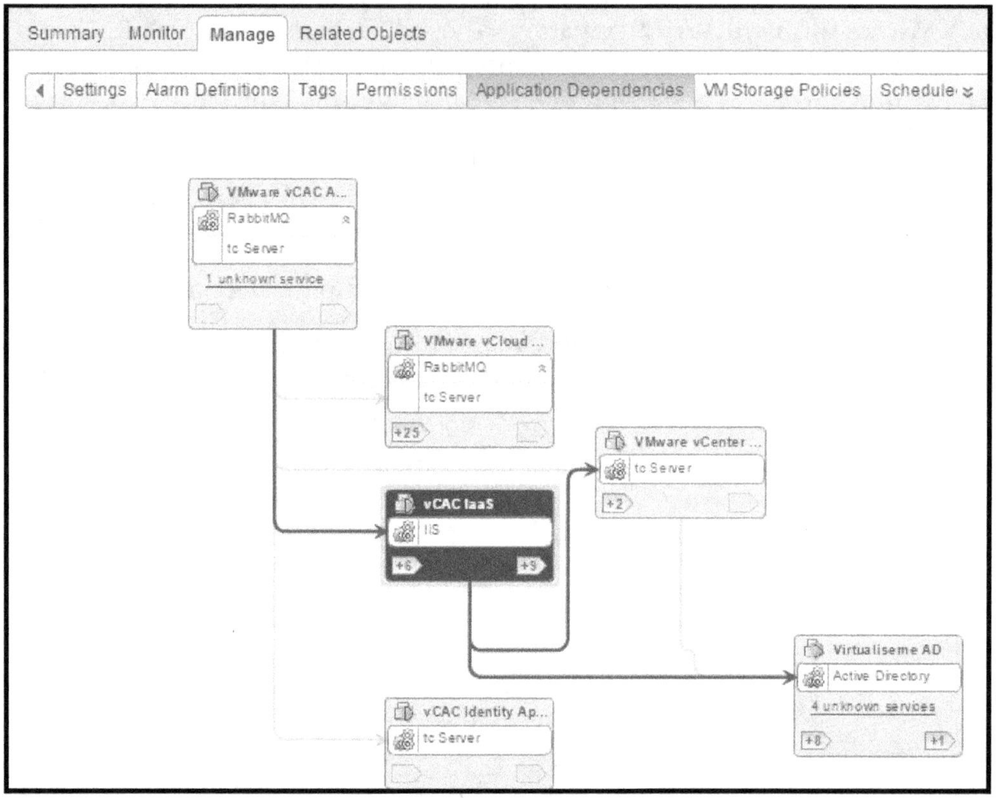

2. Now, hold the *Ctrl* button and click on all the VMs that you want to make a part of the application. They will be highlighted in dark blue if selected (don't worry if not all are visible, we can manually add them later.)

3. Then, click on the create application button, which is highlighted in the following screenshot:

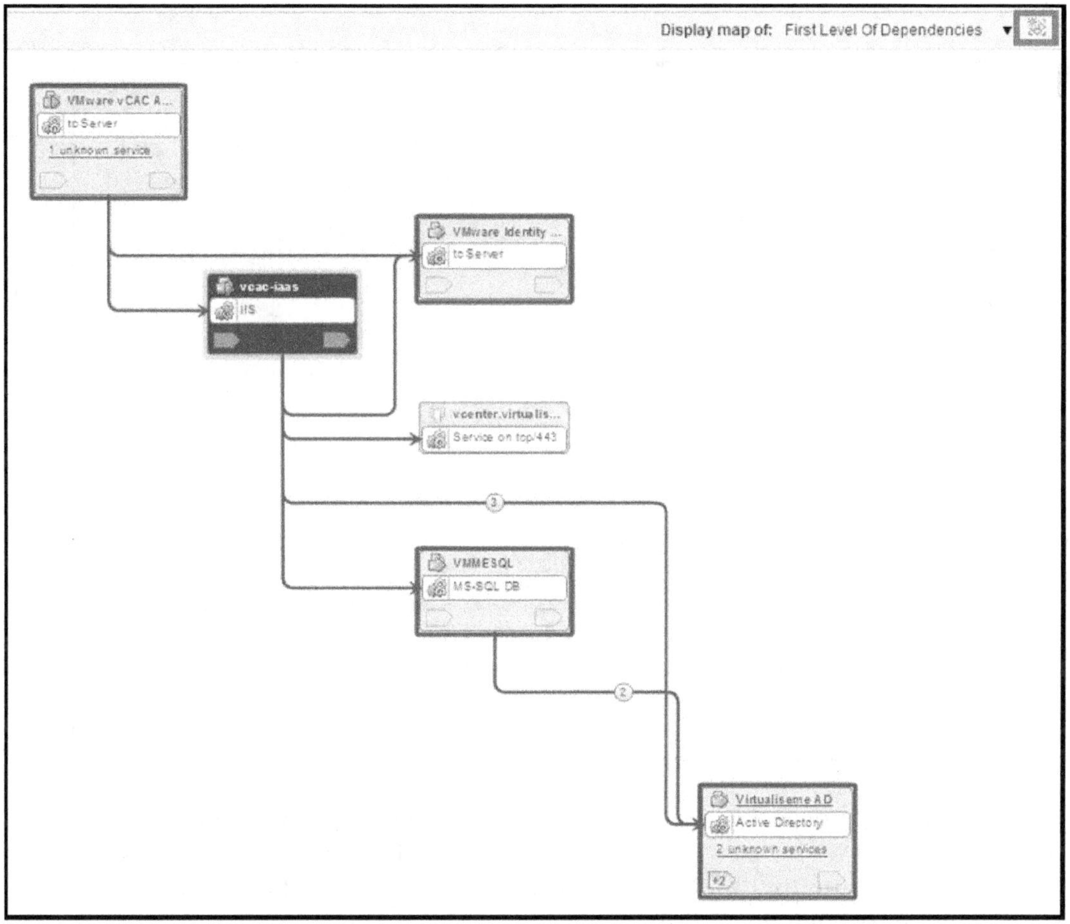

4. We are then prompted to enter a name. Enter a name and click on **OK** to create the application.

Within vROps, there will now be two different types of applications; the inbuilt application, which we created earlier, and the VIN-sourced application that will appear as a custom group in vROps, as shown in the following screenshot:

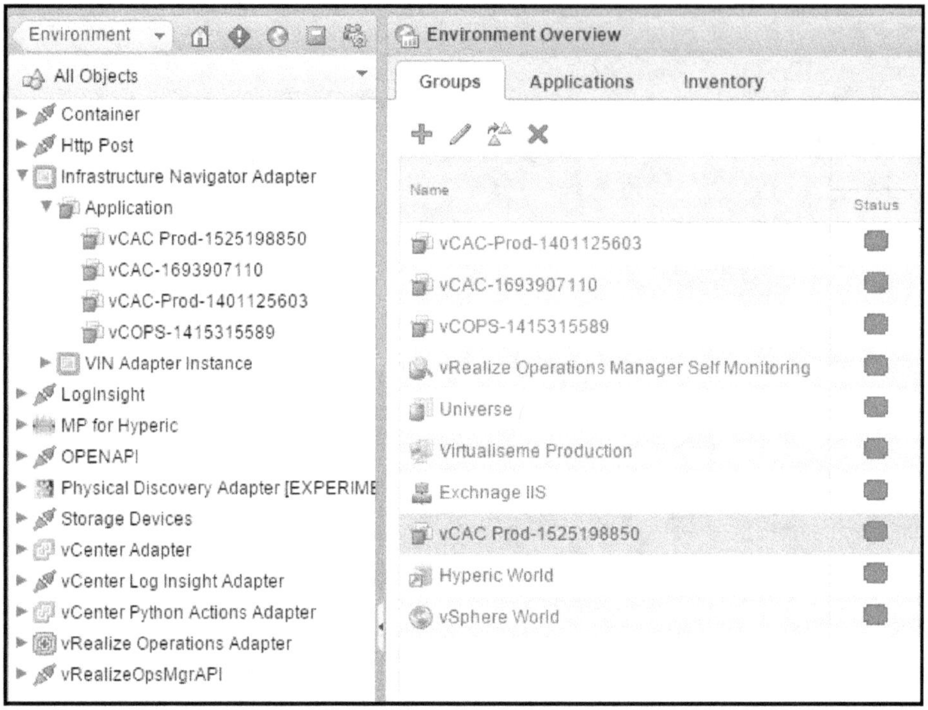

VIN comes with two preinstalled dashboards from the VIN solution that uses the topology widget to give us a mapping of the application. This also provides us the applications that run in the VM with their associated ports and dependencies. One such example is shown in the following screenshot:

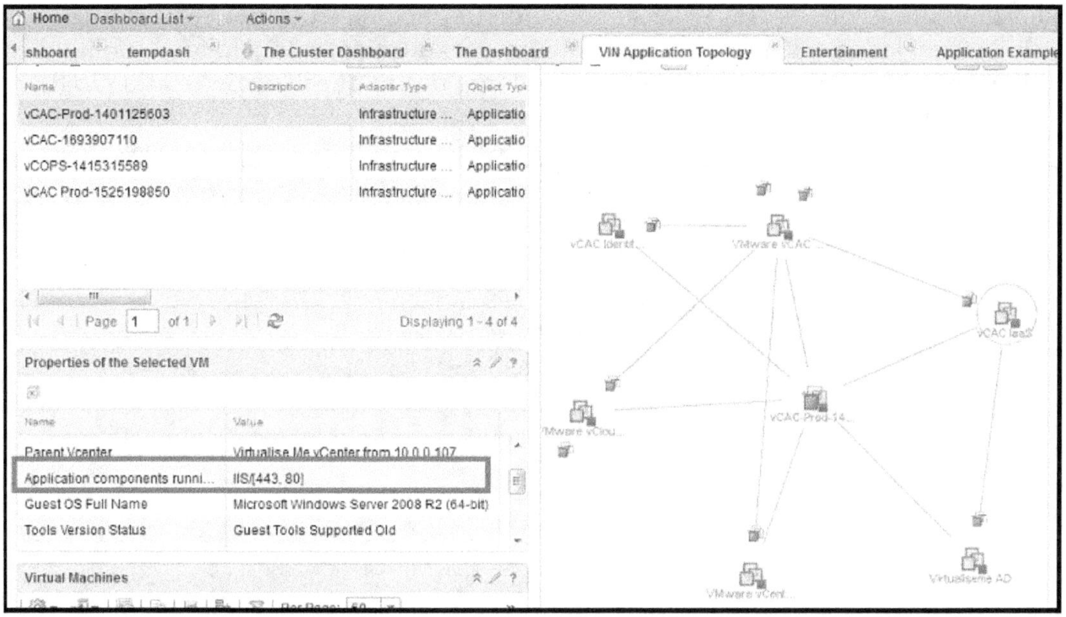

While this chapter is really an extension of *Chapter 11, Expanding vROps with Solutions*, it shows us how we can create applications as a logical grouping. This allows the vROps administrators to create application-specific dashboards, such as the Exchange dashboard or vRealize Automation dashboard, shown in the following screenshot. Then, it allows us to assign these logical groupings and dashboards to the relevant applications teams.

This dramatically decreases tickets and incidents of being stuck in a forwarding loop between teams. It also frees up more time for administrators to focus on how to improve the environment, rather than fielding health questions in relation to the application's performance.

Summary

In this chapter, we focused specifically on the creation of applications with vROps and how they can be enhanced with the use of the vRealize Hyperic solution and VMware Infrastructure Navigator solution.

In the next chapter, we will move on to alerts and recommendations that can be used in conjunction with what has been shown in this chapter.

13
Alerting, Actions, and Recommendations

One of the weaker aspects of vCOps 5.x is its ability to customize alerting, particularly if the standard version is used. These alerts focus on the major and minor badges and, with the exclusion of faults, often struggle to relay the actual issue to the administrator, apart from the obvious degraded badge status.

Actions and recommendations are new for vROps 6.0. Some argue that there were recommendations in the previous versions that were really tied up in the alert information or an output of a report. However, the recommendations that vROps 6.0 can produce are rule-based, 100 percent configurable, and in near real time.

In this chapter we will look at:

- How to configure our own alerts
- How to configure symptoms
- How to create and use our own recommendations and attach an action

Symptoms, recommendations, and actions

Symptoms, recommendations, and actions combine to give alerts. In the following figure, we can see where they all fit when it comes to alerts:

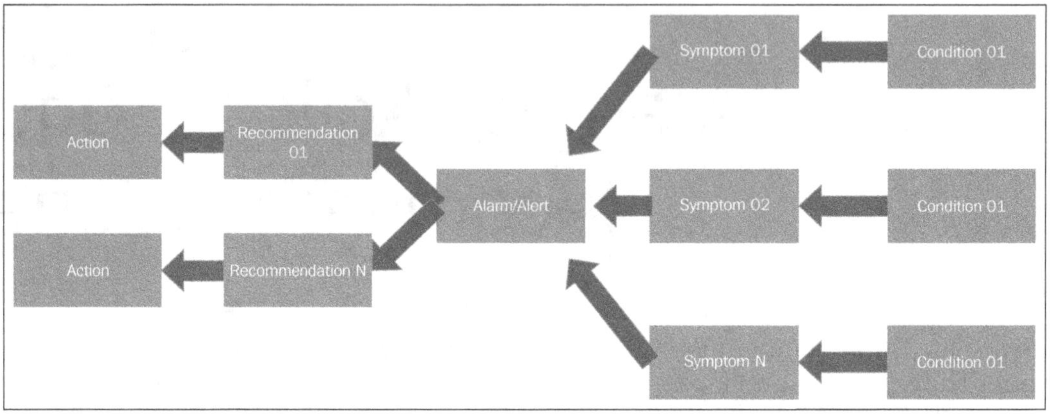

Symptoms

Symptoms are made up of a single condition. Conditions can be based on metric conditions, such as when the CPU usage is greater than 90 percent, or property conditions, such as when the DRS/HA is fully automated.

Symptoms can be used just to highlight an issue that directly affects the score of the associated badge, such as Health. Alternately, a symptom can be a part of a greater problem, which in this case is an alert.

Any symptom that is triggered will appear as an issue within the vROps UI under the related badge and object.

Alerts

Alerts are made up of one or many symptoms. Alerts can be configured in such a way that either all symptoms must be true or only a single symptom must be true to activate the alert.

This can be broken down further by creating multiple symptom sets, where either one or all symptoms in that set must be true to activate the symptom set. Then the alert can be configured to be activated with either one symptom set to true, or all of them set to true.

Recommendations

Recommendations are used to supply information on how to fix the alert that has been triggered. There are plenty of built-in recommendations but these can be created manually based on your organization policies and procedures, KB links, and contacts. A recommendation can be a single line of text, or pages of text telling a person how to fix the issue at hand.

When assigning recommendations to an alert, the recommendations are given priorities, as it is commonly known to any administrator that there can be a number of issues that represent the same symptom, so, we can prioritize which recommendation will more likely fix the issue, based on the environment knowledge.

Actions

Actions are a new feature of vROps 6.0 that requires the vCenter python solution to be configured. The number of actions are fixed and additional ones cannot currently be created. The out-of-the-box actions offer simple solutions to remedy some problems, for example, remove a snapshot, add a vCPU, add memory, remove a vCPU, and so on. Only a single action can be assigned to a recommendation but this is completely optional.

An example scenario of how this fits together is shown in the following figure:

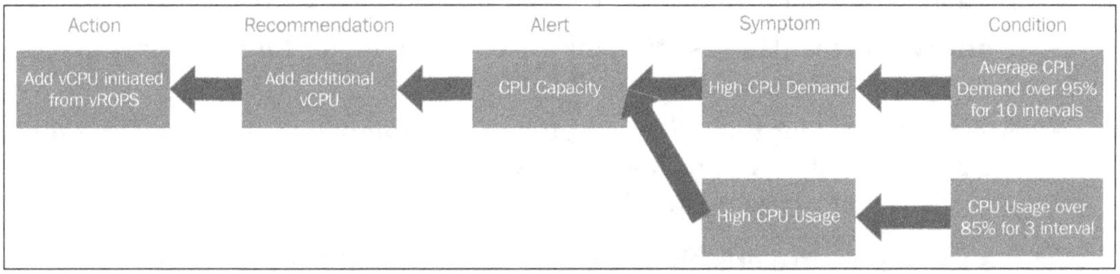

All these pieces come together to create one neat way to troubleshoot in an environment, especially when a good catalog has been created or modified to fit in with the environment.

Think about it: we have a known issue in the environment and we know the symptoms. This can be something like when MSCS RDMs are set to round robin and do not use PowerPath VE, the storage latency will peak in bursts as it switches paths and waits for the switch back, or we notice that when the server's BIOS power settings have not been correctly configured, and we get specific CPU performance issues.

We can supply all the data needed to fix an issue as well as additional suggestions within a recommendation, so that when an alarm is triggered, and if the SME of the environment is not there, the lone junior server engineer can fix the issue as the resolution is right there in black and white.

Creating symptoms and recommendations

Let's look at what is involved in creating an alert. We will work backwards as we need to add symptoms and recommendations to an alert, so it makes sense to create them first before putting everything together.

Let's take a quick look at the symptoms. There are five different types of symptoms, these are as follows:

- **Metric/Supermetric symptom**: These are metric-based symptoms, for example, when the virtual machine CPU usage is greater than 75 percent
- **Property symptom**: These are configuration settings, for example, when the DRS is not fully automated.
- **Message event symptom**: These are event-based symptoms, for example, notifying that the vCenter license will expire soon. This type is based on regular expressions for text in event messages.
- **Fault symptoms**: These symptoms are based on faults, for example, vCenter "Lost Network Redundancy" fault in vCenter.
- **Metric event symptom**: This symptom type straight out-of-the-box is really only targeted at hard threshold events in vROps, which are based on the threshold that we set on metrics.

Symptoms are the key to alerts; they are the conditions that have to be met to trigger an alert. To know where all these are kept, navigate to the **Content** section and go to the fifth option in the navigation pane where we will see **Metric Event Symptom Definitions**. If we select this, we can then see all the symptom types on the navigation pane to the left and the symptoms for each type to the right, as shown in the following screenshot:

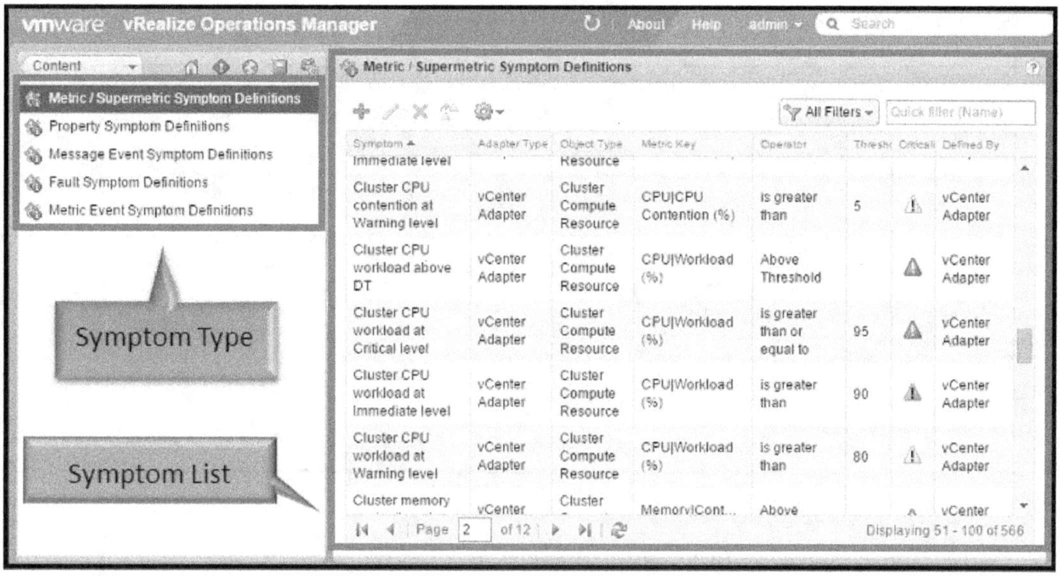

As we can see, there are a large number of symptoms that come out-of-the-box and most will cover the bulk of what anyone would want in their environment. More symptoms can and will be added with additional solutions installed:

We can edit all symptoms except the badge-driven symptoms, which we cannot change. We are free to modify anything based on raw metrics, as follows:

1. Creating a new symptom is similar to making many of the other additions we have done throughout this book, which is clicking on the little green plus icon. This will open up the **Add Symptom Definition** window. This is where we select our base object type and the metric we are after.
2. As shown in the following screenshot, we can then select a metric and drag it over to the right-hand side pane to create a new symptom.
3. In this pane, we first give the metric a name followed by an error level. Then, we select the condition at which this symptom is activated. When using metrics this will generally be "is greater than" or "equal to" a value.

   Then, in the next line, we can see the wait cycle and cancel cycle. This shows how long a condition has to be true or false, in order to first activate and then to cancel the condition.

4. Once you are happy with the symptom(s), click on **Save**.

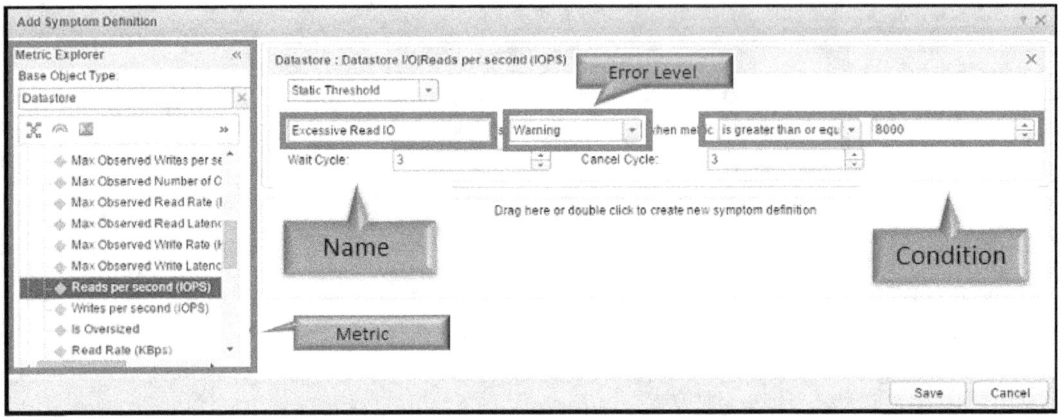

> The symptom type that was selected will determine what condition options will be presented.

Since actions are fixed and cannot be modified or added for the time being, we will now look at recommendations. These are, so far, the simplest to create and are really just text in a box.

1. Navigate to the content section and select **Recommendations**, as shown in the following screenshot:

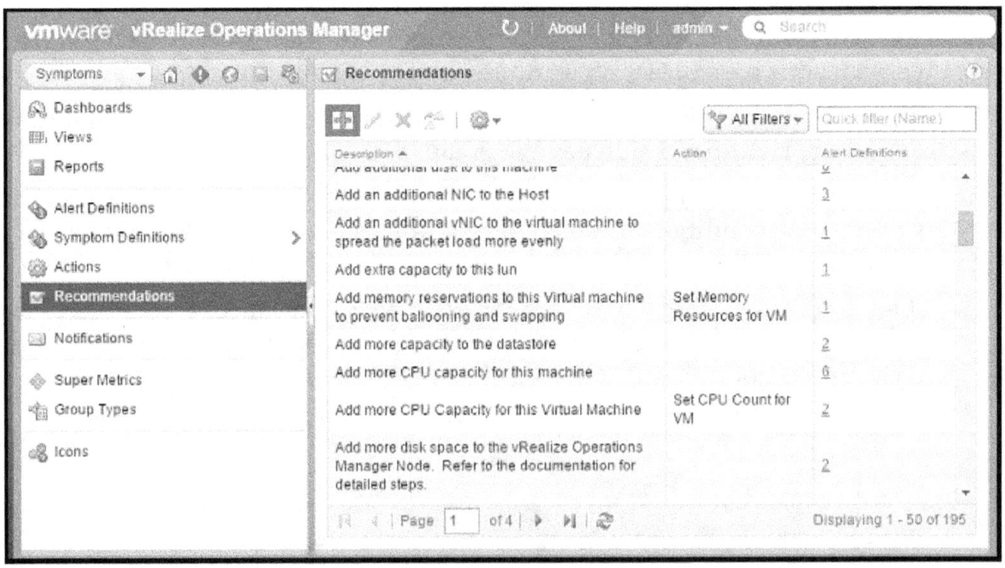

2. Click on the little green plus icon, which will open up the **New Recommendation** window. In here, we enter the text we want and associate the recommendation to an action from the drop-down list of actions, of which one meets the recommendation.
3. Once happy with the recommendation, click on **Save**.

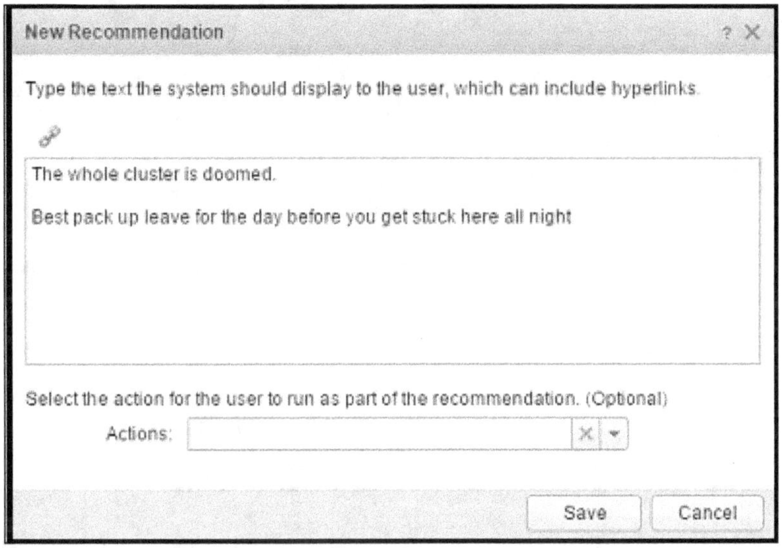

That is all there is to it. In the following sections, we will add the recommendation we have made to an alert.

Creating alerts

As discussed in the beginning of this chapter, alerts are a combination of symptom definitions. Any single symptom appearing as true can cause an alert to be activated or, alternatively, we can specify that all the symptoms need be true for the alert to be activated. This is completely up to how we configure it.

1. Navigate back to the content section and select **Alert Definitions** in the navigation pane; we can then see the alerts on the right-hand side. Here, we can tweak existing definitions, or create our own. Let's create our own so that we can see what goes into an alert. Click on the little green plus icon, as shown in the following screenshot:

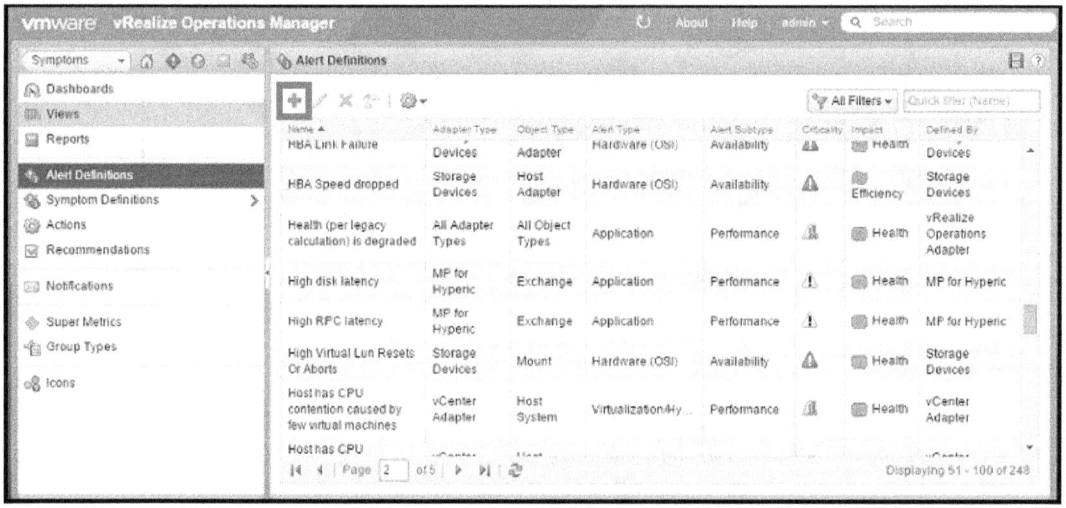

2. This then opens up the **Alert Definition Workspace** window, which is very similar to the policy creation window. We need to first enter the name and description, as shown in the following screenshot:

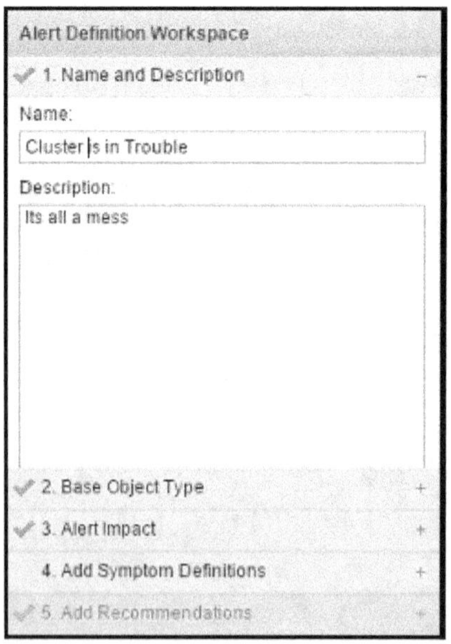

3. Now, we click on the **Base Object Type** bar wherein there is only a single thing to select, which is the base object to which this alarm will be associated. The **Cluster Compute Resource** option can be selected as could the host, VM, datastore: any object from any solution can be chosen.
4. Next, we click on the **Alert Impact** bar. In this section, we choose the following:
    - **Impact**: This is the major badge that will be affected, which can be one among **Health**, **Risk**, or **Efficiency**.
    - **Criticality**: This is a type of alert that can be classified as info, warning, immediate, critical, and symptom-based. The symptom-based type will take the criticality of the symptoms into consideration to decide the alert's value.
    - **Alert Type and Subtype**: There are quite a number of values in here to select but the main types are **Application**, **Virtualization/ Hypervisor**, **Hardware**, **Storage**, and **Network**. This will categorize the alert where it fits.
    - **Wait Cycle**: This is the number of cycles we need to wait for in order for the symptoms to be triggered , so as to then trigger the alarm.
    - **Cancel Cycle**: This is the opposite to wait cycle; it is the number cycles for which the alert remains active when the conditions are not met.

The following screenshot illustrates how this could be configured:

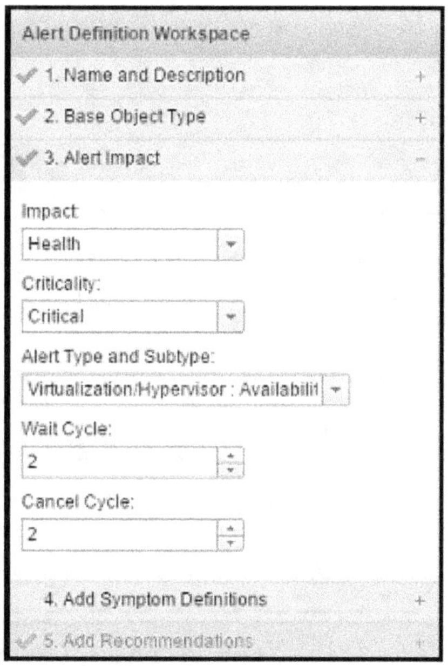

5. Click on the **Add Symptom Definitions**. This is where the magic happens. In this section, we can choose on what level we want the symptoms to be applied. We have selected **Self**, which in this case is a host or parent, for example, a datacenter,
6. We then need to choose a symptom or 10. From the drop-down list, select the **Symptom Definition Type** and then, under it, select a symptom and drag it over to the right.

   We can drag and drop symptoms on top of each other to nest them; this is called a symptom set, in which case, we will see multiple numbered symptoms in one box. Alternately, we can drag and drop symptoms into the dotted outlined area to create a new symptom set.

   From the following screenshot, we can see all the previous data we entered at the top right-hand side and, under it, we can see the metric symptoms we dragged over it.

   Each set of symptoms has the drop-down option to say if all or any of the symptoms need to be true to set the symptom to true.

7. At the top of the symptom sets, we have a **Match** value, which can be set to all or any of the symptoms sets to be true, to activate the alert.

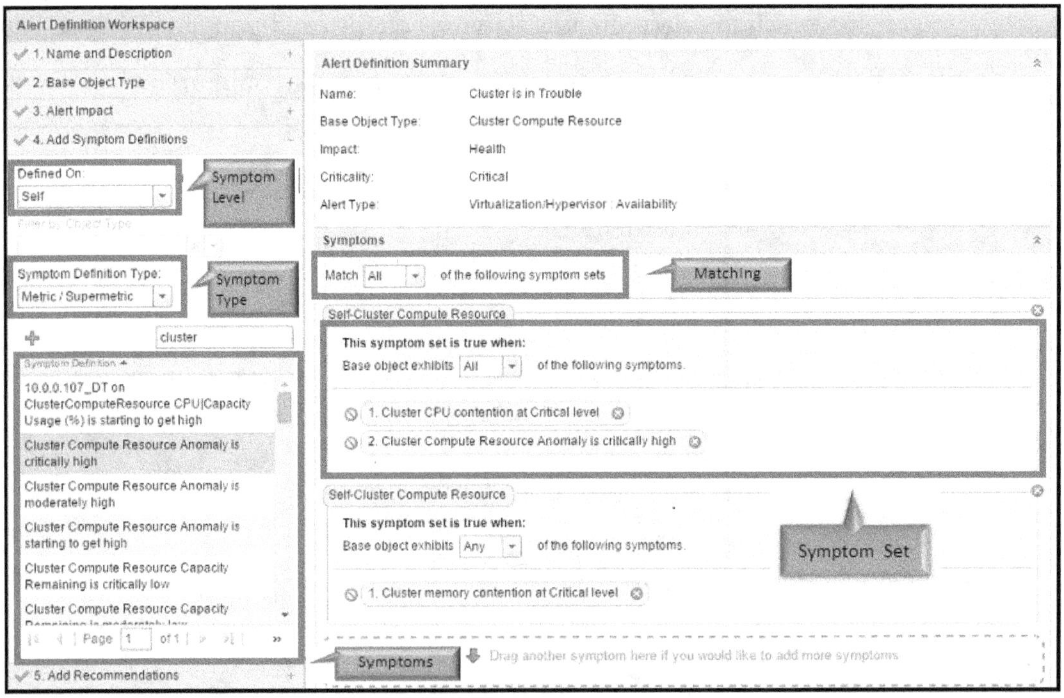

8. The last step is to add recommendations. This is optional when creating an alarm, but I highly recommend you do this as it can save time, especially when you are not there to fix an issue. Click on the **Add Recommendations** bar and search for the recommendation that you require, then drag and drop that recommendation from the left to the right.

   What you can also do is drag multiple recommendations over and give them a priority, so if you know that a particular symptom you have chosen can have multiple courses of action, put all of them in here. This is shown in the following image:

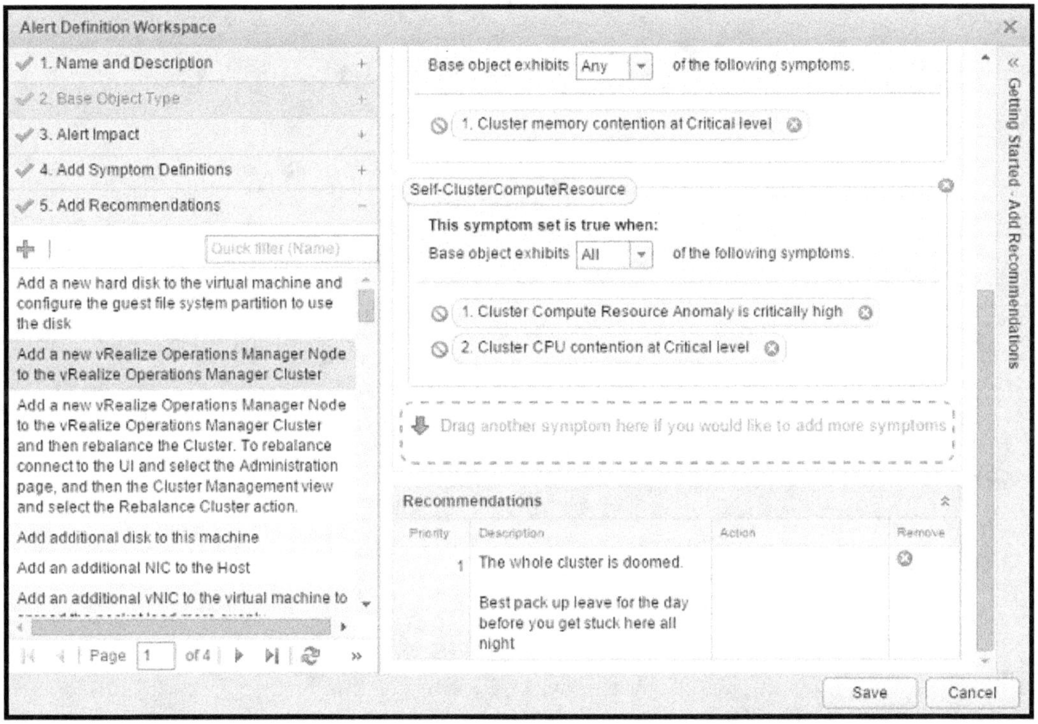

9. Click on the **Save** button, and this is how we create an alert.

From this very simple example, we can see just how powerful the new alerting system is when it's made up of multiple items. It allows us to become very specific with the alerts we want, while providing guidance on how to fix an issue.

Summary

In this chapter, we looked at what symptoms and recommendations are. We discussed how to create and bundle them together to create fine-tuned granular alerting that meets the environment's requirements. No need to make do with out-of-the-box alerting anymore.

14
Just Messing Around

All the previous chapters in this book are entirely business-oriented. They are structured to give you knowledge so that you can use them when you are having a hard time fixing your environment. However, what about a little fun? In this chapter, we will take a look at how we can mix work and pleasure on a single screen.

There is a great little widget called the text widget, which allows us to display content in either HTML or text, and can be pointed to either a URL or a file.

If your vROps instance has access to the internet, you can display your sports news, blogs, or even media streaming services.

From the following screenshot, you can see that I am catching up on some TV, looking at my blog, and keeping an eye on the environment's health:

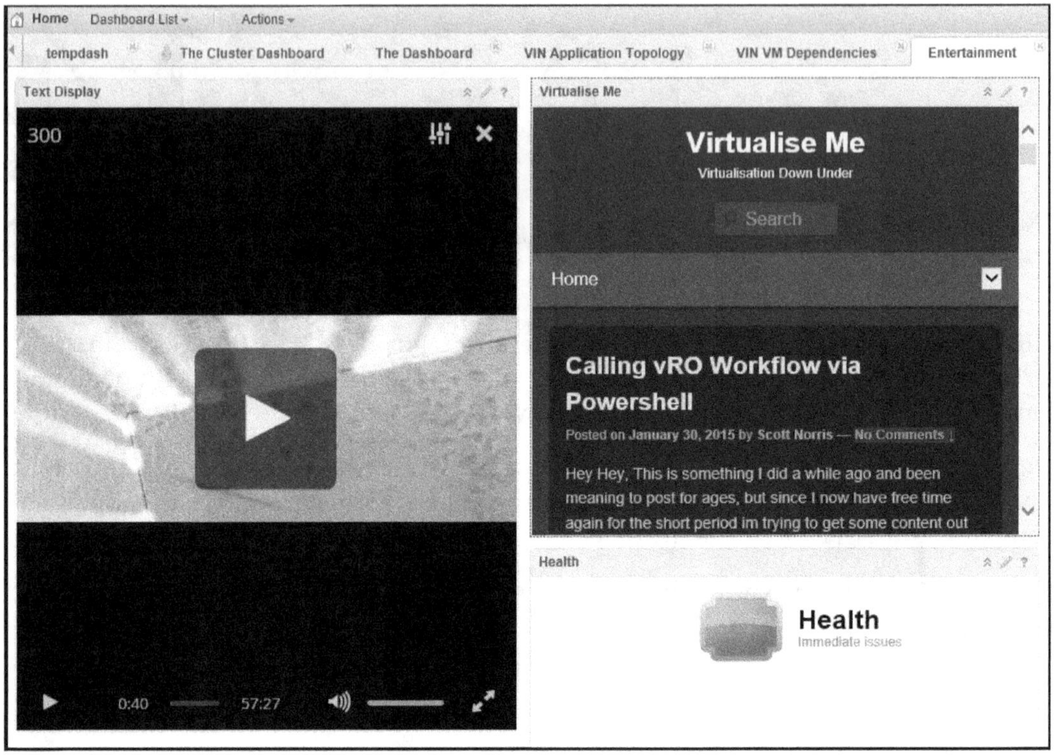

On a slightly serious note, this can also be used to display web interfaces for other monitoring systems—maybe even your ticketing system. There is only one restriction, however, that the site or webpage that is being displayed must be able to run in an iframe. Due to security reasons, some websites do not allow this.

Here is an example of running Applications Services:

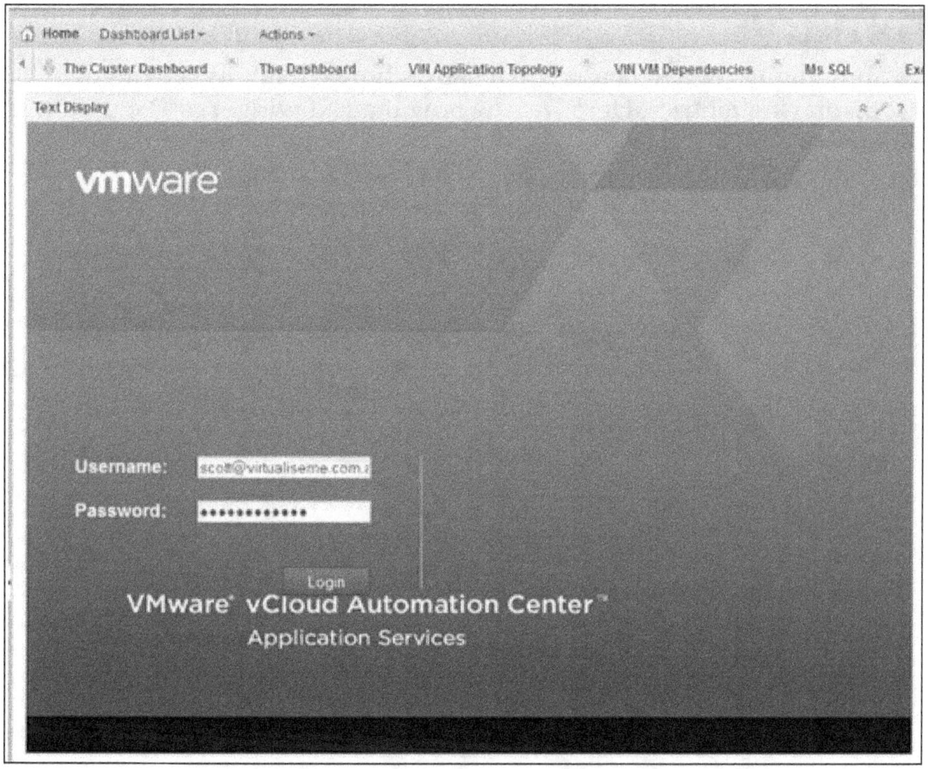

The settings for this widget are very straightforward, as shown in the following screenshot. We have the **View mode**, which allows us to choose between text and HTML, with the choice of attaching a URL or a file. If a text object is selected when pointing to a web page, it will display the HTML source for that page.

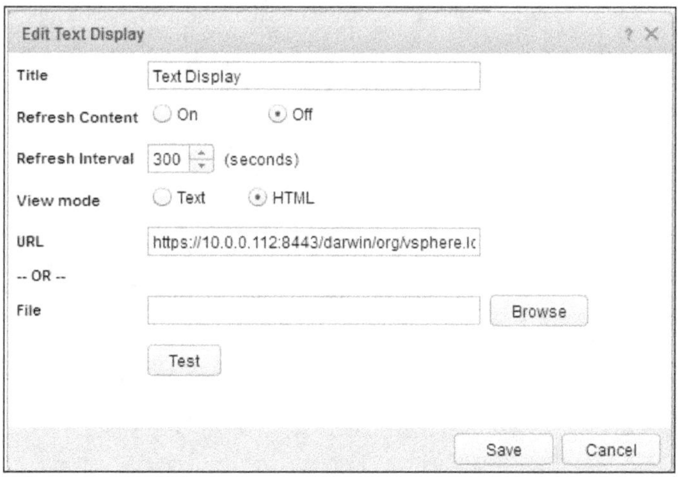

Summary

This is a short, light-hearted chapter that shows how we can use a widget to do more than just displaying metrics. Here we saw how the text widget can be used to display other web-based content.

Index

A

B

C

D

E

F

G

H

I

L

M

N

O

P

R

S

T

U

V

W

[PACKT] enterprise
professional expertise distilled
PUBLISHING

Thank you for buying

Mastering vRealize Operations Manager

About Packt Publishing

Packt, pronounced 'packed', published its first book, *Mastering phpMyAdmin for Effective MySQL Management*, in April 2004, and subsequently continued to specialize in publishing highly focused books on specific technologies and solutions.

Our books and publications share the experiences of your fellow IT professionals in adapting and customizing today's systems, applications, and frameworks. Our solution-based books give you the knowledge and power to customize the software and technologies you're using to get the job done. Packt books are more specific and less general than the IT books you have seen in the past. Our unique business model allows us to bring you more focused information, giving you more of what you need to know, and less of what you don't.

Packt is a modern yet unique publishing company that focuses on producing quality, cutting-edge books for communities of developers, administrators, and newbies alike. For more information, please visit our website at `www.packtpub.com`.

About Packt Enterprise

In 2010, Packt launched two new brands, Packt Enterprise and Packt Open Source, in order to continue its focus on specialization. This book is part of the Packt Enterprise brand, home to books published on enterprise software - software created by major vendors, including (but not limited to) IBM, Microsoft, and Oracle, often for use in other corporations. Its titles will offer information relevant to a range of users of this software, including administrators, developers, architects, and end users.

Writing for Packt

We welcome all inquiries from people who are interested in authoring. Book proposals should be sent to `author@packtpub.com`. If your book idea is still at an early stage and you would like to discuss it first before writing a formal book proposal, then please contact us; one of our commissioning editors will get in touch with you.

We're not just looking for published authors; if you have strong technical skills but no writing experience, our experienced editors can help you develop a writing career, or simply get some additional reward for your expertise.

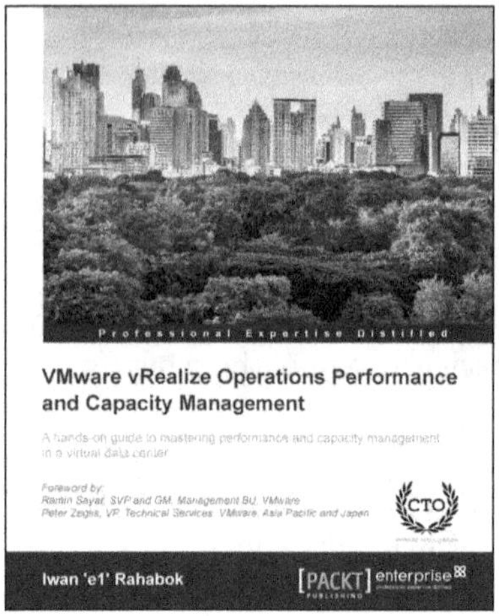

VMware vRealize Operations Performance and Capacity Management

ISBN: 978-1-78355-168-2 Paperback: 276 pages

A hands-on guide to mastering performance and capacity management in a virtual data center

1. Understand the drawbacks of traditional paradigm and management that make performance and capacity management difficult in SDDC.
2. Master the counters in vCenter and vRealize Operations by discovering what they mean and their interdependencies.
3. Build rich dashboards using a practical and easy-to-follow approach supported with real-life examples.

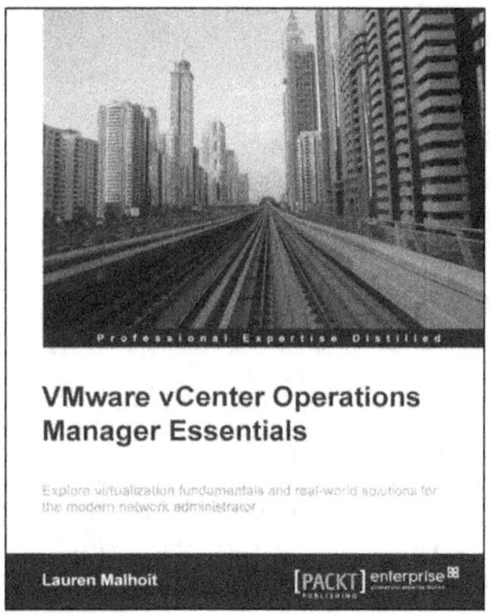

VMware vCenter Operations Manager Essentials

ISBN: 978-1-78217-696-1 Paperback: 246 pages

Explore virtualization fundamentals and real-world solutions for the modern network administrator

1. Written by VMware expert Lauren Malhoit, this book takes a look at vCenter Operations Manager from a practical point of view that every administrator can appreciate.
2. Understand, troubleshoot, and design your virtual environment in a better and more efficient way than you ever have before.
3. A step-by-step and learn-by-example guide to understanding the ins and outs of vCenter Operations Manager.

Please check **www.PacktPub.com** for information on our titles

[PACKT] enterprise
professional expertise distilled
PUBLISHING

Hyper-V Network Virtualization Cookbook

ISBN: 978-1-78217-780-7 Paperback: 228 pages

Over 20 recipes to ease the creation of new virtual machines in the networking layer using Hyper-V Network Virtualization

1. Create, configure, and administer System Center 2012 R2 virtual networks with Hyper-V.
2. Design practical solutions to optimize your network solutions.
3. Learn how to control who can access a VM on a specific port to enhance the security of your virtual machine.

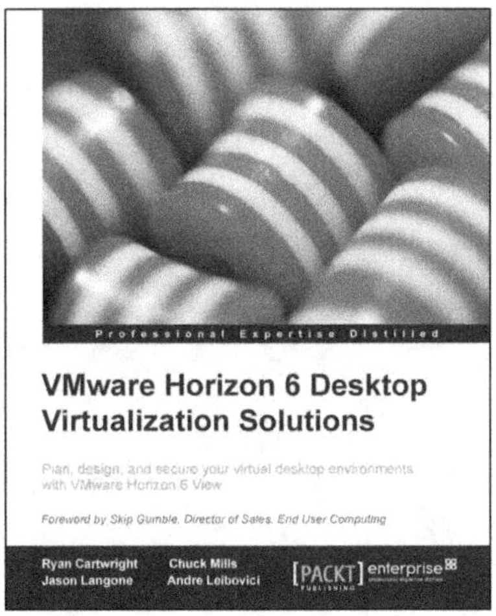

VMware Horizon 6 Desktop Virtualization Solutions

ISBN: 978-1-78217-070-9 Paperback: 362 pages

Plan, design, and secure your virtual desktop environments with VMware Horizon 6 View

1. Design a successful solution to deliver Windows desktops and applications as a service.
2. Provide redundancy for components and design a backup solution and disaster recovery plan to protect your investment and to keep your users productive.
3. A learn-by-example-based approach that focuses on key concepts to provide the foundation to solve real-world problems.

Please check **www.PacktPub.com** for information on our titles

www.ingramcontent.com/pod-product-compliance
Lightning Source LLC
LaVergne TN
LVHW080039210926
848481LV00011B/3234
* 9 7 8 1 7 8 4 3 9 2 5 4 3 *